Border images, border narratives

Manchester University Press

RETHINKING BORDERS

SERIES EDITORS: SARAH GREEN AND HASTINGS DONNAN

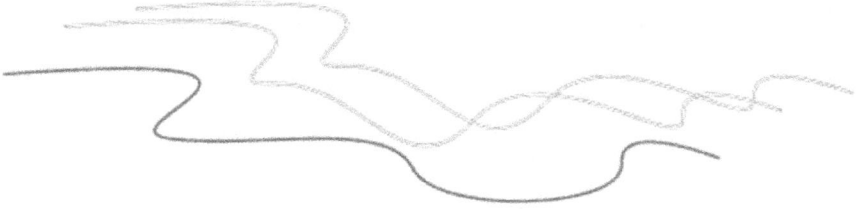

Rethinking Borders focuses on what gives borders their qualities across time and space, as well as how such borders are experienced, built, managed, imagined and changed. This involves detailed and often richly ethnographic studies of all aspects of borders: finance and money, bureaucracy, trade, law, new technologies, materiality, infrastructure, gender and sexuality, even the philosophy of what counts as being 'borderly', as well as the more familiar topics of migration, nationalism, politics, conflicts and security.

Previously published

Migrating borders and moving times: Temporality and the crossing of borders in Europe
Edited by Hastings Donnan, Madeleine Hurd and Carolin Leutloff-Grandits

The political materialities of borders: New theoretical directions
Edited by Olga Demetriou and Rozita Dimova

Border images, border narratives

The political aesthetics of boundaries and crossings

Edited by
Johan Schimanski and Jopi Nyman

MANCHESTER UNIVERSITY PRESS

Published by Manchester University Press
Oxford Road, Manchester M13 9PL
www.manchesteruniversitypress.co.uk

British Library Cataloguing-in-Publication Data is available

ISBN 978 1 5261 4626 7 hardback
ISBN 978 1 5261 7189 4 paperback

First published by Manchester University Press in hardback
2021

This edition first published 2023

The publisher has no responsibility for the persistence or accuracy
of URLs for any external or third-party internet websites referred
to in this book, and does not guarantee that any content on such
websites is, or will remain, accurate or appropriate.

Typeset by New Best-set Typesetters Ltd

Contents

Part III: Crossing the border (migrations)

Figures

Notes on contributors

Anne-Laure Amilhat Szary is Professor of Political Geography at Grenoble-Alpes University, member of the Institut Universitaire de France, and Head of the CNRS *Pacte* multidisciplinary social sciences research centre. Her comparative analysis of border dynamics in Latin America and Europe has led her to formulate the notion of 'mobile border'. Her recent research concerns the interrelationships between space and art, in and about contested places. She is a founding member of the 'antiAtlas of borders' science-art collective and initiated the Performance Lab dedicated to structuring practice-based research in France. Recent books include the co-edited collection *Borderities: The Politics of Contemporary Mobile Borders* (2015).

Chiara Brambilla is Assistant Professor of Anthropology at the Department of Human and Social Sciences, University of Bergamo. Her research focuses on anthropology, critical geopolitics and epistemology of borders; the Mediterranean border-migration nexus; borders in Africa; colonialism and post-colonialism. She co-edited the volume *Borderscaping: Imaginations and Practices of Border Making* (2015). Brambilla is Associate Member of the Nijmegen Centre for Border Research, member of the Association for Borderlands Studies, and Regional Editor of the *Journal of Borderlands Studies*.

Patricia García is an Associate Professor in Hispanic and Comparative Literature at the University of Nottingham. Her research focuses on narrative spaces and their intersection with representations of the supernatural. She has co-ordinated the British Academy project *Gender and the Hispanic Fantastic* and is a member of the Spanish Research Group on the Fantastic (GEF, Grupo de Estudios de lo Fantástico). Her most notable publications include *Space and the Postmodern Fantastic in Contemporary Literature: The Architectural Void* (2015).

Karina Horsti is a media and migration scholar whose work focuses on refugees, migration, memory and cultural representations. She is Senior

Lecturer in Cultural Policy at the University of Jyväskylä, Finland. Her current work focuses on memory politics on migrant deaths at Europe's borders. She is completing a book that examines the afterlife of the 3 October 2013 disaster in Lampedusa, and she is the editor of *The Politics of Public Memories of Forced Migration and Bordering in Europe* (2019).

Zhiding Hu is a Professor of Geography at Eastern China Normal University in Shanghai. Professor Hu received his PhD from Beijing Normal University and has also taught at Yunnan Normal University where he maintains an affiliation. He has been successful in receiving the prestigious Chinese research award, and he is widely regarded in China for his research and writing on Chinese geopolitics. Professor Hu is author of numerous articles in Chinese, and recently has co-authored several publications in English.

Victor Konrad teaches Geography at Carleton University in Ottawa. He is author and editor of more than one hundred publications in cultural geography, border studies and Canadian studies including *Beyond Walls: Re-inventing the Canada–United States Borderlands*, and *North American Borders in Comparative Perspective*; *Culture, Borders in Globalization*, and *Canada's Borders* was published in 2020. Professor Konrad is past-president of the Association of Borderlands Studies and the Association for Canadian Studies in the United States, and recipient of the Donner Medal. In recent years he has been a visiting professor at universities in China, the United States, Finland and the Netherlands.

Tuulikki Kurki is a Senior Researcher in Cultural Studies and Deputy Director at the Karelian Institute, University of Eastern Finland. Her recent research interests have focused on borders from a cultural point of view, border- and mobility-related traumas and literature at the Finnish–Russian borderlands. As a principal investigator, she has managed two international research projects studying literature, cultural practices and traumas at borders and borderlands in the contexts of Finland, Estonia and Russia. Her ongoing project examines mobility and border crossing experiences through objects that people carry with them. Her recent publications include the monograph *Rajan kirjailijat: Venäjän Karjalan suomenkieliset kirjailijat tilan ja identiteetin kirjoittajina* (2018) analysing border, space and identity in Finnish-language literature from Russian Karelia.

Wolfgang Müller-Funk is a literary scholar, cultural philosopher, essayist, lyricist and cultural critic. He completed his Habilitation at the University of Klagenfurt (1993) and has been Professor of Cultural Studies at the Universities of Birmingham (UK) and Vienna, and visiting professor/researcher in India, Ireland, Croatia, USA, Germany and Italy. His research interests include cultural theory, narratology, Central European studies, Austrian literature, Romanticism, avant-garde and essay studies. Ehrenkreuz of the Republic of Austria for Science and Art (2013). Recent monographs include *Theorien des Fremden* (2016), a commentary on Sigmund Freud's *Das Unbehagen in der Kultur* (2016), *Die Dichter der Philosophen* (2013) and *The Architecture of Modern Culture* (2012).

Jopi Nyman is Professor of English and Vice Dean at the School of Humanities, University of Eastern Finland, Joensuu Campus. He is the author and editor of several books in the fields of anglophone literary and cultural studies, most recently of the monographs *Equine Fictions: Human–Horse Relationships in Twenty-first-century Writing* (2019), *Displacement, Memory, and Travel in Contemporary Migrant Writing* (2017) and the co-edited anthologies *Mobile Narratives: Travel, Migration, and Transculturation* (2014), *Animals, Space and Affect* (2016) and *Racial and Ethnic Identities in the Media* (2016). His current research interests focus on transcultural literatures and border narratives, as well as the environmental humanities.

Holger Pötzsch is Associate Professor in Media and Documentation Studies at UiT – The Arctic University of Norway. He has published on the relationship between media and war (in particular war films and games), on material aspects of digital networks and on border culture and technologies. Pötzsch currently leads the academic networks WARGAME and ENCODE. His most recent publication is the volume *War Games: Memory, Militarism, and the Subject of Play*, co-edited with Phil Hammond.

Johan Schimanski is Professor of Comparative Literature at the University of Oslo and Head of Research at the Department of Literature, Area Studies, and European Languages there. While working on this book he also held a position as Professor of Cultural Encounters at the University of Eastern Finland. His research focuses on borders in literature, Arctic discourses and literary exhibition practices. At present he leads a NOS-HS workshop on *Temporalities and Subjectivities of Crossing*. Recent books include *Passagiere des Eises: Polarhelden und arktische Diskursen 1874* (co-author 2015), *Border Aesthetics* (co-editor 2017) and *Living Together* (co-editor 2019).

Ilaria Tucci is a theatre practitioner (BA in Acting) and peace scholar (BA, MA in Peace Studies). During the last ten years, she has been developing her own applications of theatre as a tool of dialogue among people, participation, peacebuilding and empowerment. She is a doctoral researcher at Tampere University, Finland, in the Peace and Conflict Studies Program doing interdisciplinary research combining ethnography, applied theatre, and peace research. For her doctoral project, 'Activist Theatre at the Border of Europe: Militarization and Migration Industry in Lampedusa', she has facilitated a community-based theatre experience within the militarised context of Lampedusa.

Stephen F. Wolfe has taught at UIT, The Arctic University of Norway; University of Alberta and York University in Canada; and in colleges in the United States. He has co-coordinated research projects on border aesthetics in Norway, and within the EU FP7 project EUBORDERSCAPES. He has co-edited, with Johan Schimanski, the volumes *Border Poetics Delimited* (2007) and *Border Aesthetics: Concepts and Intersections* (2017). Recent publications focus on border-crossing narratives in British modernist writers; he is currently researching the early modernist photo essays of John Berger and Edward Said for their representations of migrants and refugees.

Acknowledgements

We should like to thank the following institutions and individuals for their help in the project. Financial support from the University of Eastern Finland and its School of Humanities made possible the symposium where several of the chapters in this book were first presented. We also wish to thank the University of Oslo for editing expenses. We are also grateful to the series editors, Professor Sarah Green and Professor Hastings Donnan, for accepting the book in the series. We would like to thank the external reviewers for their helpful feedback, and our editor Tom Dark at Manchester University Press for all his help.

An earlier version of Anne-Laure Amilhat Szary's chapter 'Borders: The topos of/for a post-politics of images' has appeared as 'Les frontières, lieu/locus d'une post-politique des images' in *Les Carnets du Bal*, 7 (2016): 63–81. This text is a translated and extended version, and the translation is by André Crous.

We should like to thank the following for permissions to reproduce the images which appear in this book: Sabine Funk-Müller (Figure 1.1), Trevor Paglen and *The Intercept* (Figure 3.1), Chiara Brambilla (Figures 4.1, 4.2 and 4.3), Victor Konrad and Zhiding Hu (Figure 6.1), Yuli Liu (Figure 6.2), Adrien Missika (Figures 7.1 and 7.2) and Humanist forlag (Figure 10.1).

Introduction: images and narratives on the border

Jopi Nyman and Johan Schimanski

The aesthetics of borders

In the first chapter of this volume, Wolfgang Müller-Funk reminds us of Georg Simmel's pioneering work in border theory around the beginning of the twentieth century. As a sociologist, Simmel used borders, limits and thresholds as ways of understanding society, but also involved them in his numerable essays on aesthetics. Often, social and aesthetic boundaries cross ways in his work, such as when he compares the boundaries of a social group with the frame of a painting (1997b: 141), and it seems natural to see Simmel as a precursor also of the field to which we see this book contributing: that of border aesthetics.

Müller-Funk refers to various texts by Simmel, among them 'Brücke und Tür' ('Bridge and Door', 1997a). This short text, on the way in which we see our world through both borders and connections, considers a short series of central figurations of the divisions and joinings between different spaces: the path, the bridge, the door (and implicitly the threshold) and the window. These are conceptual metaphors, ways of grouping a range of border phenomena not necessarily named as such in terms of a concrete image. In each case, Simmel emphasises the necessity of making these figures tangible, even of seeing them as images or as if they were paintings, in order for them to function. People can wander to and fro, but it is only when their wandering becomes fixed and repeatable as a visible path that places are 'objectively connected' (Simmel, 1997a: 171). The bridge attains aesthetic value in its transformation of dynamic movement and the joining of divided river banks into something visible and enduring (171). Simmel compares it to a timeless 'portrait' and a 'work of art', even pointing to the fact that a bridge will give to a landscape a '"picturesque"' quality (172);

he is emphasising the importance of both bridges and doors as artistic motifs.

Whilst Simmel is not specifically concerned with one important form of border-crossing, migration, his series of images might evoke it as an underlying 'master narrative'. One could say that migrants follow routes (paths), they pass through crossing points (bridges), they are excluded and have to wait outside selective barriers in order to enter (doors), and they can see a better life on the other side of the border (windows). For the most part, Simmel however reduces any potential narratives of movement to images. To him, the bordering process itself is precisely a form of aesthetic fixing in static images. His reference to the aesthetic in this essay is solely to visible forms and to the art of painting; nowhere in this essay does he mention literary narratives or other senses. Only at one point in his mainly explicative essay does he tell a story, though in a minimal form. A variant of the door, the window, gives a teleological feeling (Simmel, 1997a: 173). The openings of Romanesque and Gothic cathedrals, when they use repeated ornamental frames to narrow in on the actual doors of the building, draw us in, and rows of pillars point us towards the altar – the fact that we usually leave again in the opposite direction Simmel characterises as 'accidental' (173). Simmel states that entering the cathedral symbolises our journey from life to death, since it privileges the uni-directional before free movement in all directions (174). He thus evokes a narrative of border-crossing.

This book explores both images and narratives as integral parts of bordering processes and border-crossings as they impact on our world. Borderlands – experienced by their inhabitants amongst others – and border-crossings – such as those carried out by migrants – are present both in public discourse and in more private, everyday experience. As they are mediated through various stories, photographs, films and other forms, narratives and images are part of the borderscapes in which border-crossings and bordering processes take place, contributing to the negotiation of borders in the public sphere and constructing new configurations of belonging and becoming (Brambilla, 2015: 24). This means that these aesthetic forms are central to the political process, the latter being characterised by the philosopher Jacques Rancière as a *partage du sensible*, a 'distribution of the sensible' (2004) or, to retain the ambivalence of the original wording, a 'sharing/division of the sensible'. What narratives and images make possible is identifying various top-down and bottom-up discourses to be heard, and they also open up the diverse experiences of different minority groups and constituencies. In so doing, they contribute to the act of making visible the experience of those who live with and cross borders, especially ethnic and cultural minorities and migrants. This visibility, in the view of Hannah Arendt, is necessary so as to provide them with political agency, since the world for her is a public 'space of appearance' (1958: 199) where visibility is necessary to achieving political participation and recognition.

This book is a contribution to the interdisciplinary discussion of the role of images and narratives in different borderscapes through contributions by researchers in various disciplines, including literary studies, cultural studies, media studies, social anthropology and political geography. This interaction between the humanities and the social sciences, producing a multilayered understanding of various borderscaping phenomena through the use of shared theoretical concepts and heightened focus on images and narratives as means of approaching the border, is our response to calls for interdisciplinarity in border studies, where humanities perspectives have been underrepresented (Brunet-Jailly, 2005; Newman, 2006a, 2006b; Schimanski and Wolfe, 2009; Wilson and Donnan, 2012; Scott, 2012; Szary et al., 2016; Rosello and Wolfe, 2017). The chapters in this volume combine theory and specific case studies in order to attend to three pressing issues as to how images and narratives contribute to a political aesthetics of borders, through their focus on key sites where migration and borders remain highly topical, ranging from France to China, including, but not limited to, the Mediterranean and Calais, and the border between Mexico and the United States. At a more general level, the chapters thus aim to address the following three key questions.

First, how does the choice of *form, medium, genre and aesthetical strategies* help form and potentially transform the borderscape? Do images negotiate borders, borderlands and border-crossings in a different way from narratives? What differing temporalities, epistemologies and sensual perceptions involved in bordering do images and narratives afford? How do images and narratives combine to create different ways of figuring borders in specific contexts?

Second, how do these different forms, discourses and genres cross the borders into the *public sphere*? How do they mediate between realities and imaginaries in their act of bordering? Do images and narratives of borders, borderlands and border-crossings function differently on different levels of discourse (literary, artistic, cinematic, journalistic, political, juridical etc.) in the public sphere? What different discourses organise the representation of borders politically and historically? How is cultural memory appropriated in border imagery?

Third, what paradoxes can problematise simple perceptions of *making visible* and *giving voice*? Is making visible or audible always an act of empowerment for minority constituencies? Can some images and narratives block out others, and be used to block out others?

In discussing these questions, the contributors acknowledge the hybrid nature of media forms and genres, as they deal with, e.g., textual imagery, performance, participatory video, border art, novels, drama, photography, installations, short story cycles, life-stories, documentaries, data clouds, maps, monuments, ethnography and the fantastic. Specific aesthetic categories (e.g., metaphor, the grotesque) and specific motifs (e.g., horizontal vertigo, windows, cul-de-sacs) are also examined for both their visual and their narrative potentials.

The third set of questions, with its focus on paradox and ambivalence, needs perhaps some elaboration. The spectacularisation and memorialisation of borders, borderlands and border-crossings that we often find in the news media and the heritage industry appear an immediate source of border knowledge, but often simplify heterogeneous and contested borderscapes and mobilities (De Genova, 2012; Mazzara, 2019). Maps of borders and migration routes can seem informative, but are often a source of misinformation, and are the heirs of a long genealogy of military and colonialist violence (Bueno Lacy and Houtum, 2015; Houtum and Bueno Lacy, 2019). Borderlands and border-crossings can often be connected with wars and migration movements, and thus with trauma; and we know that trauma is connected to an inability to narrate, and to the blockage of narrative memory by limited sets of fixed, timeless images (e.g., Kolk, 2002; Langås, 2015: 25; Schimanski, 2019). Borderscapes can be the sites of pathological regimes of 'in/visibility' in which people are made 'publicly invisible' and excluded from politics at the same as they are made 'naturally visible' as ethnicised or racialised others, but they can also be transformed sites in which people are made 'publicly visible' (and audible) and be allowed the privacy to be 'naturally invisible' (Borren, 2008; Brambilla and Pötzsch, 2017). Where migrants are concerned, sympathetic representations in the media can de-ethnicise or de-racialise others, whilst surveillance and criminalisation are often countered by clandestinity and discourses of 'crimmigration' (Woude et al., 2018).

In responding to all three questions, the chapters in this book, along with our epilogue, follow a transnational and interdisciplinary methodological approach, working beyond and across borders and cultural contexts on the basis of border theory, so as to highlight new approaches to imagining borders and crossings, and their representation in the media, literature, the arts and politics more generally. In such an approach, an understanding of borders as fixed and merely geopolitical markers of division and control has been replaced by a more dynamic conception emphasising the social and cultural constructedness of borders through acts of bordering, as well as their extensive character as borderscapes. A border, as the border theorist Henk van Houtum has suggested, is 'not a noun but a verb' (2013: 173). Such an understanding of the multiple effects of and responses to borders inspires current work by boosting the potentiality of interdisciplinarity and sharing of concepts by scholars representing both the humanities and the social sciences. In so doing, they rely and comment on recent debates in border studies, as addressed in the following section.

The concepts framing our discussion in this book are informed by theories of borders and liminality in general, but also by developments within border studies, a field originating in research on borders within political geography. Two ongoing turns have come together in the 2000s, a 'cultural turn' in border studies and a 'border turn' in cultural studies. On the one hand, border studies has gone beyond a narrow understanding of borders as singular dividing lines between nations. It has been becoming aware of borders as not only contingent, ongoing processes with dimensions stretching beyond the geopolitical boundary line, and this redefinition of the object of study has been reflected in the proliferation of terms such as 'bordering', 'b/ordering', 'de/rebordering', 'border work', 'mobile borders', 'borderlands' and 'border zones'. Border studies has also begun to see how geopolitical borders are caught in a relational net of power and meaning, connecting territorial boundaries to the borders between economies, classes, genders, ethnicities, languages, classes, genders, cultures, mobilities, discourses and so on. It has increasingly acknowledged the need for investigation of the cultural and symbolic dimensions of borders, including calls for research on border narratives (Newman, 2006b). The 2010s have seen the development of thinking around the terms 'borderscape' and 'borderscaping' (Strüver, 2005; Rajaram and Grundy-Warr, 2007; Brambilla, 2015; Brambilla et al., 2015; dell'Agnese and Amilhat Szary, 2015; Schimanski, 2015; Krichker, 2019), signifying a both physical and imagined space connecting up all aspects of the bordering process including policing, barrier-building, passport regimes, international law, citizenship, political rhetoric, news media spectacle, popular culture, literature, art and everyday experience.

On the other hand, a border turn in the humanities reaches back to the focus on margins and transgression in such thinkers as Jacques Derrida and Michel Foucault and has been strengthened by the impact of post-colonial theory and Chicanx studies, the latter connected to the borderlands of the Mexico–USA border. Indeed, the conceptual shift away from studying territorial border lines to exploring a more symbolic idea of 'borderlands' can partly be traced back to Gloria Anzaldúa's seminal work of Chicanx cultural theory, *Borderlands / La Frontera: The New Mestiza* (1987; see also Calderón and Saldívar, 1991; Arteaga, 1994; Saldívar, 1997; Saldívar-Hull, 2000; Sadowski-Smith, 2008). The larger border turn has resulted not only in the production of an ever-increasing number of publications on borders and literature and other art forms, but also in the formulation of a field of 'border theory' within cultural studies and critical theory (Michaelsen and Johnson, 1997; Castillo, 1999), and the development of a 'border poetics', a theory and methodological approach that was initially focused primarily on the analysis of literary narratives of successful and failed border-crossings and was connected topographically not only to symbolic but also to temporal, epistemological and textual or media borders (Schimanski, 2006; Schimanski and Wolfe, 2007). This border turn in cultural studies has also cross-pollinated with a parallel liminality turn; 'threshold studies' and 'liminality studies' have come into being as academic fields in their own right (Aguirre et al., 2000; Benito and Manzanas, 2006; Kay et al., 2007; Viljoen and van der Merwe, 2007; Lund, 2012; Nuselovici et al., 2014; Jørgensen, 2019).

The cultural turn and the border turn have brought border studies and border theory or border poetics into dialogue in a time when we see the multiplication of cultural production – novels, films, music, artworks, border wall art – focusing on borders. One result of this has been the development of a field of 'border aesthetics' (dell'Agnese and Amilhat Szary, 2015; Schimanski, 2015; Schimanski and Wolfe, 2017a; Mazzara, 2019; Ganivet, 2019; for a glossary, see Schimanski and Wolfe, 2017b), often closely connected with thinking around the borderscape concept, in/visibility and Rancière's beforementioned *partage du sensible*. As the EU politician Guy Verhofstadt said in 2017 concerning Brexit and the question of the Irish border, with reference to the art of René Magritte, '[a] border is visible otherwise it isn't a border' (Rankin and Asthana, 2017); borders have material components (Demetriou and Dimova, 2018; Green, 2018), and Svend Erik Larsen (2007: 97) has argued that every boundary must have an aesthetic component. Questions about how borders make themselves tangible through aesthetic forms have been connected with the investigation of the in/visibility of border-crossers, in particular migrants. While aesthetic culture is traditionally identified with the imaginary, aesthetic forms always imply material components (even when these forms seem to belong to the virtuality of cyberspace, as Holger Pötzch underlines in his contribution to this volume, Chapter 3). Debra Castillo's concept of the 'border umbilical object' (Castillo, 2007) points specifically to the way in which migrants use cultural objects to make imaginary connections across borders. Aesthetic objects belong to a number of 'material flows', including remittances, food and goods, between migrants and their places of origin (Bon, 2017). A number of central figurations of the border bring questions of aesthetics to the fore, e.g., border trauma, border spectacle, border landscape, border walls and border surveillance. The aesthetic practices connected to these figurations can be highly mobile (as in the case of border novels), or fixed in place (as in the case of site-specific border art, Amilhat Szary, 2012), but they always, like borders themselves, have a material base.

Image and narrative

We argue that border aesthetics must engage with the three questions we pose above, on the difference between aesthetic strategies, the way in which they connect private experience to the public sphere, and their paradoxical ambiguities. Some answers to these questions will be found in the rest of the book; in this introduction we wish only to prepare the grounds for the overarching tension or potential for combination represented by two dominant aesthetic strategies where borders are concerned: image and narrative.

Image and narrative have existed in an uneasy relationship in European culture since the introduction of one of the major text-based religions, Christianity. The focus on the Bible as a written book has created a certain scepticism to images and privileging of narrative, resulting in iconoclastic debates and recurring 'iconophobia'. A key text in the aesthetic tradition, Gottfried Ephraim Lessing's *Laokoön oder Über die Grenzen der Malerei und Poesie* ('Laocoon, or On the Borders of Painting and Poetry', 1874 [1767]), attempts a truce by saying each to its own. A literal translation of Lessing's alternative title might be 'On the Borders [or Limits] of Painting and Poetry', and, as the prominent iconologist W.T.J. Mitchell reminds us, Lessing explicitly compares the difference between art and poetry to a territorial border (2015: 173). By essentialising painting as 'figures and colours in space' and poetry (primarily the narrative epic) as 'sounds in time' (1874: 149), Lessing sets the stage for a form of normative thinking in which the image is defined as spatial and narrative is defined as temporal, and where each should avoid focusing on the other's main dimension. In spite of this attempt to police a border between image and narrative, forms combining the two physically (illustrated stories, cinema, comics, phototextual novels, magazines, newspapers and so on) have continued to proliferate after Lessing's time, and major narrative genres such as the novel clearly allow for the insertion of descriptions and verbal images (including metaphors and ekphrases) in their narratives. One can indeed argue, as the fictional character Daniel Gluck does in Ali Smith's recent border novel *Autumn*, that images and narratives are always hybrid forms, containing each other: 'One. Every picture tells a story. Two. Every story tells a picture' (Smith, 2016: 72).

The term 'narrative' is sometimes used fairly loosely, especially in mass media and political contexts, where it could almost mean the same as 'image'. In other contexts it is too narrowly reduced to the idea of the minimal narrative based around a temporal ordering: a character experiences some kind of transformation dividing an earlier from a later situation. In his book *Basic Elements of Narrative* (2009), the post-classical narratologist

David Herman shows the richness of the concept of narrative, identifying its four basic characteristics: embedding in 'a specific discourse context or occasion for telling', presentation of 'a structured time-course of particularized events', focus on 'some sort of disruption [...] into a storyworld' and the conveying of 'the *experience* of living through this storyworld in flux' (xvi; emphasis original). For Herman, these elements are found not only in fictional or literary narratives, but also in more private and ethnographic narratives. They have several aspects that might bring borders into play, not least the idea of crossing borders as a form of disruption in a life-narrative, but their main contribution to border aesthetics is that they each contain a multiplicity of nuanced possibilities for revealing and hiding dimensions of private experience in a complex way.

Herman also touches upon an important distinction when dealing with narratives. Whilst arguing that narratives are more narrative-like when they are particular than when they are general, he touches upon a difference between, first, actual concrete acts of narration in the form of story-telling, documentary accounts or literary fictions, and, second, the underlying and sometimes not directly expressed master narratives that make up dominant collective discourse and contribute to hegemony, spectacle, doxa and ideology. Indeed, the particularity of 'actual' narratives is that they often offer what he calls a 'counternarrative' (Herman, 2009: 57, 187). By extension, images are also subject to the same distinction, encapsulated in two common but slightly different meanings of the word, one orientated towards concrete pictures, and the other towards general perceptions. Mitchell has called this the 'image/picture' distinction (2015: 16–18). One attempt to address images in literature, imagology, has for the most part focused not on visual images but on the composite perceptions of national characters and other imaginings of others and selves (Leerssen, 2016).

As suggested before, the image has had to struggle with negative associations with superficial surfaces, the decadence of the art market and mass media spectacle. This would be to deny the image its potential for narrative and complexity, and to pretend also that its competitor narrative cannot also be simplistic and superficial. Border images can indeed convey simplistic, spectacular images, but they can also provide (much like counter-narratives) 'counter-images' to dominant perceptions, and mobilise different perspectives, focuses and rhetorical figures (such as visual metaphor and metonymy) in order to create either empathy or othering (Šarić, 2019). The frames of images and their surfaces can also provide us with concrete approaches to connecting images to borders, as can the association of drawing with borders: Mitchell reminds us that borders are 'drawn' and 'erased', and indeed that they are images, often with a graphic element (2015: xi, 167).

Parts and chapters of this book

The chapters in this collection engage with the critical concerns addressed so far. In the different case studies, the contributors follow an interdisciplinary methodology that understands both social and cultural phenomena as part of the borderscape, as performatives (Butler, 1990) that are involved in acts of bordering, rather than merely reflecting them. In this sense the narratives and images – the various languages and forms of representation used to tell the story of the borderscape – are part of the aesthetics of the borderscape and its political phenomena ranging from migration and mobility to sense of place and cross-border co-operation. This general method of approaching the border has been operationalised in various ways by the contributors, who rely on ethnographic, textual and visual methods, and also seek to develop novel ways of analysing digital and visual borders and borderscapes. Their ideas renew our current thinking on issues of territoriality and spectacularisation, reveal a need to negotiate perceptions of borders as binary constructs, underline acts of resistance to both political and representational hegemonies, and emphasise the idea that borders travel with border-crossers through extended borderscapes. Ranging from literary fiction and memoirs to interviews, installations, documentaries and border culture from various parts of the world, the multifaceted materials explored show that the border is actually a 'kaleidoscopic looking glass' (Brambilla, 2014: 221) rather than a binary, enabling multiple border constellations.

The volume is divided into three parts. Part I develops theoretical and conceptual frameworks for thinking the border, whilst Parts II and III focus, respectively, on issues linked with living in the proximity of the border, and experiences of migration and border-crossing.

Part I: The border (forms)

The first part of the volume focuses on developing the theory of the border by examining the theoretical and philosophical underpinnings of the concept of border and its representation.

In Chapter 1, Wolfgang Müller-Funk presents a novel interpretation of the concept of liminality on the basis of the work of Georg Simmel, one of the discursive founders in this field, and in doing so challenges the view that borders are always somehow negative phenomena. The chapter provides new perspectives on the ontology and anthropology of the border, showing that life at the border always involves a need to negotiate between the territorial, cultural and linguistic demands of the different spaces, revealing the instability and ambivalence of liminality. The chapter provides an in-depth investigation of various border figurations associated with limits and thresholds – often marked symbolically as bridges, staircases, windows and doors – which are part of an aesthetics of the border and also function to connect two aspects of cultures that are central for the dynamic of cultural processes. A concluding analysis of the film *Babel* (2006), by the Mexican director Alejandro González Iñárritu, shows the potential of the theoretical frame for the study of border narratives and images. Müller-Funk suggests that the multilocational and multicultural encounters of the film set in locations ranging from Japan to the United States and Mexico testify to global cultural entanglements and embedding of border-crossings in globalisation, countered by the closed space of the tourist bus accommodating the motley crew of international tourists in Morocco. A border figure that offers an alternative, utopian version of hypermodern globalisation and reconstructs the notion of bordering is that of the membrane, capable of being both a barrier and an entrance.

In the second chapter, Patricia García examines the aesthetics of the border by examining spatial border figures in situations where the sense of borders as constructs that articulate spatial frames and generate an impression of realism fails to provide this function. Focusing on a set of twentieth-century fantastic narratives by Spanish, French and British writers that mediate between realities and imaginaries in their treatment of borders, García examines their discourse of boundaries at three levels: ontologically, narratologically and thematically. What is of particular interest is the function of two specific tropes that transgress the 'realistic' system of boundaries, operating according to the physics and logics of our extratextual world: horizontal vertigo – a loss of the border that puts an end to a physical space – and spatial psychasthenia – a fusion of the body with space. Following Mieke Bal's (2002) concept-based methodology, the analysis traces the itinerary of these border tropes across disciplines, from human geography and urban studies to literary and film studies. Through analyses of fantastic texts by J.G. Ballard, Rosa Chacel and the TV episode 'El asfalto' based on a short story by Carlos Buiza, García shows the relevance of the fantastic for understanding of these border figures as well as border narratives and the configuration of human spatiality more generally.

Part II: Living with the border (zones)

The second part of the volume presents four case studies that address socio-cultural responses to the dilemma of living with the border, both on the global level and within specific borderlands. What unites the contributions is a focus on the ways in which the different forms and discourses cross borders and enter the public sphere. Through studies discussing topics such as data clouds and their capability of transgressing conventional border zones and their territoriality, spectacularisation and agency in Mediterranean borderscapes, border trauma in narratives of the Finnish–Russian border, and discursive and lived representations of and responses to China's borderlands policy with its South-East Asian neighbours, the part opens up new ways of addressing borders and borderscapes in different social, historical and cultural contexts.

In Chapter 3, Holger Pötzsch examines the problem of territoriality and borders in the digital age through an investigation of the geographies of data clouds, as well as their artistic representation by the US artist and activist Trevor Paglen. Starting from the ambiguity of the idea of capturing clouds, raised in the title of the chapter, Pötzsch investigates the materiality of digital networks and shows how notions of borders and agency change in an era of increasingly ubiquitous cloud computing. What and how do data clouds capture? Are these clouds themselves captured both in physical infrastructure, ownership, state conduct, and through artistic responses to their inherent dynamics? Following Amoore's (2018) distinction between two different geographies of data clouds, the chapter asks where the capturing clouds behind US National Security Agency (NSA) bulk surveillance materialise, and whether they fundamentally challenge spatial notions of state sovereignty and borders. Is there space for resistance? In an analysis of Paglen's artworks visualising the material underbelly of NSA surveillance, Pötzsch shows how he reconnects the apparently fluid and ephemeral nature of digital technology and surveillance with its often classified physical and institutional basis. In doing so, Paglen combines forensic expertise with an awareness of both pedagogical and performative effects of cultural expressions, both conveying knowledge and enabling concrete acts of resistance.

In her contribution, Chiara Brambilla examines the spectacularisation of Mediterranean borderscapes evident in the dramatic staging of refugee crises and migrant deaths in the Mediterranean, but also in the discursive framing of terrorism, migration pressures and religious conflict. According to Brambilla, the border spectacle is predisposed through various culturally and technologically mediated forms of in/visibility that frame processes of in/exclusion, legitimising particular instances of b/ordering and the border regimes that these b/orderings engender. Spectacularisation is a part of a 'politics of in/visibility' (cf. Arendt, 1958) that frames political subjects as either relevant or negligible through processes of making in/visible at the shifting threshold between what is worthy of being seen and what is not, which is evidenced in the limited agency and public visibility of migrants and refugees, as well as of civil society, groups and individuals inhabiting Mediterranean borderscapes. On the basis of collaborative ethnographic research with young people in the Italian/Tunisian borderland, the chapter shows the benefit of mixed collaborative visual methods as means to outline possible 'tactics' for negotiating regimes of in/visibility in an attempt to restore public visibility to young people. Reimagining this borderscape around young people's border imaginations and experiences favours new forms of political participation and subjectivity that call for a more nuanced analysis of the working of border regimes, as well as for the inclusion of the plurality of agencies at work in the ordinary complexity of border sites and the multiplicity of their border narratives, images and practices. In this way, Mediterranean borderscapes emerge as a space of political becoming where new forms of performative political participation can be developed.

In Chapter 5, Tuulikki Kurki addresses in/visibility in the context of border-related trauma narratives through a discussion of the representation and reception of border crossers' traumas in literature dealing with Finnish–Russian national borderlands in the twentieth and twenty-first centuries, by writers including Boris Cederholm, Kirsti Huurre, Arvi Perttu (Finland), Nikolai Jaakkola and Antti Timonen (Soviet Union). The chapter reveals how historical and political discourses related to border-crossers and their experiences have influenced discourses on migrants and their traumatic experiences up to the current day. The public reception of the earlier narratives tended to evaluate them according to their truth-value and documentary value, ignoring their affective and emotional aspects of the narratives, i.e., their role as trauma literature. In Finland, the reception denied the traumas of border-crossers because their trauma narratives, memoirs and life-stories were neither 'ours' nor those of 'the other'; they were not part of the nation's narrative. Similarly, on the Soviet side of the border, critics condemned biographical works attempting to discuss trauma and argued that fiction is supposed to narrate only ideologically correct, heroic deeds. During the post-Soviet era, trauma narratives by the border-crossers have applied elements of fictional genres, such as Russian postmodernism and grotesque, and become increasingly intertextual and layered. Affect, personal experiences and inner reflections play central roles, suggesting that aesthetic strategies, rather than merely documentary ones, now play an important role in mediating and narrating the trauma of the border. Kurki shows how the marginalised experience of the border trauma has gradually gained visibility, transforming public perception of the past.

In Chapter 6, Victor Konrad and Zhiding Hu focus on China's encounters and negotiations across its borders with Myanmar, Laos and Vietnam, where cross-border interaction and enhanced mobility play an increasingly more important role. The chapter shows how narratives and imaginaries of border-crossings and processes contribute to border negotiation in the public sphere, and, particularly, how these aesthetic forms deliver a range of top-down and bottom-up discourses between national interests and a richly intertwined tapestry of minorities in the region. In so doing, it places particular emphasis on how form, medium and genre contribute to the understanding of borders and borderscapes in the South-East Asian context in particular and in globalisation more generally. On the basis of field research in the localities of Ruili, Kokang and Dalou/Mongla along the China–Myanmar border, the China–Laos border at Mohan/Boten and the China–Myanmar border at Hekou, the chapter shows how images and narratives of borders and borderlands may function differently at different levels of discourse in the public sphere, but also that border space allows these diverse discourses to co-exist, particularly if border spaces accommodate plural cultural memories. Also, in most of the research sites, it is evident that making visible and giving voice through border images and narratives is a strong act of empowerment for minority constituencies, and are allowed as long as the local images and narratives do not eclipse national discourse. The process of 'borderation', the authors suggest, lets the border function as a catalyst for mediating and merging of various border narratives as well as negotiations in the borderlands.

Part III: Crossing the border (migrations)

Part III shifts the focus to contemporary migration and border-crossings by exploring topics such as visual and performative crossings in the arts, post-colonial identity negations in black British culture, narrative representation of the 'Jungle' refugee camp in Calais, France, imagological aspects of migrant representations to journeying to Norway and the act of witnessing in the context of migrant deaths in the Mediterranean. The contributions address both visuality and textuality, as well as their simultaneous presence in cultural texts. In this section, particular attention is paid to issues of aesthetic form and its role in approaching the borderscape. Several chapters suggest that border texts are not characterised merely by their topicality: the use of particular aesthetic strategies that problematise established ways of representing the border generates works whose aesthetics are also political. In this sense, the changing aesthetics of the border can be compared with Michael Rothberg's (2006) critique of the dominance of the realist mode in representing the Holocaust: trauma may be represented in ways that go beyond the documentary. Similarly, border narratives and images, as the contributors note, do not have to be realist but may rely on postmodernist and non-representational conventions and in so doing are involved in 'doing politics' (Rancière, 2011: 8).

In the chapter opening this part of the volume, Anne-Laure Amilhat Szary addresses the recent proliferation of border-related visual art and the problem of resisting political power in particular. For Amilhat Szary, border art is a medium that is both aesthetic and political, addressing borderscapes and bordering processes through images. It can also make visible and even subvert experiences and expectations related to the border. She reviews critically several instances of border art from Europe to the United States and Canada, showing that in contemporary border art borders are a topos, that is, the anchor point of a multi-sited message. In so doing, it also highlights the links between the different aesthetic productions at the borders at the global level. Amilhat Szary argues that, if we understand border art as a form of 'alternative spatiality' offering potential for subversion and critique, new reflection on the relationship between aesthetics and politics is necessary. She focuses on works that critique the medium and are non-representational as powerful means with which promote non-consensual understandings of borders in the visual arts.

In Chapter 8, Stephen F. Wolfe shows how migrant writers from 1950 to 2013 have addressed the experience of border-crossing into the city of London, their collective experience of migrancy within that city and their 'burden of representation' of themselves within the current boundaries of the European Union. He examines border-crossing narratives and representations of migrant crossings and how they have expressed feelings of displacement created from their imaginative geographies of space and place in the home land, the host land and the context of contemporary public history. He also shows how migrant writers use aesthetic strategies peculiar to border narratives, such as the trope of the threshold and other border figures such as passages. The first section addresses the border-crossing narrative as a cultural expression for a community of 'black writers and artists' such as George Lamming, Sam Selvon, Caryl Phillips and Hanif Kureishi in Britain in the period ranging from the 1950s to the 1980s. Wolfe focuses on their border-crossings via passages aboard ship, or at entry points, as well as in private settings in which migrants lived, or within the working communities in London. In his second section he examines the aesthetic representation of 'the British Isles' and how the physical coastline has come to be policed by a 'Border Force' that moves borders to crossing points at ports and airports and into the urban spaces of the major cities, causing a shift that emerged as a response to the migrant crisis of 2013. Here he analyses the play *Routes* (2013) by the British playwright Rachel De-lahay and its exploration of migration, borders and power. The final section revisits the idea of the threshold to explore the migrant's border-crossing into Europe, across the Mediterranean, and argues for a need to create a 'politics of presence' (De Genova, 2010) where their visibility and voice are accepted in the public sphere.

In the following chapter Jopi Nyman examines the representation of forced migrants at the borders of Europe in the recent short story collection

Breach (2016), by the Nigerian German writer Olumide Popoola and the Southern African author Annie Holmes. Focusing on fictional narratives telling of forced migrants travelling towards and inhabiting the originally temporary and notorious refugee camp known as the 'Jungle' on the outskirts of Calais, France, home to ten thousand people at the time of its closing and known for its poor conditions, the collection addresses diverse aspects related to migration to Europe and Britain. The stories emphasise how the refugee camp in Calais is linked with contemporary global mobility towards Europe and Britain in particular. The space imagined is a borderscape where identities are formed and negotiated in conditions that offer moments of both 'belonging' and 'becoming', following Brambilla's (2015) definition of the concept. In addition to addressing the thematic of borders and border-crossings, the chapter contributes to border aesthetics by suggesting that the form of the collection, the short story composite, is a way of narrating the borderscape. It both unites the stories, functioning as the site where the cultural encounters between migrants and hosts take place, but also underlining the characters' diverse affiliations and transforming identities – their belongings and becomings – unique to each story and individual. By challenging acts of bordering and refusing to fix the identities of the subjects narrated, *Breach* voices the transnationalism of the experience of forced mobility as a sign of resistance. While the borderscape as a setting uniting the collection is full of ambiguity and precariousness, it is through mobility that the migrants of the collection may gain glimpses of a better future and become members of communities providing safety and hope, as well as opportunities for visibility and voice.

In Chapter 10, Johan Schimanski brings together the concerns of border aesthetics and 'post-national' imagology. Setting out to map images of Northernness in contemporary migrant literature that features viewpoints originating from the global 'South', he discusses the border processes implied by stereotypical images of the other and of the self. He addresses a number of fictional or autobiographical public narratives written in Norwegian by migrants arriving in Norway as children or young adults, including testimonial narratives by the child refugee Amal Aden and 'illegal' migrant Maria Amelie, along with semi-autobiographical novels by Romeo Gill and Sara Azmeh Rasmussen. Migrant narratives negotiate discourses of arcticity, winterliness, nordicity and so on, known from imagological research on Northernness (Chartier, 2007). The chapter asks to what degree various topoi of Northernness contribute to the bordering processes in the texts, or whether these narratives produce new images of Northernness and new vocabularies for addressing the border-crossing. Schimanski suggests that the narratives deploy chiastic switchings between North and South, circling disorientations, entropic whiteouts, and liberating and destructive verticalities in order to figure the border in new ways at different points of their physical and symbolic journeys. The ambivalence of these images, Schimanski suggests, shows that they are not related merely to borders but also to the epistemological borders negotiated.

In the final chapter of Part III, Karina Horsti and Ilaria Tucci address problems related to the study of the much-publicised disaster that occurred in the proximity of the island of Lampedusa, Italy, in October 2013, leading to the death of hundreds of mainly Eritrean migrants at sea. The chapter has both methodological and empirical aims: in addition to discussing responses to the disasters, it also seeks to counteract established ways of reporting such disasters where fatality metrics and distantiation are dominant modes of representation. In contrast, Horsti and Tucci argue for more ethical and reciprocal approaches in research, placing emphasis on narrative testimonies by those who have witnessed the incident at first hand. The chapter reports on the formation of embodied knowledge that would foreground the human aspects of the disaster, in a process in which Horsti and Tucci worked together with survivors and witnesses. In this process, they saw acts of telling and listening as suitable ways for achieving such knowledge because of the more balanced and horizontal relationships created between researchers and their interviewees. Two testimonies – 'performances of a story' – by an Eritrean survivor and an Italian rescuer were presented as parts of memory workshops and provide individual responses to the event by first-hand witnesses. In so doing, they show the role that narratives and images – since their project also involved documentary films – have in transforming the borderscape and despectacularising migration and the disaster in particular. More significantly, however, the chapter strengthens our understanding of border representations in the public sphere. Rather than giving voice to the migrant, Horsti and Tucci underline the act of listening to their story. Trust and commitment, they claim, are central for achieving such effects.

The volume closes with an Epilogue – 'Border images and narratives: paradoxes, spheres, aesthetics' – where the editors examine how the individual contributions to this volume answer our three basic questions about different aesthetic strategies, how they enable crossings from private experience into the public sphere, and the various paradoxes they involve. The ways in which contributors answer these questions help us connect the different chapters with each other. Here the editors also suggest possible ways forward for future research, or themes that need a closer focus. They argue that, besides the need to broaden the focus to other forms of aesthetic experience than those prototypically characterised as 'images' and 'narratives', we have to examine in more detail how border images and narratives act in the world, focus on the temporalities of such images and narratives, and also explore their emotional dimensions.

References

Aguirre, M., R. Quance and P. Sutton (eds) (2000) *Margins and Thresholds: An Enquiry into the Concept of Liminality in Text Studies*. Madrid: The Gateway.

Amilhat Szary, A.-L. (2012) 'Walls and border art: The politics of art display', *Journal of Borderlands Studies*, 27(2): 213–28.

Amilhat Szary, A.-L., J. Cristofol and C. Parizot (2016) 'Introduction: Science-art explorations at the border', *antiAtlas Journal*, 1: 1–9.

Amoore, L. (2018) 'Cloud geographies: Computing, data, sovereignty', *Progress in Human Geography*, 42(1): 4–24.

Anzaldúa, G. (1987) *Borderlands / La Frontera: The New Mestiza*. San Francisco: Aunt Lute Books.

Arendt, H. (1958) *The Human Condition*. Chicago: The University of Chicago Press.

Arteaga, A. (ed.) (1994) *An Other Tongue: Nation and Ethnicity in the Linguistic Borderlands*. Durham, NC: Duke University Press.

Bal, M. (2002) *Travelling Concepts in the Humanities: A Rough Guide*. Toronto: University of Toronto Press.

Benito, J., and A.M. Manzanas (eds) (2006) *The Dynamics of the Threshold: Essays on Liminal Negotiations*. Madrid: Gateway Press.

Bon, N.G. (2017) 'Silenced border crossings and gendered material flows in southern Albania', in H. Donnan, M. Hurd and C. Leutloff-Grandits (eds), *Migrating Borders and Moving Times: Temporality and the Crossing of Borders in Europe*. Manchester: Manchester University Press, pp. 140–56.

Borren, M. (2008) 'Towards an Arendtian politics of in/visibility: On stateless refugees and undocumented aliens', *Ethical Perspectives: Journal of the European Ethics Network*, 15(2): 213–37.

Brambilla, C. (2014) 'Shifting Italy/Libya borderscapes at the interface of EU/Africa borderland: A "genealogical" outlook from the colonial era to post-colonial scenarios', *ACME: An International E-Journal for Critical Geographies*, 13(2): 220–45.

Brambilla, C. (2015) 'Exploring the critical potential of the borderscapes concept', *Geopolitics*, 20(1): 14–34.

Brambilla, C., and H. Pötzsch (2017) 'In/visibility', in J. Schimanski and S.F. Wolfe (eds), *Border Aesthetics: Concepts and Intersections*. New York: Berghahn, pp. 68–89.

Brambilla, C., J. Laine, J.W. Scott and G. Bocchi (eds) (2015) *Borderscaping: Imaginations and Practices of Border Making*. Farnham: Ashgate.

Brunet-Jailly, E. 'Theorizing borders: An interdisciplinary perspective', *Geopolitics*, 10(4): 633–49.

Bueno Lacy, R., and H. van Houtum (2015) 'Lies, damned lies & maps: The EU's cartopolitical invention of Europe', *Journal of Contemporary European Studies*, 23(4): 477–99.

Butler, J. (1990) *Gender Trouble*. London: Routledge.

Calderón, H., and J.D. Saldívar (eds) (1991) *Criticism in the Borderlands: Studies in Chicano Literature, Culture, and Ideology*. Durham, NC: Duke University Press.

Castillo, D.A. (1999) 'Border theory and the canon', in D.L. Madsen (ed.), *Post-Colonial Literatures: Expanding the Canon*. London: Pluto Press, pp. 180–205.

Castillo, D.A. (2007) 'Borders, identities, objects', in J. Schimanski and S. Wolfe (eds), *Border Poetics De-limited*. Hanover: Wehrhahn, pp. 115–48.

Chartier, D. (2007) 'Towards a grammar of the idea of North: Nordicity, winterity', *Nordlit*, 22: 35–47.

De Genova, N. (2010) 'Migration and race in Europe: The Trans-Atlantic metastases of a post-colonial cancer', *European Journal of Social Theory*, 13(3): 405–19.

De Genova, N. (2012) 'Border, scene and obscene', in H. Donnan and T.M. Wilson (eds), *A Companion to Border Studies*. Chichester: Wiley-Blackwell, pp. 492–504.

Dell'Agnese, E., and A.-L. Amilhat Szary (2015) 'Borderscapes: From border landscapes to border aesthetics', *Geopolitics*, 20(1): 4–13.

Demetriou, O., and R. Dimova (2018) 'Introduction: Theorizing material and non-material mediations on the border', in O. Demetriou and R. Dimova (eds), *The Political Materialities of Borders: New Theoretical Directions*. Manchester: Manchester University Press, pp. 1–15.

Ganivet, E. (2019) *Border Wall Aesthetics: Artworks in Border Spaces*. Bielefeld: transcript.

Green, S. (2018) 'Lines, traces and tidemarks: Further reflections on forms of the border', in O. Demetriou and R. Dimova (eds), *The Political Materialities of Borders: New Theoretical Directions*. Manchester: Manchester University Press, pp. 68–83.

Herman, D. (2009) *Basic Elements of Narrative*. Chichester: Wiley-Blackwell.

Houtum, H. van (2013) 'The border as a moral design: "Over there lies a land, another land"', in M. Eker and H. van Houtum (eds), *Borderland*. Eindhoven: Blauwdruck, pp. 172–83.

Houtum, H. van, and R. Bueno Lacy (2019) 'The migration map trap: On the invasion arrows in the cartography of migration', *Mobilities*, 1–24.

Jørgensen, D. (2019) 'Limit and threshold: Knowledge and ethics in the making', in A. Cooper and S. Tinning (eds), *Debating and Defining Borders: Philosophical and Theoretical Perspectives*. Abingdon: Routledge, pp. 138–51.

Kay, L., Z. Kinsley, T. Phillips and A. Roughley (eds) (2007) *Mapping Liminalities: Thresholds in Cultural and Literary Texts*. Bern: Peter Lang.

Kolk, B. van der (2002) 'Trauma and memory', *Psychiatry and Clinical Neurosciences*, 52(51): S52–S64.

Krichker, D. (2019) 'Making sense of borderscapes: Space, imagination and experience', *Geopolitics*, 1–19.

Langås, U. (2015) *Traumets betydning i norsk samtidslitteratur*. Bergen: Fagbokforlaget / Landslaget for norskundervisning.

Larsen, S.E. (2007) 'Boundaries: Ontology, methods, analysis', in J. Schimanski and S. Wolfe (eds), *Border Poetics De-limited*. Hanover: Wehrhahn, pp. 97–113.

Leerssen, J. (2016) 'Imagology: On using ethnicity to make sense of the world', *Iberic@l*, 10: 13–31.

Lessing, [G.E.] (1874) *Laocoon*, trans. R. Phillimore. London: Macmillan and Co.

Lund, J. (2012) 'The threshold returns the gaze: Border aesthetics in disciplined space', in H.V. Holm, S. Lægreid and T. Skorgen (eds), *The Borders of Europe: Hegemony, Aesthetics and Border Poetics*. Aarhus: Aarhus Universitetsforlag.

Mazzara, F. (2019) *Reframing Migration: Lampedusa, Border Spectacle and Aesthetics of Subversion*. Bern: Peter Lang.

Michaelsen, S., and D.E. Johnson (eds) (1997) *Border Theory: The Limits of Cultural Politics*. Minneapolis: University of Minnesota Press.

Mitchell, W.J.T. (2015) *Image Science: Iconology, Visual Culture, and Media Aesthetics*. Chicago: The University of Chicago Press.

Newman, D. (2006a) 'Borders and bordering: Towards an interdisciplinary dialogue', *European Journal of Social Theory*, 9(2): 171–86.

Newman, D. (2006b) 'The lines that continue to separate us: Borders in our "borderless" world', *Progress in Human Geography*, 30(2): 1–19.

Nuselovici, A., M. Ponzi and F. Vighi (eds) (2014) *Between Urban Topographies and Political Spaces: Threshold Experiences*. Lanham, MD: Lexington.

Rajaram, P.K., and C. Grundy-Warr (eds) (2007) *Borderscapes: Hidden Geographies and Politics at Territory's Edge*. Minneapolis: University of Minnesota Press.

Rancière, J. (2004) *The Politics of Aesthetics: The Distribution of the Sensible*, trans. G. Rockhill. London: Continuum.

Rancière, J. (2011) 'The thinking of dissensus: Politics and aesthetics', in P. Bowman and R. Stamp (eds), *Reading Rancière*. London: Continuum, pp. 1–17.

Rankin, J., and A. Asthana (2017) 'May to make "important intervention" on Brexit, says Verhofstadt', *The Guardian* (online ed., 4 September 2017), www.theguardian.com/politics/2017/sep/04/may-to-make-important-intervention-on-brexit-verhofstadt-predicts. Accessed 27 November 2019.

Rosello, M., and S.F. Wolfe (2017) 'Introduction', in J. Schimanski and S.F. Wolfe (eds), *Border Aesthetics: Concepts and Intersections*. New York: Berghahn, pp. 1–24.

Rothberg, M. (2006) *Traumatic Realism: The Demands of Holocaust Realism*. Minneapolis: University of Minnesota Press.

Sadowski-Smith, C. (2008) *Border Fictions: Globalization, Empire, and Writing at the Boundaries of the United States*. Charlottesville: University of Virginia Press.

Saldívar, J.D. (1997) *Border Matters: Remapping American Cultural Studies*. Berkeley: University of California Press.

Saldívar-Hull, S. (2000) *Feminism on the Border: Chicana Gender Politics and Literature*. Berkeley: University of California Press.

Šarić, L. (2019) 'Visual presentation of refugees during the "refugee crisis" of 2015–2016 on the online portal of the Croatian public broadcaster', *International Journal of Communication*, 13: 991–1015.

Schimanski, J. (2006) 'Crossing and reading: Notes towards a theory and a method', *Nordlit*, 19: 41–63.

Schimanski, J. (2015) 'Border aesthetics and cultural distancing in the Norwegian–Russian borderscape', *Geopolitics*, 20(1): 35–55.

Schimanski, J. (2019) 'Migratory angels: The political aesthetics of border trauma', in K. Horsti (ed.), *The Politics of Public Memories of Forced Migration and Bordering in Europe*. Cham: Palgrave Pivot, pp. 37–52.

Schimanski, J., and S.F. Wolfe (eds) (2007) *Border Poetics De-limited*. Hanover: Wehrhahn.

Schimanski, J., and S. Wolfe (2009) 'Introduction: Cultural production and negotiation of borders', *Nordlit*, 24: 5–8.

Schimanski, J., and S.F. Wolfe (eds) (2017a) *Border Aesthetics: Concepts and Intersections*. New York: Berghahn.

Schimanski, J., and S.F. Wolfe (2017b) 'Intersections: A conclusion in the form of a glossary', in J. Schimanski and S.F. Wolfe (eds), *Border Aesthetics: Concepts and Intersections*. New York: Berghahn, pp. 147–69.

Scott, J.W. (2012) 'European politics of borders, border symbolism and cross-border cooperation', in T.M. Wilson and H. Donnan (eds), *A Companion to Border Studies*. Chichester: Wiley-Blackwell, pp. 83–99.

Simmel, G. (1997a) 'Bridge and door', trans. M.R.D. Frisby, in D. Frisby and M. Featherstone (eds), *Simmel on Culture: Selected Writings*. London: Sage, pp. 170–4.

Simmel, G. (1997b) 'The sociology of space', trans. M.R.D. Frisby, in D. Frisby and M. Featherstone (eds), *Simmel on Culture: Selected Writings*. London: Sage, pp. 137–70.

Smith, A. (2016) *Autumn*. London: Hamish Hamilton.

Strüver, A. (2005) *Stories of the 'Boring Border': The Dutch-German Borderscape in People's Minds*. Münster: Lit Verlag.

Viljoen, H., and C.N. van der Merwe (eds) (2007) *Beyond the Threshold: Explorations of Liminality in Literature*. New York: Peter Lang.

Wilson, T.M., and H. Donnan (2012) 'Borders and border studies', in H. Donnan and T.M. Wilson (eds), *A Companion to Border Studies*. Chichester: Wiley-Blackwell, pp. 1–25.

Woude, M. van der, V. Barker and J. van der Leun (2018) 'Crimmigration in Europe (Introduction)', *European Journal of Criminology*, 14(1): 3–6.

Part I

The border (forms)

1

Phenomenology of the liminal

Wolfgang Müller-Funk

Introduction

This chapter presents a modified understanding of borders and boundaries. Liminality, a term created by the anthropologist Victor Turner (1964; 1977), is seen as an umbrella term that refers to various aspects of constructing relations between individuals, as well as between groups and collectives. Liminal phenomena are not limited to visible barriers, but also include invisible constellations. Moreover, borders and boundaries are not simply spatial issues, but always entail temporary and dynamic moments, such as opening and closing. Developing a more general understanding of the liminal, the chapter reappraises some of Georg Simmel's mini-essays (1993a, 1993b, 1993c) which deal with phenomena such as the door, the window, the frame and the bridge. In this cross-disciplinary approach it becomes evident that liminal phenomena have an anthropological foundation that could be connected to Turner's and van Gennep's conceptions of *'rites de passage'* (Turner, 1970; Gennep, 1960; Ruthner, 2012: 36), although the frame of limitation is here formulated as a broader issue. The German word *Grenze* (a linguistic import from Slavic languages) includes many and various limitations – borders, boundaries, barriers, frontiers, frames, including the invisible limits in a social but also existential or cultural sense, such as a *Grenzsituation* (Jaspers, 1971: 20). There are limits to power, to understanding; there are 'boundaries' between different symbolic and linguistic entities. It was Simmel who defined *Grenze* as a relation between individuals, but also between groups or collectives (1992: 698). Boundary lines can also be seen as a compromise in a conflict between two rival elements.

As Simmel points out (1992: 699), every boundary may be understood as the spatialisation of a sociological, psychological or cultural phenomenon, generating clarity and safety by fixing it to a line in space. But this spatial and therefore visible '*Investierung*' (investment) has a problematic aspect that Simmel calls '*Erstarrung*' (solidification) – that which undermines the dynamic and temporal aspect of meeting and dividing (1992: 699). Going beyond Simmel, one could argue that certain barriers have a magic surplus. The Iron Curtain that marks the boundary between a theatre play and its audience, and which later became a metaphor for the strict border between the capitalist West and communist East, is/was such a magic liminal element. These borders bear similarities to the fetish which suggests that it is the sheer materiality that has the power of separating peoples and individuals from each other. It functions in a similar way to sexual fetishes for Freud or money for Marx (Böhme, 2006: 14, 449). What all these cultural 'investments' have in common is that human power and abilities appear and are experienced here as foreign, objective, independent and transcendent entities and powers.

Liminality and constructing boundaries are seen as central issues for the understanding of 'culture'. Creating limits is a central human activity that creates, socially and symbolically, a system of cultural structures. In contrast to traditional concepts of culture that define culture as work on nature, one can show that it is based here on the activity of creating relations. Constructing borders is one such central cultural activity on a social as well as on a symbolic level. In this respect, the analysis of borders and boundaries enriches our understanding of culture as a permanent process of opening and closing, of homogenisation and 'heterogenisation'. What we call 'third spaces' (Bhabha, 1994: 55) is a symptom of a process that characterises 'culture', which could be understood, refering to Bakhtin (1981: 84–5), as a chronotope of an instable situation, and not a fixed space. To some extent, one might say that the visible border, for example between different nation states, is only a very specific instance of something much more general.

The following section of the chapter is a rereading of short texts by Georg Simmel (1993a, 1993b, 1993c) in which he develops a new understanding of liminality (even though he does not make use of the concept) and furthermore a new understanding of culture beyond his own programmatic definitions (1993b). In the section after that I shall also refer to thinkers such as Massimo Cacciari, Bernhard Waldenfels and Zygmunt Bauman, whose understanding of liminality has similarities to that of Simmel. In the fourth and fifth sections I shall depict a poetry (I use this term to make it clear that not all poetic elements are automatically poetic in a narrow sense) of the space beyond, presenting examples from literature and the arts.

The sixth section is a short analysis of Alejandro González Iñárritu's film *Babel* (2006). This may be understood as an application of the theoretical work presented in the first part of this text, but at the same time it provides new insights into the border poetics embedded in the wide frame of liminality. The chapter will end with some conclusions about the film *Babel*.

Three Simmel theorems

The term 'border-crossing' might suggest that transgression is something which runs counter to the logic of demarcation and in opposition to it. In its logic, however, transgression is always included in demarcation. This brings me to the consideration of the phenomenology of very different manifestations, along with the manifestations of boundaries: two methodological premises that could be useful as a key to understanding my presentation. Although Simmel never used the term 'liminality', I refer to him as a discourse founder of a concept of borders and boundaries who deals with various liminal elements such as the door and the bridge, the window and the frame.

What I would call the first Simmel theorem is the argument that borders of any kind always carry both elements within themselves, namely separation and joining, opening and closing (Simmel, 1993c: 55, 60–1). As is the case in remembering and forgetting, the respective conceptual pairs are not binary oppositions but poles of a dynamic process. One could even imagine an understanding of the macro phenomenon 'culture', in which the opposing tendencies of borders to present themselves as obstacles and as preconditions for the possibility of networking and interference.

Liminality is a phenomenon that can be located at different levels: at the individual level, for example. It is precisely at this level that it is obvious that the one-sided negative connotation of the word 'border' is misleading. Social communication works in successful everyday life when certain limits are respected and recognised in the game of proximity and distance. Intimacy and privacy are possible only if certain protection mechanisms work. In this respect, border violation is as ambivalent as the border itself. In art, for example, it opens the perspective to something new that has been possibly tabooed by an aesthetic rule, but it also contains, in an extreme case, the moment of violence: every kind of human rights violation can be described as a border crossing, as an attack on the body and soul.

Even in social groups such as minorities this kind of liminal phenomenon is at work, ensuring the physical and symbolic integrity of groups within a never homogeneous culture. Similarly – as a keyword in international law – the liminal can also be found in the handling of various national or transnational macrostructures. The first Simmel theorem can also be formulated as follows: from an anthropological point of view, borders are inevitable, and every crossing, positive or negative, always presupposes the phenomenon of the border. Furthermore, different systems of rule including, presumably, an economic one, adhere to various forms of logic in or of space and borders.

While empires and colonial powers, as well as the capitalist economy, tend to cross borders and transitions, nationalist and homogenising regimes claim to postulate natural boundaries which go hand in hand with the concept of the constant and essentialist nature of the nation and the idea of natural borders.

The second Simmel theorem follows on from the first and conveys that the causes of *liminality* are not visible devices or natural obstacles, such as mountains, rivers, lakes or valleys; liminality is rather caused by invisible anthropological constellations, which Simmel describes as connecting and separating, as opening and closing (1993c: 55–6, 58). The implication is that culture is understood as a dynamic and non-closable process, in which boundaries and the ways of dealing with them change, without ever completely disappearing. What we understand as boundaries make liminality visible, but they are not its cause.

The third Simmel theorem (which is taken from his short essay on the framing of paintings) states that framing is not something peripheral (1993a). Culture needs such frameworks to function as a social and symbolic-cultural procedure. Like the boundary that reverses the space, it is the periphery which constitutes the centre and not, as commonly assumed, the other way around. Such a conception of boundary and space can be very well combined with post-colonial and post-imperial approaches, in which a clear shift of focalisation and perspective has taken place from the centre to the periphery.

Liminality and space

> The new world different from the old with new jewels to be consumed, new frontiers to be won, and much more love to be given.
> Eric Burdon, *Winds of Change* album cover (1967)

There is a certain central discourse about borders, frontiers and all sorts of liminal phenomena that is older than the current discourse on globalisation and post-colonialism. It appears to date back to the very beginnings of classical modernism and suggests the idea or, rather, the promise of overcoming all sorts of limitations and restrictions. Friedrich Schlegel's famous 116th Athenaeum fragment points to this narrative behind modernism and avant-garde movements: the Utopia of delimitation and the unification of the heterogeneous (1972: 37). In this specific cultural and philosophical context, freedom and delimitation become synonyms. This may be seen as the core of the eroticism of modern aesthetics.

The postmodern virtual space constructed by the new digital media seems to be the material fulfilment of this desire. The promise of ubiquity, of living in a space as infinite and boundless as the ocean, is attractive. It goes hand in hand with the fantasy of an unlimited subjectivity. This dream is based on the phantasma of being able to be everywhere – like God. The heroes of the old myths, but also those in modern movies, can be characterised by the fact that they overcome borders, disregarding barriers and ignoring dividing rules.

At first glance, borders, barriers and limitations are suspicious, especially from a liberal political perspective. But how could a world exist in which the territorial, social or symbolic space is, to borrow from Deleuze and Guattari (1987), uncut and plain? Is it possible to have a world which is only a rhizome; a netting without any centrings; intersections, limits and margins in which all and nothing is the limit?

Borders are space dividers, dividing rules and frames in at least three dimensions: space, time and symbolism. A house is an artefact that not only protects you from wind and weather but also gives you a feeling of security, and moreover a certain kind of identity. If it has no openings, as the house in Erich Kästner's children's book *Die Schildbürger* (1976), it becomes from the inside a prison and from the outside a space one cannot enter. The quality of living and dwelling in it is real, as in a metaphorical sense it is always connected with limitation and accessibility. As the Italian philosopher Massimo Cacciari has pointed out, borders are never only *limes* (Latin: 'boundary'), borders, fences or walls: rather, at the same time, they are also spaces between contact zones (2002: 73–84). This brings me to the following conclusion: that the disappearance of borders makes contact impossible. Moreover, the dream of boundlessness proves ultimately to be totalitarian.

Human space is always constructed by limitation, which has a strong, double and irreducible function. It means separation and connection at once. What is important and decisive here is to bring these two functions into an artful balance. If border is only *limes*, habitability is destructed and abolished, because we are either imprisoned or locked out. If there are no borders we also lose habitability, because there is no possibility of security and no contact in any emphatic sense.

People living at territorial, linguistic and cultural borders always live life as a balancing act (for examples, see the contributions of Chiara Brambilla, Tuulikki Kurki and Victor Konrad and Zhiding Hu, Chapters 4, 5 and 6 below). They are importers and exporters from one space to the other. Because of their mobility they achieve, at least internally, what human existence is not able to achieve: to be inside and outside at the same time. Because they are located in a space in between, that which is their own and that which is strange are connected in a remarkable way. Metaphorically speaking, there are many crossers of borders in our times: migrants, diplomats, translators, importers of what is foreign and exporters of what is their own. If there is any Utopian figure in our contemporary cultural life then it is the 'hybrid', the man or woman who seems to ignore frontiers, especially metaphorically, like Peter Handke's protagonist Kobal in the novel *Die Wiederholung* (*The Repetition*), who moves with one leg in one space and the other in a second space. Looking at Kobal's new passport, the Yugoslav soldier on the border at Jesenice talks to him about his Slavic family name, which refers to a singular space and also to a person with one leg on the one side and the other leg on the other side:

> After a glance at my newly issued Austrian passport, the border guard in Jesenice spoke to me in his language. When I failed to understand, he told me in German that Kobal was a Slavic name, that the word meant the span between parted legs, a 'step', and consequently a person standing with legs outspread, so that my name would have been better suited to him, the border guard.
>
> (Handke, 1988: 3)[1]

He is in neither the first nor the second space: to quote the song by Mick Jagger and Keith Richards, he is 'Sittin' on a Fence' (1967). Whether this is really the third space is an interesting question. There are some kinds of spaces in between, nowhere lands and stairwells, but they seem to be, to use Marc Augé's terminology, *non-lieux*, non-places (1995: 75–115). The third space has a strong temporal aspect. In other words, 'hybridity' is unstable. Hybridity and the idea of a third space (Bhabha, 1994: 55, 245) are quite often linked to the hidden Utopia, converting non-places into places for living – dwelling – in a space in between.

In my view, the idea that globalisation – which is mainly an effect of economy – and modern and new media and migration will wipe out all borders and limitations is problematic. Likewise the strange, which incidentally is also the result of a cultural construction, does not disappear. It is not very probable, for example, that European countries will lose their specific profiles and differences. What becomes homogeneous is very often the surface – which is a lot, but not everything. If it is true that we need borders to cross them in order to create human space in a temporal and semiotic sense as well, then we have to expect a new drawing-up of borders.

The adventure of modern times is based on the fact not that our world is becoming borderless but that borders have become more mobile, and moreover invisible, like the wall (which is also a frameless window at the same time) in Marlen Haushofer's novel *Die Wand* (1963; *The Wall*, 2012). This proves to be a strange combination of a wall and a window. Thus, the female main figure can see the other side to which she is not able to cross

(Chovanec, 2014: 15–30). Many limitations are no longer seen as objective, evident or irrefutable. We begin to understand that we are the creators of all those spaces because we draw borders and barriers. Culture can be defined to some extent by human capability and necessity, drawing borders and developing cultural techniques and concepts to make use of them. Probably not all is probable, but it could be true that Robert Musil's *Möglichkeitssinn*, 'sense of possibility', in *Der Mann ohne Eigenschaften* (*The Man without Qualities*, 1980), which is more of a sense of the impossible than of the possible, has been converted into *Realitätssinn*, 'sense of the real' (Musil, 1980: Chapter 4). Transgressing, moving and changing borders may sometimes be dangerous but at the same time, as the text of the Eric Burdon *Winds of Change* album cover of 1967 suggests, stimulating. In contrast with fashionable fantasies of dissolving, it might be necessary to rehabilitate such phenomena as limits, thresholds and borders. One could also pose the question as to what configurations limits may take (Waldenfels, 1990: 28–40)

There is strong support from two sides, firstly from philosophy, especially from phenomenology, and secondly from Freud's psychoanalysis. In *Culture and Its Discontents*, Freud argues against Roman Rolland's idea of an oceanic feeling that is close to Friedrich Schleiermacher's and connected to the modernist idea of disintegration (Freud, 2001: 72; Freud, 2016: 51). This oceanic feeling is seen as a form of infantile borderless existence. Freud's scepticism goes hand in hand with the argument that there is a need for human beings to develop certain forms of internal barriers to create an individual identity separate from the mother and father.

Poetry and the poetics of the space beyond

Modifying the famous title of a famous book, Gaston Bachelard's *The Poetics of Space* (1969), I shall depict outlines of the poetry of a space in between, of different modes of limitations such as the threshold, the bridge, the door, the wall, the fence and the barrier. It is quite clear that they differ in their functional logic, but also in their temporal logic, that is, in the dialectical relation between opening and closing. Quite clearly a bridge places a strong emphasis on connecting separated spaces on all levels, but bridges can also be used for controlling access to the 'other' space beyond. A threshold is an in-between which is associated with danger, and therefore it is also a metaphor for a central aspect of liminality, for all rites of initiation.

Briefly speaking, and starting with the 'real' spatial aspect, one can roughly differentiate between three kinds of in-between situations. The inside–outside contrast can be related to the phenomenon of entering and initiation. The here (on this side) and the there (on the other side, beyond) may refer to transgression, and up and down fits together with the idea of overcoming on the vertical plane: it is the ladder that takes the biblical Jacob up into another, divine world (for this vertical dimension of the border, see also the contributions by Patricia García and Johan Schimanski, Chapters 2 and 10 below).

The door, the bridge and the staircase are the classical representative elements of these three situations. With reference to Waldenfels (1990: 33–5), they may be said to have something in common, an asymmetrical situation, since as a human being you are always only on one side – mainly outside, here on this side and downstairs. Waldenfels here (1990: 33–5) calls our attention to an asymmetry that is decisive for thresholds, but also for all kinds of space-marking. We can never be inside and outside at the same time. This is central to the famous scene between Oedipus and the Sphinx. He is the man standing outside and she is the female monster positioned at the threshold that separates inside from outside, man from woman. The Sphinx is also the imaginary product of the male eye. The female space behind the threshold is dark and invisible (Müller-Funk, 2014: 167–84).

This story can hardly be reversed. From the perspective of the Sphinx, she herself would disappear, including the uncanny that is part of her monstrosity. The Sphinx is the threshold of the man, Oedipus. Like all threshold keepers, be they male or female, human or animal, the Sphinx is dumb and gives no answer. In the standard story she poses just a single riddle.

In the case of Waldenfels and psychoanalysis, this famous figure could also be discussed as the figure on the threshold, as gatekeeper, in charge of policing and access to another space. From the male point of view, the code of this space of otherness has a double function. It is the space of the other sex, the female, but it is also the space of another state, of the unconscious. Thus the location of Sphinx is in between the male and the female, in the space between the conscious and the unconscious. And this kind of principal limit – *eros* and *thanatos* – is what creates metaphors and symbols (Macho, 1984). I also want to mention the idea of understanding female genitalia as a bodily space for the sexual other, the man: it contains aspects of a threshold and, from the perspective of the man, it is a strange place. Incidentally (hetero-)sexual coitus is a good example of Waldenfels's idea of the inside–outside asymmetry that is so central to all spatial phenomena. One can argue that the Greek version of the story has replaced the original Egyptian version, in which the Sphinx is male and protecting a space in which power is guaranteed and legitimated by religion.

On the one hand, limits are created and established by human existence, but on the other hand there is an irreducible moment in all these limitary phenomena. Such philosophers as Merleau-Ponty and Waldenfels, with a keen interest in the body and its phenomena, have concentrated on thinking about these paradoxical issues. The way they approach borders, thresholds and limits cautiously can be contrasted with the deconstruction and its basic figure, suggesting a transgression of binary oppositions which as such result from obvious limits. To work beyond this binary, in cultural reality as well as in thinking, has become a Sisyphean task. Dissolving frontiers has become an influential slogan in postmodern cultural life. The contemporary debate about limits, borders and frontiers is characterised by this dichotomy: either to acknowledge or to overcome limitations and limits. The threshold can be seen as that element which is in the impossible middle.

Limits seem to be timeless. In contrast to all these fixations, thresholds entail a temporal dynamic from the very beginning. Standing in front of the controlled entrance, one has the choice: you may cross over the dangerous threshold, but you also can move back because of fear. Or – and this might be the worst-case scenario – you are fixed, you are not able to move, as is the case in 'Before the law', Kafka's famous parable about the doorkeeper and the poor chap from the countryside who spends all his time waiting in front of the door. This implies absolute standstill. Maybe there is still a fourth possibility: the human being in front of a threshold can also circle the barrier. Maybe he or she becomes a writer.

The membrane: Sabine Müller-Funk

In his study on modernity and ambivalence, Zygmunt Bauman (1990) discusses the differences between the enemy and the stranger. The figure of the enemy is based on 'the master-opposition between the inside and the outside'; the stranger, however, 'rebels' against this conflict-torn collusion of friends and enemies (Bauman, 1990: 53, 55). Whereas the enemy is constructed by the logic of either/or, the stranger is seen as ambivalent. Quoting Simmel, Bauman states that '[t]he stranger represents an incongruous and hence resented "synthesis and remoteness"' (Bauman, 1990: 60).

One could argue that Bauman's enemy is – following Carl Schmitt (1991: 22, 33–7) – to some extent the immutable version of a stranger whose position is outside or on the other side (Müller-Funk, 2016: 147–9). In other words, it is the foreigner, the person beyond the (national) border. But such a comment makes it clear that there is a strong connection between all forms of otherness and liminal phenomena.

This connection becomes quite clear when Bauman, quoting Derrida (1981), interprets the stranger as a 'member of the family of *undecidables*', 'unities that [...] can no longer be included within philosophical (binary) opposition, resisting and disorganizing it, *without ever* constituting a third term, without ever leaving room for a solution in the form of speculative dialectics' (1990: 55, emphasis original). Bauman mentions three such 'members of the family of *undecidables*' in Derrida's *Dissemination* (1981): firstly the *pharmakon*, a term that can signify remedy or recipe, but also poison or drug (Bauman, 1990: 55); secondly the *hymen*, which is on the one hand 'both membrane and marriage' but also signifies 'for this reason' 'at the same time virginity'; and thirdly the *supplement*, which can be understood as an addition, but also as a replacement (55–6). All these undecidables do not follow the binary opposition of either/or but are embedded in the contrast of neither/nor. One could also say that they follow the logic of 'as/as' or 'and'. The *supplement* may be an addition and a replacement, the *hymen* a symbol of virginity but also of marriage and the *pharmakon* is medicine and poison. The stranger can be the object of fascination and of fear. It depends on the context. The border can be a *limes* (boundary) and a *limen* (threshold).

Quite evidently these three 'members of the family of *undecidables*' do not work at the same level of logic. The two meanings of *supplement* are overlapping. If the addition becomes the main part, the work is overshadowed by it. The meaning of *pharmakon* is based on the paradox that something can also mean its opposite. The *hymen* has a magic meaning in sexual intimacy and is, as Bauman (1990) points out, part of an initial rite. It is not a membrane in a strict sense, but a unique boundary that disappears after the first border-crossing. The invisible borders that are so enormously important in sexual intimacy remain. They are connected to the physical qualities of female and male bodies. As Luce Irigaray has shown (2006: 247), the female genitals are experienced – by the man as well as by the woman – as a threshold from inside to outside (birth) and from outside to inside (coitus) (see Müller-Funk, 2016: 253–65). In all these examples it is not clear what is the 'real' and what is the metaphorical boundary. A hymen is quite certainly a physical reality combined with blood, but it also refers to a dramatic psychic event, a 'reality'.

Cacciari's differentiation between *limes* and *limen* is also part of the *undecidable*. For decades, the Iron Curtain (or the Berlin Wall) worked more or less as a barrier that made it impossible to leave the territory of a state. But in 1989 it proved to be a *limen*, an invitation to a border-crossing. Today the old borders have not disappeared but they have lost their former meaning. They are part of the European structure and orientation.

Within the 'family of *undecidables*' the membrane has a specific position. It is a unique *limen/limes*, because the membrane can be absolutely permeable, although it need not be symmetric. Skin, too, has similar qualities. The membrane is the limitation in which *limes* = *limen*. In contrast to other 'undecidable' issues, the very specifics of this organic phenomenon are that the membrane is, at one and the same time, barrier and entrance. The French psychoanalyst Didier Anzieu (2019) has described human skin as a membrane that is and must be open to its environment (as an organ for breathing and touching) but which works at the same time as a boundary of the body, guaranteeing its physical cohesion.

The artist Sabine Müller-Funk uses the membrane in a metaphorical sense by using meshes. Like glass, meshes are transparent. To some extent they work in her installations as glass plus skin. You come in contact with the other. They establish a 'contact zone' (Pratt, 1991, 34; Schimanski, 2018, 101–3). The artist makes use of the concept of the membrane especially in the case of intercultural experiences. In 2011, she created the installation *Teheran-Membranen* ('Tehran Membranes', see Figure 1.1) which was the result of a visit as artist in residence to Iran, where she was confronted with an unknown 'strange' country – but it also refers to meetings with colleagues. She comments on her installation with the words: 'Through the membrane of your words I am looking at you – through the membrane of my view, I am walking into the world' (Müller-Funk, 2011).

Globalisation and new borders: *Babel* (2006)

The film *Babel* (2006), created by the Mexican film director Alejandro González Iñárritu, is interesting in two respects with regard to its narrative matrix. On the one hand, the film unfolds a narrative matrix, which is described as the butterfly effect. An action in one corner of the globe evokes other unintended, unexpected and unpredictable consequences. On the other hand, Iñárritu has already dealt with the subject of (border) narratives in two previous films: *Amores Perros* (2000) and *21 Grams* (2003). By multiplying a story using several narrative variants he thus directs our attention to the narrative construction of 'reality'. In his third film, Iñárritu has projected this process on to a global space represented by Japan, Mexico and Morocco, as well as an American middle-class apartment and a tourist bus. The multicultural group of actors – Brad Pitt, Cate Blanchett, Said Tarchani, Gael Garcia Bernal, Adriana Barraza and Rinko Kikuchi – correspond to the ambition of symbolising the entanglement of people from different local and cultural traditions in a global context.

But Iñárritu's film is also one about various liminal dimensions. I shall try to sum up the phenomena of borders in the film. They fit together with the three different geographical places in the film: Mexico and the United States; a mountain region in Morocco; and the urban space of Tokyo. At the same time, these spaces are connected by a globalising plot that transcends the traditional system of liminality: firstly, the visible border between the United States and Mexico; secondly, the visible and invisible border between

1.1 Sabine Müller-Funk, 'Teheran-Membranen' (Installation, 2011). One part of an installation consisting of four membranes (each 220 cm × 90 cm, with text made of garden soil) and video projections: a moving mouth speaking the written words and a moving eye looking.

the world of a nomadic people in Morocco and that of the Western tourists; thirdly, the border between the young people and the adults in the Japanese narrative.

The action begins with the purchase of a much-admired Winchester rifle, a wonder from another world, a violent instrument, which connects the rooms and stories like a hinge. The spectator walks with the rifle and the two brothers through the Moroccan mountains, which constitute a first symbolic space. The two brothers shoot with the gun until a road with a bus enters the frame; when a shot hits the bus the invisible camera changes. The recipient enters a second symbolic space, the world of an American tourist couple, Susan and Richard, played by Cate Blanchett and Brad Pitt.

Here, the bus is a strange space: to a certain extent it represents a specific chronotope. It forms a mobile space *sui generis*; it is a mobile and temporary Western diaspora in another, non-European culture. The bus is not only a means of transport, a transport medium, but also a social and symbolic shelter. It contains a clear liminal aspect but also two openings, real (doors) and visual (windows), which are to some extent risky with regard to safety. The purpose of a tourist trip is not primarily to make contact with another symbolic world but to remain separate from it, not to come into contact with people from the other side.

However, the actual telos of the couple's trip has nothing whatever to do with the foreign symbolic space, since it is about overcoming a marriage crisis and the family left behind, more precisely their children, who are supposed to be being cared for at home. The woman's annoyance indicates how superfluous she finds this excursion, not only because she is more eccentric than the man but because she is thoroughly distrustful of the strategy of a long-distance journey as a means of re-establishing a relationship. She shows how much she is frustrated by the hardships of this long-haul trip.

The tourist is a cultural voyeur who, through a glass pane, looks at the strange landscape and briefly descends to take in a so-called sightseeing. The bus, a space–time divider, is a separate symbolic cosmos, a safety device that prevents the encounter of cultures, and does not, at least at the beginning of the story, create a third space. Thus, the technically hypermodern bus, a kind of chronotope and a space-in-time approach to a modern and possibly futile journey, establishes a border that is as relevant to globalisation as the fortified boundaries of prosperity in the south of the United States and in the east and south of continental Europe.

The shot from a Western gun (imported from Japan) in the hands of an innocent Berber boy, who immediately sets the terrorist narrative in motion in a way that proves to be a statistically unlikely coincidence, transforms the trivial holiday into an adventure of cultural encounter, a third space of negotiation. As a result, the husband is propelled into the lead role because he has to negotiate with the bus driver, as well as with the village doctor who turns out to be a veterinarian. He also has to deal with unwilling fellow-travellers who regard the interruption of their journey as a threat to their safety and well-being, and want to sustain the logic of tourist apartheid.

It is an accident that, in a completely involuntary and tragic-ironic way, overrides the separation of cultures and the logic of symbolic separation on which modern tourism is based. At the end, the husband reaches the goal which the standard planned package trip would never have brought about: reconciliation with his wife, to whom he would never have been able to prove his love on the planned package holiday.

The involuntary adventure, the violation of the borders, provokes the power of evidence. For not only does the life-threatening – in the sense of cathartic – injury act in the sense of the Aristotelian narrative theory: rather, the man proves, through his courageous commitment and risking of dialogue with the other culture, as well as the confrontation with the fellow travellers, that for the woman he is the right man, who is helping and loving, in the right place.

There are two 'Utopian' scenes: the encounter between the American husband and the doctor and their helplessly touching attempt to get in contact with each other – across all cultural barriers – as well as the silent exchange of views between the injured wife and an old, monstrous-looking village dweller, who plays the role of the premodern miracle hero and exotic witch. At this point, a respectful encounter takes place: For a short time, the 'membrane' as a contact zone seems to function (Hanna, 2019: 96).

At first, the American lady is horrified by the ugly countenance of the woman who stands for the monstrosity of the stranger as outlined by Kristeva (1990: 208–9). But the possibility of seeing through the distortions of the stranger – the face of the other – and recognising her or him as an alter ego flashes to the point that it becomes a help and not a threat.

The film, however, is not illusory and idyllic. Iñárritu leaves no room for doubt in the post-colonial dilemma of the two symbolic spaces. The imperious tone of the husband, who commands and threatens the native man, corresponds with the circumstance in which the life of an American woman is much more worthy than that of the natives who are oppressed and humiliated by a statehood which is submissive to the culture from which the temporary migrants come.

An American television report which the audience sees in the symbolic space of Japan makes the woman and her accident a temporary citizen of the state. Telephones, televisions, helicopters and buses are just like the rifle-relevant media that connect the heterogeneous cultures of the globe in a surprising, but uneven way. With regard to liminality, they seemingly transcend traditional borders but confirm them in a second step.

The second line of action also contains a split symbolic space. It is firstly the home of Susan and Richard, the space that the couple have temporarily left to find their marital love again in romanticism. But this space contains a foreign element in the form of the Mexican nanny, working illegally in the USA. She lives symbolically in an ethnoscape in the sense of Appadurai (1996). When a relative appears to take her to a wedding in Mexico she agrees after some hesitation and takes the children of the American couple with her.

Unlike the long-distance travel of American tourists, this trip has a clear telos: home, territorial homecoming on time. In contrast with the Western tourists, however, there is no air-conditioned bus to protect the inmates from the dangers of the other culture. On the contrary, the two American children come into contact with the relatively unknown world of Mexican culture: disturbing experiences with irritating violence (chickens fighting), and sexual and ecstatic moments take place – the well-ordered American middle-class world has preserved the children until now from such aspects of life – and this is the real borderline in the film.

It is the strongly stereotyped symbolic space of Mexico, however, that forms a post-colonial counter-world to the West. Exuberance, ecstasy, physicality and direct corporeal contact with one another are those elements that mark boundaries which seem to be at least ambivalent, if not attractive, from the child's perspective. In a reversal of the first narrative, the accident – a traffic accident – occurs only at the end of the partial narrative. This has to do with the inequality of one and the same limit. It is easy to pass the boundaries from north to south, from the United States to Mexico; it can be a huge obstacle to pass the border in the other direction, especially if you do not have the right papers and two American 'white' children in the car.

For Amelia, the housekeeper, there is no happy ending in the film, for she is ultimately deported from the privileged symbolic space. The self-image of a global world without borders is undermined in this narrative segment as well. In view of a culturally multi-fragmented world, with visible and invisible boundaries, symbolic pavilions, and exclusions and inclusions, the self-image of globalisation as a cheerful colourful mixture in the style of a Benetton advertisement turns out to be a false romance that hides the power asymmetries and the structural violence of this global world.

The third narrative, in turn, is assigned to a specific symbolic space, the urban space of modern Japan. Interiors, such as a sports hall, correspond with megalomaniac architecture and the street noise of Tokyo. The fact that the main character, the Japanese girl Chieko, is deaf is understood in the sense of a secondary metaphorical meaning, a 'dense description'. This fact reads as a very critical finding of a society that lives from the contradiction of being more 'Western' and global than the Western world itself, and at the same time sustaining traditional Japanese hierarchical structures.

There is a strong aspect of strangeness in the Japanese narrative. Chieko is unable to handle social boundaries. She has no cultural techniques to balance the opposition between nearness and distance in her social environment. Chieko's father represents this world; Chieko resents him, and, whilst superficially on her first sexual adventure, in reality she is longing for love and security that she does not find. The third segment of action reports the disturbances of that globalisation in an outwardly perfectly modern metropolis, more perfect than the Western 'original'. The confinement of this sequence of actions results from the focalisation, which is mostly that of the deaf without speech girl, from whose disturbed perspective the cold glittering world of modern Japan becomes visible.

Here, too, the stereotyping can grate, but the film leaves no doubt that it is transporting images of globalisation and is not a film about real globalisation. Rather, it is a picture of Japan in a global panorama which, by contrast with Morocco and Mexico, first acquires its visual power. It is the montage technique that takes the relations between the symbolic contrasts to a further semiotic level.

It becomes evident only very late on that Chieko's rich father, a global tycoon, is the original owner of the rifle, which has reached the hands of the two Moroccan shepherds (later, at the level of the narrated time, but earlier at the level of the narrative discourse). He gave it to his guide on a big-game expedition, as a hunting weapon; it later became the dangerous plaything of the Moroccan youngsters. The death of his wife, which is clearly a cause of the life crisis of the pubertal girl, remains unsolved. Here, too, it is a globalising medium that brings the crossover context to light. The dramatic event in Morocco is reported on Japanese television and the fact that a Japanese weapon is involved comes into play.

Iñárritu's film does not expose a great narrative of globalisation: it introduces the global world as a network of small narratives obscurely intertwined. It is postmodern in that it is ambivalent. Critical aspects are inseparably mixed with Utopian moments, beauty with repulsive elements. It contains no analysis of globalisation by cinematic means: the political dimension of the global world becomes visible as a framework and the economy is manifested in the metropolis of Tokyo, as well as the global periphery in its own way in Mexico and Morocco. What the director supplies is picture material of a hypermodern world whose heterogeneous fragmentation contrasts with the homogenising tendencies of space grabbed via various media. He also lends a voice to those who, like the deaf without speech Chieko, are otherwise dumb.

It is not at all easy to say for whom this film is made and where the symbolic space of the narrative community lies. Presumably it is that space which is not symbolically edited in the film itself. It is more or less spared. But it is quite clear that it is an international audience of individuals who do not all move in the same way, and not exclusively in the spatial touristic quarantine of a bus tour through strange worlds. The film is a virtual alternative chronotope to that of the motorised vehicle, to the seemingly safe tourist bus. The journey which the director undertakes by cinematic means may be understood as a counterpart to the conventional long-distance journey of the Western tourist, even though the stereotypes presented by the film can be attributed to those images from catalogues which those tourists take, to be able to feel good again in the strange land, and as a couple. As mentioned, the film introduces these images and yet does not quite provide them, because it contains precisely what I have described as a second reflection (see Müller-Funk and Budňák, 2013), which goes hand in hand with advanced, modern and postmodern aesthetics.

Perhaps the thesis that the film does not contain a grand narrative of globalisation must ultimately be revised, or at least limited. The title comes with a mythical narrative from the Old Testament, which is effective as a matrix of today's globalisation. The Babel narrative is a narrative about the creation of dimension and difference, heterogeneity and confusion, which has played a decisive role in today's discourse on translation, from Jorge Luis Borges to George Steiner to Jacques Derrida (see Müller-Funk, 2016: 311–42). The population of the city of Babel wanted to build a tower pointing to the heavens, and because God disliked this megalomania he dispersed them by making many out of their one language. To that extent, this story is the biblical explanation of why there are so many different languages in our world. If the film title, as a peritext, brings this meaning into play as a suggestion for self-interpretation it is probably in the revisionary intention to score through the original story at a decisive point.

The film's title establishes a new level of sense, generated by the implicit relationships of the different spaces, a transition, an in-between, which sometimes opens, but is often closed. At the same time, the film, as I have said, forms a virtual space, a 'globe' – in contrast with the closed space of the tourist bus, which is a symbolic enclave on foreign territory, enclosed by glass and air-conditioning.

The only God who is at work in the film is a cinematic narrator, an organiser who, thanks to the most modern media techniques and semiotic mixtures, creates a global world that is Babylonian from the very beginning and remains so. These connections remain hidden from the individual actors, in contrast to the film viewer.

Returning to the differentiation between *limen* and *limes*, one could say that this double aspect of liminality is constructed on hypermodern globalisation in an unequal way. Whereas media suggest a principal possibility of overcoming borders at least virtually (the window), there is a renaissance of building borders with the idea of a permanent and not a temporary closure (the door). To that extent, the membrane represents a positive, maybe Utopian model of another globalisation, in which reciprocal acknowledgement is in-written.

Globalisation means, to vary Eric Burdon's statement from 1967, not the disappearing but the raising of new borders. Whether this is a win or a loss, that is the question. The membrane is a plea not for a borderless world but for a world with another use of borders, of barriers. The magic surplus of *Babel* is that it shows many different aspects of border phenomena, visible and invisible aspects of bordering and border-crossing, the importance of time and context, the instability of borders and boundaries, and the dynamic of opening and closing.

Note

1 'Der Grenzsoldat in Jesenice redete mich freilich, nach Blick in meinen frischaus-gestellten österreichischen Paß, in seiner Sprache an. Als ich nicht verstand, sagte er deutsch, Kobal sei doch ein slawischer Name, "kobal" heiße der Raum zwischen den gegrätschten Beinen, der"Schritt" und so auch ein Mensch, der mit gespreizten Beinen dastehe' (Handke, 1978: 7–8).

References

Anzieu, D. (2019) *The Skin-Ego: A New Translation by Naomi Segal*. London: Routledge.
Appadurai, A. (1996) *Modernity at Large: Cultural Dimensions of Globalisation*. Minneapolis: University of Minnesota Press.
Augé, M. (1995) *Non-Places: Introduction to an Anthropology of Supermodernity*. Trans. J. Howe. London: Verso.
Bachelard, G. (1969) *The Poetics of Space*. Trans. M. Jolas. Boston: Beacon Press.
Bakhtin, M.M. (1981) 'Forms of time and of the chronotope in the novel', in *The Dialogic Imagination: Four Essays by M.M. Bakhtin*, trans. Caryl Emerson and Michael Holquist. Austin: University of Texas Press, pp. 84–258.
Bhabha, H.K. (1994) *The Location of Culture*. London: Routledge.
Bauman, Z. (1990) *Modernity and Ambivalence*. London: Sage.
Böhme, H. (2006) *Fetischismus und Kultur: Eine andere Theorie der Kultur*. Reinbek: Rowohlt.
Burdon, E. (1967) *Winds of Change*. MGM Records.

Cacciari, M. (2002) 'Wohnen. Denken: Essays über Baukunst im Zeitalter der völligen Mobilmachung', in *Grossstadt. Baukunst. Nihilismus: Essays*. Trans. R. Kacianka. Klagenfurt: Ritter, pp. 73–84.

Chovanec, J. (2014) 'Marlen Haushofers "Die Wand" als Thirdspace', *Sprachkunst*, 44(1): 15–30.

Deleuze, G., and F. Guattari (1987) *A Thousand Plateaus: Capitalism and Schizophrenia*. Trans. B. Massumi. Minneapolis: University of Minnesota Press.

Derrida, J. (1981) *Dissemination*. Trans. B. Johnson. London: Athlone Press.

Freud, S. (2001) 'Civilization and its discontents', in J. Strachey (ed. and trans.), *Sigmund Freud: The Standard Edition of the Complete Psychological Works of Sigmund Freud*. London: Vintage, vol. XXI, pp. 57–145.

Freud, S. (2016) *Das Unbehagen in der Kultur: Herausgegeben und kommentiert von Wolfgang Müller-Funk*. Vienna: Vienna University Press.

van Gennep, A. (1960) *The Rites of Passage*. Trans. M.B. Vizedom and G.L. Caffee. London: Routledge & Kegan Paul.

González Iñárritu, A. (2000) *Amores Perros*. 153 minutes film. Mexico.

González Iñárritu, A. (2003) *21 Grams*. 124 minutes film. USA.

González Iñárritu, A. (2006) *Babel*. 142 minutes film. France / USA / Mexico.

Handke, P. (1978) *Die Wiederholung*. Frankfurt am Main: Suhrkamp.

Handke, P. (1988) *Repetition*. New York: Farrar, Straus & Giroux.

Hanna, M. (2019) 'The cinematic borderlands of Alejandro González Iñárritu's *Babel*', in M. Hanna and R.A. Sheehan (eds), *Border Cinema: Reimagining Identity through Aesthetics*. New Brunswick, NJ: Rutgers University Press, pp. 81–98.

Haushofer, M. (1963) *Die Wand: Roman*. Gütersloh: Mohn Verlag.

Haushofer, M. (2012) *The Wall*. Berkeley: Cleis Press.

Irigaray, L. (2006) 'Der Ort der Zwischenraum: Eine Lektüre von Aristoteles: Physik IV, 2–5', in J. Dünne and G. Stephan (eds), *Raumtheorie: Grundlagentexte aus Philosophie und Kulturwissenschaften*. Frankfurt am Main: Suhrkamp, pp. 46–70.

Jagger, J., and K. Richards (1967) 'Sittin' on a Fence', on The Rolling Stones, *Flowers*. ABCK.

Jaspers, K. (1971) *Einführung in die Philosophie*. München: Piper.

Kästner, E. (1976) *Die Schildbürger / The Schildburghers*. Munich: Deutscher Taschenbuch Verlag.

Kristeva, J. (1990) *Fremde sind wir uns selbst*. Frankfurt am Main: Suhrkamp.

Macho, T. (1984) *Todesmetaphern*. Frankfurt am Main: Suhrkamp.

Müller-Funk, S. (2011) 'Teheran-Membranen'. *Sabine Müller-Funk*, www.sabine.muellerfunk.com/teheran-membranen.php. Accessed 7 April 2019.

Müller-Funk, W. (2014) 'The Sphinx as a threshold figure: About the limits between the sexes', in F. Vighi, A. Nuselovici and M. Ponzi (eds), *Between Urban Topographies and Political Spaces: Threshold Experiences*. Lanham, MD: Lexington Books, pp. 167–84.

Müller-Funk, W., and J. Budňák (2013) 'Die zweite Spiegelung: Jiří Gruša als der Andere in Eduard Glodstückers Werk: Prozesse: Erfahrungen eines Mitteleuropäers/ Vzpomínky', *Brücken: Germanistisches Jahrbuch Tschechien Slowakei*, 21(1–2): 139–55.

Müller-Funk, W., in collaboration with J. Chovanec (2016) *Theorien des Fremden*. Tübingen: A. Francke.

Musil, R. (1980) *The Man without Qualities*. New York: Perigree Books.

Pratt, M.L. (1991) 'Arts of the Contact Zone', *Profession*, 91: 33–40.

Ruthner, C. (2012) 'Phantastik und/als Liminalität', in W. Amthor, A. Hille and S. Scharnowski (eds), *Wilde Lektüren: Literatur und Leidenschaft: Festschrift für Hans Richard Brittnacher*. Bielefeld: Aisthesis.

Schimanski, J. (2018) 'Grenze (Glas, Schrift, Körper)', in B. Höller, M.C. Holter and W. Müller-Funk (eds), *Bruch – Spur – Zeichen: Die Kraft der Semiose: Sabine Müller-Funk and Friends*. Vienna: Sonderzahl, pp. 101–3.

Schlegel, F. (1972) *Schriften zur Literatur*, ed. W. Rasch. Munich: Deutscher Taschenbuch Verlag.

Schmitt, C. (1991) *Der Begriff des Politischen: Mit einem Vorwort und drei Corollarien von 1963*. Hamburg: Duncker & Humblot.

Simmel, G. (1992) *Soziologie: Untersuchungen über die Formen der Vergesellschaftung*. Frankfurt am Main: Suhrkamp.

Simmel, G. (1993a) 'Der Bildrahmen: Ein ästhetischer Versuch', in R. Kramme, A. Rammstedt and O. Rammstedt (eds), *Aufsätze und Abhandlungen 1901–1908: Band I*. Frankfurt am Main: Suhrkamp, pp. 101–8.

Simmel, G. (1993b) 'Vom Wesen der Kultur', in O. Rammstedt and H.-J. Dahme (eds), *Aufsätze und Abhandlungen 1901–1908: Band II*. Frankfurt am Main: Suhrkamp, pp. 363–73.

Simmel, G. (1993c) 'Brücke und Tür', in R. Kramme, A. Rammstedt and O. Rammstedt (eds), *Aufsätze und Abhandlungen 1901–1908: Band I*. Frankfurt am Main: Suhrkamp, pp. 55–61.

Turner, V. (1964) 'Betwixt and between: the liminal period in rites de passage', in J. Helm (ed.), *Symposium on New Approaches to the Study of Religion: Proceedings of the 1964 Annual Spring Meeting of the American Ethnological Association*. Seattle: University of Washington Press, pp. 4–20.

Turner, V. (1970) 'Betwixt and between: the liminal period in *rites de passage*', in E.A. Hammel and W.S. Simmons (eds), *Man Makes Sense: A Reader in Modern Cultural Anthropology*. Boston: Little, Brown and Company, pp. 335–69.

Turner, V. (1977) 'Liminality and communitas', in *The Ritual Process: Structure and Anti-Structure*. New York: Cornell Paperbacks, pp. 94–130.

Waldenfels, B. (1990) *Der Stachel des Fremden*. Frankfurt am Main: Suhrkamp.

2

Horizontal vertigo and psychasthenia: border figures of the fantastic

Patricia García

Introduction

The boundary, border or frontier is a dominant feature of how we understand ourselves in space: self and other, here and there, belonging and not-belonging are structured and arise through the awareness and affirmation of a border that very often has a material presence and geopolitical, cultural and existential implications. In narrative worlds, boundaries are also key in constructing articulated spatial frames that generate an impression of realism. However, what happens when these boundaries fail to fulfil this articulating function? Fictions of the fantastic offer interesting aesthetic responses to this question.

The chapter starts by approaching the fantastic as a spatial form, outlining its fixation with borders. It then engages with two versions of the same spatial transgression found across several cultural texts from the second half of the twentieth century. These aesthetic phenomena, which I approach as 'border figures' following Johan Schimanski (2016), invite us to reflect on the sociopolitical and existential implications of the destabilisation of our sense of (normal, natural, logical) boundaries articulating human spatiality.

The first one, *horizontal vertigo*, portrays the absence of the border that marks the end of a physical space. I trace the itinerary of this concept across disciplines and cultural contexts, from its metaphorical use to refer to the Argentine pampas to its presence in postmodern urbanism. In the literary domain, I focus on J.G. Ballard's literary representation of this border figure as criticism of the expansion of the built environment in tourist areas. The second border figure, which I call *spatial psychasthenia*, concerns the fusion of the body with its surrounding material space. My analysis builds on Roger Caillois's explanation of this term in reference to some animal species that mimic their environment for survival, whilst I also refer to its use in urban studies designating a spatial pathology related to the absence of boundaries in the megalopolis.[1] I study this border figure in two texts: the short story 'Fueron testigos' (2008 [1952]), by the Spanish writer Rosa Chacel, and the TV episode 'El asfalto' (*Historias para no dormir*, 1966) based on a short story by Carlos Buiza; both texts were written during Franco's dictatorship and address the suppression of the individual by totalitarian regimes.

In line with Mieke Bal's concept-based methodology (2002), on the grounds that concepts travel across disciplines and that each disciplinary border-crossing adds a new dimension to these concepts, in the next sections I set out to trace how their epistemological and aesthetic discourse on borders mutates according to the different fields in which they have been employed.

The fantastic and liminality

The texts of the fantastic are constantly engaging with borders, border-crossings, border-crossers and border beings. In this section, I discuss two different forms in which the fantastic engages with border theory: first, by exploring its limits as an aesthetic form against other non-mimetic narratives and second, thematically, by identifying recurrent tropes that are related to the liminal.

The fantastic is understood in this chapter as Roger Callois has described it as 'the breach of the known order, the eruption of the inadmissible in the midst of the unalterable legality of everyday life'.[2] As a narrative form, it developed by the end of the eighteenth century within the predominant scientific positivism model of thought and as a reaction to the over-confidence in reason as the primordial explanation for the world that characterised the Enlightenment. Its evolution is marked by short stories by E.T.A. Hoffmann, Théophile Gautier, Edgar Allan Poe, Guy de Maupassant, H.P. Lovecraft, Jorge Luis Borges and Julio Cortázar, with canonical novels of the fantastic including *The Castle of Otranto* by Horace Walpole, Mary Shelley's *Frankenstein*, Bram Stoker's *Dracula* and Shirley Jackson's *The Haunting of Hill House*, to name but a representative few. In contrast to the all-inclusive North American paradigm of the fantastic as an umbrella term for any deviation from realism, with a scope that includes myths, fairy tales, magical realism and science fiction, European theorists such as Pierre-Georges Castex (1951), Roger Caillois (1965), Tzvetan Todorov (1975 [1970]), Irène Bessière (1974), Rosalba Campra (2008), Roger Bozzetto (2005) and David Roas (2018), among others, have set out to define the specific boundaries of the fantastic on the basis that not all narrative forms featuring a supernatural element are constructed in the same way.

Todorov, one of the founders of this restricted approach to the fantastic, argued already in 1970 that '[w]e cannot conceive a genre which would regroup all works in which the supernatural intervenes and which would thereby have to accommodate Homer as well as Shakespeare, Cervantes as well as Goethe. The supernatural does not characterise works closely enough, its extension is much too great' (1975: 34). As is well known, his theory is based on the premise that the fantastic is different from other modes of the supernatural: it creates a moment of hesitation on the part of the reader, a moment between the acceptance of the supernatural as possible within the fictional universe and the denial of this possibility. In this respect, the fantastic would occupy a liminal space, identified by the reader as oscillating between a realistic and a marvellous text: 'The person who experiences the event must opt for one of two possible solutions: either he is a victim of an illusion of the senses, of a product of the imagination – and laws of the world remain what they are; or else the event has indeed taken place, it is an integral part of reality – but then this reality is controlled by forces unknown to us. The fantastic occupies the duration of this uncertainty' (Todorov, 1975: 25). As later noted extensively in scholarship, the problem lies in the fact that this definition of the fantastic as a moment of suspension is of little use in understanding the functioning of the form: the fantastic would be a genre defined by its neighbouring genres. Furthermore, whilst the premise of fantastic as hesitation is applicable to a particular type of the fantastic that is based on an ambiguous denouement (Henry James's *The Turn of the Screw*, for example), it does not encompass other canonical works in which the supernatural is perceived and presented as impossible. The characters of Count Dracula and Dr Frankenstein's monster are not rationalised with a logical explanation nor do they fall within a magical universe.

Like the aforementioned post-Todorovian critics, here I understand the term 'fantastic' to refer to a specific form of the supernatural in fiction: namely, texts that present a realistic literary world that operates within the physical laws of our world and in which an impossible exception irrupts. This inevitably creates a problematic coexistence between the natural and the supernatural and, as such, the supernatural is presented and perceived as impossible by the reader and the characters of the narrative world.

Narrative passages that focus on the exceptional nature of the events that are about to be told are frequent in fantastic stories. As illustrative examples, consider the following quotations from Rosa Chacel's 'Fueron testigos' (2008 [1952]), a story discussed later in this chapter: 'the questions of those men, who couldn't not attain the full understanding of the event, were being lost without answers, like mere signs of an inefficient reality'; '[i]llogical effects, so they seemed, unpredictable from whichever external point of view they were regarded'.[3] These passages show how the discursive presentation of the supernatural differs from, for example, fantasy or the marvellous. These two other non-mimetic forms introduce the supernatural as being normalised in their narrative world. In them talking animals, ghosts, miracles or elves are extraordinary, but not impossible (Roas, 2018: 5). The fantastic, in contrast, represents an ontological and epistemological impossibility: a clash, a seizure, a fracture of our idea of the real and possible. This definition highlights one of the elements that makes the fantastic a narrative form 'preoccupied with limits' (Jackson, 2003: 48): it always implicitly refers to an ontological boundary (and thus to the effect of realism) that the impossible creature or occurrence will transgress. Accordingly, it is not surprising to find the figure of a border transgression in theorisations of the fantastic; see for example the title of one of the most recent volumes, *Behind the Frontiers of the Real: A Definition of the Fantastic* by David Roas (2018).[4]

The fantastic needs this ontological limit in order to be able to operate, in an echo of the Foucauldian idea of the interdependence between limit and transgression: 'the limit and transgression depend on each other for whatever density of being they possess: a limit could not exist if it were absolutely uncrossable and, reciprocally, transgression would be pointless if it merely crossed a limit composed of illusion and shadows' (Foucault, 1980: 34). Wolfgang Müller-Funk similarly refers to this phenomenon in Chapter 1 above: 'transgression is always included in demarcation'. As paradoxical as it may seem, realism is therefore a premise of the fantastic as it allows the latter to operate as a transgression: only by creating a realistic world that we as readers identify as being similar to our world can there be an ontological transgression by an impossible element.

This connects to a further point on the importance of borders within the fantastic: that of the importance of spatial referents in constructing the initially-required effect of realism. Philippe Hamon reminds us that narrative space plays a central role in the generation of a realistic environment in the text, in particular the architectural frames that structure the setting: 'As a rule architecture therefore conveniently guarantees a certain "realistic effect" to any given literary work, for it provides fiction with a recognizable frame, anchor, or background that creates its verisimilitude' (1992: 23). These architectural frames replicate well-known landmarks and boundaries (inside–outside) that we use as reference to structure our daily spatial experience. Often, narratives of the fantastic play with these architectural boundaries and subvert their structuring function. For example, we know that the interior of a house cannot be larger than its frame. Frequently, narratives of the supernatural invert this container–contained relationship in the 'little-big trope' (Clute and Grant, 1999: 586). This subversion is found in texts such as Jorge Luis Borges's 'The aleph' (1949), the aleph being a microcosmic point in the basement that condenses all temporalities and spatialities, and in Mark Z. Danielewski's expanding building of *House of Leaves* (2000), a house embodying a discrepancy between its external dimensions and its larger internal measurements.

The border also operates as a recurrent theme of liminality in the fantastic text. Thresholds, holes, tunnels and windows are some of the most common border figures of the fantastic that designate states of disorientation, in-betweenness, and physical and cultural transitioning and transformation. These liminal spaces often transcend their classical function of hosting characters and facilitating action and become elements *of* action, determining and influencing the narrated events.[5] Johan Schimanski rightly observes that any border-crossing is an act of existential negotiation and redefinition:

> there is often a strong potential for a border crossing to function as a marked boundary between two different states of being. In biographical terms, important divisions between life stages, or between life and non-life (at the borders constituted by birth and death) are often marked by topographical border crossings. (Schimanski, 2006: 47)

The fantastic gives voice to plenty of border-crossers who transition from dead to undead and vice versa, or from childhood into puberty, exemplified by Carrie's first menstruation in Stephen King's eponymous novel (1974) and clearly captured in its film adaptation by Brian De Palma (1976), in the symbolic opening scene in the showers of the school gym.

Fantastic border-crossings are highly ritualised. Evoking the explicit invitation a vampire needs to cross the threshold, the Swedish vampire film *Let the Right One In / Låt den rätte komma in* (dir. Tomas Alfredson, 2008) embeds this border ritual in its title. From the same writer, *Border / Gräns* (dir. Ali Abbasi, 2018) further illustrates the fruitful combination between the aesthetics of the fantastic and the themes of the border. Set on the Swedish border, the film voices concerns about the dangerous porosity of borders through the motif of contraband and illegal human trafficking. Most interestingly, it places a border creature at the centre of the story. Tina, its protagonist, is a customs officer who secretly suffers from an extraordinary chromosomic anomaly. Her animalistic traits transcend gender binarism and blur the distinction between human and beast. Her love story with one of the regular border-crossers, Vore, who also belongs to this type of 'troll race', will prompt a reconfiguration and acceptance of her own self. But this newfound identity will also displace her to the margins of society.[6]

To conclude this overview on the relation between border theory and the fantastic, it is worth emphasising that, after Todorov, the liminal has been and still is the cornerstone of some definitions of the fantastic. Some critics have even argued that the fantastic is per se a liminal genre, liminality being its defining trait. Three observations recur in those perspectives: the marginal position of the fantastic within the literary canon of what is conceived as 'high literature', its tendency to transgress accepted cultural and moral values in a given period and its displacement of epistemological borders by giving an aesthetic form to the unknown. However, to what extent are those theorisations on the liminal restricted to the fantastic? One could argue that most of the traits (for instance, its marginal position in the canon and its transgressive force) could also apply to many other literary forms. Still, those approximations to the fantastic and the liminal have provided interesting contributions that render it undeniable that texts of the fantastic are obsessed with (genre, moral, gender, existential) borders and their transgression. Rosemary Jackson's work (2003 [1981]), for example, defined the fantastic as a force that refers to cultural and moral limits of a given society. J.J. Cohen's famous 'monster theses' (1996) considered monsters as beings at the edge of cultural moral and values, as ontological liminalities that refuse categorisation, 'disturbing hybrids whose externally incoherent bodies resist attempts to include them in any systematic structuration' (1996: 6). Amy Ransom regarded the fantastic in parallel with the notion of the feminine, subverting established gender norms and voicing taboos: 'Liminality relates to anomaly in that objects which exceed boundaries, refuse categorisation, cannot be effectively pinned down by an act of naming. Both the Fantastic and feminine sexuality display this characteristic unrepresentability in Western masculine discourse' (1995: 38). Clemens Ruthner offered a post-Todorovian revision of the condition of liminality in the fantastic text ('*die Grenzwertigkeit der Fantastik*'), 'as a staging of liminality, or as the liminality of representation' (2012: 35). The fantastic, he argues, generates a space of productive unrest and an uncanny proximity with otherness and states of transition. Manuel Aguirre (2017), taking a generalised approach to the term *fantastic* that includes all types of non-mimetic literatures, outlined a set of 'rules of composition' that are related to liminality, as well as some liminal tropes and plot structures, for example the crossing of the threshold into the domain of the uncanny; spaces of otherness as heterotopias and hero-type plots that revolve around transitional stages or phases, which are acts of threshold-crossing.

In the next sections, my approach to the intersection between the aesthetics of the boundary and the fantastic does not seek to formulate yet another theory of this narrative form based on the potential of the undefined or liminal (i.e., as a narrative form that is in-between). Instead, I propose to explore how a problem of boundaries – in this case of absent physical frames – can generate the fantastic through the portrayal of two similar border figures.

Horizontal vertigo

Le vertige est un rappel brutal de notre humaine et présente condition terrestre.

Gilbert Durand, *Les structures anthropologiques de l'imaginaire* (1992: 124)

('Vertigo is a brutal reminder of our real, human, earthly condition')

The term *horizontal vertigo* could be considered oxymoronic, since the experience of vertigo is commonly associated in the collective imaginary with the vertical. The up-and-down axis of our experience of space evoke the fear of falling down, and in many narratives this fall is a symbolic projection of the transition from the known (dimensions and codes) to the unknown. Think for example of Alice's fall into the rabbit hole and the subsequent passages and doors that she crosses in starting her adventure into a world marked by irrational and incomprehensible codes.

The French anthropologist Gilbert Durand associates the anguish of falling with the experience of human verticality (1992: 122–9) and thus with the sense of vertigo that we inherit in our falling from the comfort of the womb or when we first rise on our feet: 'For vertical bipeds, the sense of falling and heaviness accompanies all our early autokinetic and locomotive efforts'.[7] On the other hand, the German anthropologist O.F. Bollnow remarks in his work *Human Space* (2011 [1961]) that, in addition to verticality, the experience of human space entails the horizontal spatial axis ('vertical axis and horizontal plane together form the simplest system of concrete human space', 46), which is what 'designates a tangible reality' (47). Relying on Van Peursen's essay 'L'horizon' (1954), Bollnow exposes the crucial role performed by the horizon in the human apprehension of space, differentiating it from the purely mathematical interpretation:

> The human being always extends [her] space from the centre in which [she] stands, in the frame of a limiting and unity-forming horizon, and the fact that [the human being] never reaches [her] horizon, but [her] horizon travels along with [her], shows only that the horizon belongs inseparably to the human being [...], and thus the human being always remains the centre of the space enclosed by [her] horizon.
>   [...] It is the horizon that gathers the space around [the human being] into a finite and manageable environment. (Bollnow, 2011: 74–5)

Bollnow argues that our experience of the horizon is essential in providing a structure to that which surrounds us, which otherwise would be an undifferentiated surface in all directions.[8] The necessary orientation provided by the horizon in stabilising the human body that Bollnow stresses informs what I will call here the effect of *horizontal vertigo*. In the texts that are discussed, the sense of vertigo is triggered by the (fantastic) erasure of the horizon as structuring boundary.

The concept of horizontal vertigo has featured previously in certain sociological and philosophical discourses as a metaphor that refers to an optical effect when facing an extension with no intersection of vanishing lines. One of the most well-known references is by the Argentinian writer Jorge Luis Borges, who quotes Drieu la Rochelle's metaphor of *vertige horizontal* to define the Argentine *pampa*, that vast extension of flat land where the eye meets no end (Borges and Ferrari, 2005: 247). The same metaphor has recently travelled to the 2018 Architecture Biennale in Venice (Mendiondo et al., 2018). 'Vértigo horizontal' was at the core of the artistic proposal by the Argentine pavilion, a sensorial evocation of the vastness characteristic of the Argentinian landscape:

> Horizontal vertigo proposes an optic scheme producing combined effects. First, the rupture of the spatial relations between container and content by confining the immensity of the landscape in a glass box, an architectonic act of defying perception in the manner of the countless tales of Borges. Second, the daring venture of building the vastness in the virtuality of reflections; the kaleidoscopic fragmentation of the skies and the geometrical repetition of grasses gives away the artificiality of the endeavor, breaking the mimesis but opening up new ways of perceiving space. (Dejtiar, 2018)

Moving from the natural landscapes of deserts and plateaux to the urban scene, this metaphor has acquired a negative connotation in some of the scholarship that is dedicated to the postmodern city. For example, referring to Los Angeles, the sociologist Richard T. Ford writes, '[t]he vertigo one feels in LA comes not from vertical but from horizontal distances: the multiplication of boundaries [...] makes it impossible to conceive of any absolute boundary, any sense of place. Centre and periphery become meaningless in a sweeping map of topography' (1993: 88). In an article entitled 'El vértigo horizonal: La ciudad de México como texto' ('Horizontal Vertigo: Mexico City as a Text', 2003), the Mexican writer and philosopher Juan Villoro has also used this concept to reflect upon representations of urban sprawls such as Mexico City:

> Today, Mexico, Tokyo, Calcutta, Cairo or São Paulo have no boundaries. Only in their museums do they keep the order that Ravenna once had. Their amorphous vastness is a resistance to being fully embraced [...] It is impossible

to understand the minds that created those disjointed settings, which will only stop when they asphalt the horizon.

[...] In the first decades of the twentieth century Alfred Döblin, Leopoldo Marchal, Andrei Biely and John Dos Passos wrote novels with the whole city as the protagonist. A crowded *casting*, a gallery of simultaneous voices, pronounce the names of Berlin, Buenos Aires, St Petersburg and Manhattan. The final portrait is necessarily fragmentary since it seeks to reproduce chaos [...] From the second half of the last century, a horizontal metaphor predominates: the city as an ocean, as an infinite zone of transfer.[9]

In this domain, scholars have used the trope of horizontal vertigo to refer to a sense of dislocation provoked by urban features whose shape extends endlessly.[10] Some of these features identified by postmodern urban theorists can be mapped on to the literary text. For instance, there is a sense of horizontal vertigo captured in the never-ending line of cars of 'La autopista del sur' (1966) by the Argentinian author of the fantastic Julio Cortázar. The characters of this short story are entrapped in an endless traffic jam while trying to get back to Paris on a Sunday evening. The horizontality of space also provokes the suspension of time, which in 'La sanction' (1998a [1974]) and 'Le tunnel' (1998b [1974]), by the Belgian Jacques Sternberg, becomes a metaphor of the punishing journey without end in the never-ending tunnels in which the characters are confined: 'The convict is pushed into an endless tunnel, between the rails of a railway [...] A mirage, because the tunnel has no end';[11] '[w]hen, after two days and two nights, the passengers realised that the train had not yet left the tunnel, they began to worry'.[12] This border figure is particularly important in the fantastic short story 'Having a wonderful time' (2006a [1978]), by the British writer J.G. Ballard, which is considered in detail here.

The narrative action of 'Having a wonderful time' is recounted through a series of postcards that the narrator, Diana, sends to her sister in order to tell her about their holidays at the Hotel Imperial in Gran Canaria. Diana and her partner Richard arrive at an enormous resort complex on the coast of the Canary Islands and spend two happy weeks of a perfect package holiday: sports, entertainment and cocktail parties with many other British families. However, at the end of their stay it turns out to be impossible for them to leave the compound. Their departure is eternally postponed while other guests are also kept in captivity and more and more families land on the Canary coast to be hosted in an increasing number of compounds that are being rapidly built along the extent of the coast line. Their perfect holiday bubble turns out to be a prison: there is a conspiracy between the British and Spanish authorities to build an ever-growing human reserve for the unemployed and unemployable. The text contains some of the most characteristic Ballardian tropes: a perfect sanctuary for middle-class British families is destabilised by some element (be it the arrival of a stranger, the deviant behaviour of one of its members or the breakdown of one of the elements necessary for the correct functionality of this microcosm, as with the lifts of his novel *Highrise*) and suffocated by its own inbreeding. In the case of 'Having a wonderful time', the exclusive isolation first offered by the compound gives way to the entrapment of the inhabitants. I will focus here on the effect of the increasing expansion of the built environment that the text seeks to generate as well as to criticise. This effect is configured through two main aesthetic discourses: one that describes a constant dilation of boundaries (the expansion of the horizontal axis in the visual field), and another that refers to the homogenisation of its features (people, leisure activities and buildings).

Like other Ballardian resort communities, such as Estrella de Mar in *Cocaine Nights* or Eden-Olympia in *Super-Cannes*, it is no coincidence that the action is set in Playa del Inglés, an area in the south coast of Gran Canaria (Canary Islands) well-known for being a British mass-holiday area. Right at the beginning of the short story the reader is confronted with a maze of buildings: 'I have marked our balcony on the twenty-seventh floor' (Ballard, 2006a: 473); 'I hadn't realised how vast this resort complex is' (474). This huge resort keeps on growing, becoming a saturated horizon with endless buildings and more compounds in which to jail expats. This central idea of prolongation is enhanced through the adverb *along* – 'it stretches for miles along the coast and half of it's still being built' (Ballard, 2006a: 474) – and by formulas that reflect constant building activity: 'there is a beach being built for the French' (477); 'Richard and I lost ourselves in a maze of building sites' (475).

The idea of uniformity is generated by images that echo repetition. The compound hosts the same type of families, of the same social class and nationality – 'we're all, curiously, from the West Country' (Ballard, 2006a: 474) – with the same entertainment activities. They are presented as clones in 'huge self-contained holiday complexes' (Ballard, 2006a: 476). This is strengthened through expressions that dilute any features of individualisation and difference – 'a crowd of bewildered people', 'hordes of people' (Ballard, 2006a: 475), and multiply normative behaviour exponentially, for example: 'Everywhere people were coming in on the airport buses' (474), 'There are literally hundreds of us in the same boat' (475), 'one of the thousand hotels' (478), 'every entertainment conceivable' (473), 'entertainment of every kind' (475), 'hundred and one activities' (476).

J.G. Ballard creates an aesthetic effect of homogenisation and constant expansion. Richard is the only critical character aware of this growing prison. In what is one of the most distinct Ballardian features, the short story criticises mass-produced built environments. It outlines the dangers of creating exclusive sites that initially appear to be in a (fake) state of protection by virtue of being isolated through a very strict system of boundaries. Parallels are to be found with the concept of the privatopia (McKenzie, 1994), a term that describes a type of suburban development, formed by compounds protected by boundaries that create a gated community. According to McKenzie (1994), privatopias are segregated from public zones, protected by physical, restrictive and exclusive boundaries and arise as a reaction to the dissolution of boundaries in a globalised urban space. The boundary in this sense works as a restriction, protection and definition of a similar social class. However, this segregation also works as a prison, an idea exploited literally in Ballard's text.[13]

Ballard's short story also presents the idea of mass leisure as a form of social numbness. Through the space of the ever-expanding and enclosed 'brand-new resort complex, with every entertainment conceivable, all arranged by bedside push-button' (Ballard, 2006a: 473), the text warns of the potential of the built environment to dehumanise. Its users will become victims of the environment they have themselves created. His characters are *anaesthetised*, to employ Wolfgang Welsch's concept (2003), numbed by an accumulation of sensorial input, desensitised of perceptual experience and, consequently, unaware of the political and social implications of their confinement.

In Chapter 1 above on phenomenology of the liminal, Müller-Funk reminds us that 'human space is always constructed by limitation'. In Ballard's text, the lack of discernible spatial demarcation and the disappearance of reference points, due to the massified built environment, also leads to a metaphorical loss of position of the body in space, which equates to the literal loss of presence of the characters in society. Richard dies while he tries to escape. The others stay confined to 'a kind of permanent holiday camp for the unemployables' (Ballard, 2006a: 477), as happy hostages of the ever-expanding building site that houses the outcasts of British society.

Spatial psychasthenia, or dissolutions into built space

From whichever side one approaches things, the ultimate problem turns out in the final analysis to be that of distinction.
      Roger Caillois, 'Mimicry and legendary psychasthenia' (1984: 16)

The next transgression of boundaries considered here also captures the loss of position of the subject in space; however, in this case this physical dissolution is literal. The border figure that I call *psychasthenia* designates an aesthetic effect that arises from a lack of demarcation between body and environment through a process of either mimetisation with that space or dissolution into it: in the fantastic text the character becomes the space s/he inhabits. Psychasthenia is then both the act and the effect of this distortion.

From the Greek *psykhe* (soul, mind) and *asthenia* (weakness), psychasthenia was employed as a mental pathology of the mind related to anxiety and obsessive-compulsive syndrome. Most relevant here is how this term was defined by French critic Roger Caillois in his article entitled 'Mimicry and legendary psychasthenia' (1984 [1975]). Through the study of mimetic behaviours of some species, including mechanisms such as colour-copy and adaptation to form, Caillois determines that these behaviours work as strategies for survival but also – and most importantly for my analysis here – that they refer to a disturbance in the perception of space, since the animal thinks it is the space it occupies.

Some decades later the term of spatial psychasthenia reappeared in postmodern urban discourses.[14] In *Megalopolis* (1992) Celeste Olalquiaga use this term provocatively to address a spatial pathology that occurs when the perception of distances, frames, scale and other spatial materialities break down in the city. Olalquiaga argues that this context provokes a sense of dissolution of the subject's body in urban space – a sort of disembodiment – effectuated by 'an inability to preserve a distinct body representation (body-image) in the face of the proliferation of representations in the environment' (Hansen, 2006: 127). The ever-expanding cityscape decentres the body, and body and city become co-dependent because the subject cannot demarcate her/himself from the surroundings and thus feels that s/he disappears in them.

Several literary texts employ this figure in combination with the fantastic: the lack of differentiation between body and built space leads to a total physical dissolution of one of the characters. There are two Spanish short stories that use this trope almost identically: 'Fueron testigos' (2008 [1952]), by the Spanish writer Rosa Chacel, who spent most of her career in exile during the Franco dictatorship, and 'El asfalto', by Carlos Buiza, a short story most widely known in its adaptation as an episode in the very popular Spanish TV series of horror and the fantastic *Historias para no dormir* in 1966.[15] The first of these texts tells of an ordinary man who when out walking for no explicit reason slowly dissolves into the street. In the second of these stories a man gets stuck on the over-heated pavement and slowly disintegrates into it. In both cases, no logic explains this impossible 'incomprehensible, humanly inadmissible'[16] dissolution. The psychasthenic experience of the characters is described in detail as a horrific act of depersonalisation.

The idea of the body as the basis of subjectivity is in these cases rendered problematic, since the loss of the corporeal border also entails the disappearance of the individual. This is particularly well crafted by Rosa Chacel. The unnamed man introduced at the start of the story quickly dissolves into a mass with no voice. As the following quotations show, the discourse articulates an opposition between the bounded (i.e., the human) and the boundless (non-human) entity: 'They surrounded the fallen man who was no longer a fallen man: he was not a man any more'; 'a thick mass'; 'Because the man, overall, was nothing other than that: a boundless mass'; 'He didn't retain any of the contours that corresponded with the shape he once had'; 'his lack of density rendered his boundaries irregular' (2008: 131).[17] In the TV episode 'El asfalto' the character is given a voice and explicitly expresses his painful and lonely absorption into the pavement: '– Come, please come! [...] I am a prisoner of the asphalt, help me get out, please.'[18]

The fantastic dissolution in both texts serves to direct the focus upon the witnesses and their reactions. The passers-by quickly resolve to resume their normal lives after the disappearance of the man in 'Fueron testigos'. Regarded with suspicion by the other citizens, the protagonist of 'El asfalto' is left alone to die since nobody is willing to stop and offer help: '– I am alone, alone. Please take me out of here. – But nobody could understand him; nobody came near him. And the day after, some men took away the chairs around him and repaired the street with a fresh layer of pavement.'[19] As this last sentence shows, the extraordinary nature of the event is not as prominent in the plot as is the lack of empathy of the crowd, who immediately chose to forget this act of extraordinary physical melt-down: 'They all [the witnesses] dispersed throughout the city; all except for him [the Syrian witness] returned to their usual lives and routines, some fighting the memory of it until it had washed away from their minds, others preserving it with gratitude and fear.'[20]

Several points of criticism can be read in this trope of *psychasthenia*, in particular when taking into consideration that these stories were written during Franco's dictatorship. Both texts reflect on the human choice of ignoring that which is out of the ordinary or that breaks with the parameters set by society. As soon as the protagonists get stuck on the pavement, they are stigmatised as 'others', to be looked at, laughed at, criticised and even feared. The dissolution of the body means invisibility in a society that does not tolerate alterity. The necessary return to normality by everyone else is exemplified in the end of 'El asfalto' by the symbolic act of renewing the surface that swallowed up the protagonist with a fresh layer of asphalt. The character of 'el sirio' in 'Fueron testigos', who also is an outsider, embodies, in contrast, those who are capable of seeing that which does not lie within the norm. The last passages in 'Fueron testigos' are dedicated to forging this idea: 'Only he, the man who believed in it when he saw it and screamed to wake himself up, disrupted his mundane order, alienated his life by splicing it to the branch of that belief the sense of which – hostile to reason, devoid of an exemplary nature – nurtured a sap of madness.'[21]

Parallels with these *psychasthenic* experiences are to be found in two texts by J.G. Ballard, 'Motel architecture' (2006b [1978]) and 'The enormous space' (2006c [1989]), both of which share structural and thematic convergences. The texts present characters who are secluded in their suburban homes, deliberately isolating themselves from the outside world. These spaces have the double function of acting as sanctuaries and prisons.[22] Both stories end with the same type of ecstatic dissolution of the main character within the spaces they inhabit (which can be read as a supernatural experience or as a symbolic projection of their suicide). This mental and physical fusion with the protective space of the house is presented with irony, with references to the purity and peace found in the transcendence of the self. From the characters' perspective this is a long-expected physical communion with their own Utopian foundation: 'finding at last the still centre of the world' (Ballard 2006c: 709), 'eager now to merge with the white sky of the screen' (2006b: 516), 'uncluttered by the paraphernalia of conventional life' (2006c: 705). The *psychasthenic* experience featured in these two stories raises points of criticism similar to those mentioned in the context of 'Having a wonderful time': these types of privatopias end up isolating the character to the extent that s/he is incapable of defining her/himself in relation to others. Symbolically, human form becomes ungraspable; the body camouflages itself into its microcosmic milieu and vanishes, thus reiterating the author's critique of the formation of *exclusive* communities that are at the same time *excluded* from any form of human interaction.

Conclusion

As argued in the first section of this chapter, the fantastic engages with liminal tropes and states in multiple aesthetic forms. The two border figures discussed in this chapter reflect aesthetic strategies concerning the distortion of our (logical, rational) sense of boundaries. The multiple critical dimensions of these border figures, inherited from other disciplines such as human geography and urban studies, become particularly effective in the literary text of the fantastic, a narrative form designed to destabilise our sense of the real. The effect of *horizontal vertigo* deals with the loss of the frame that the eye identifies as an end to a physical space. It emphasises the importance of the horizon as a structuring element of our human experience of space. When the horizon does not seem to be visible for the observer, the human scale is boundless and the eye meets no end point that would allow the human to apprehend its surroundings. An invisible horizon means no points of reference and thus no possible estimation of distances. *Spatial psychasthenia*, on the other hand, designates the fusion of the body with its surrounding space, when the subject cannot distinguish its own boundaries from the environment that hosts it. This metaphorical disintegration into built space resonates with totalitarian regimes: that which is different is feared, ostracised, left to die, swallowed up by the city.

Through the portrayal of the existential and the corporeal shock experienced by the absence of a material border, these texts invite us to reflect on social exclusivity and exclusion, the saturation of the built environment and of sensorial input and the spread of homogeneous architectures. Overall, by subverting our assumed notion of reality, these border figures of the fantastic highlight the importance of boundaries in the configuration of human spatiality. When these borders fail, the fantastic emerges to give voice to the unconventional, the atypical and the unnatural; to all those who lie outside the confines of the norm.

Notes

1 Following up on my long interest in sketching these two spatial tropes, this contribution develops the conceptualisation of these two border figures for the first time. Earlier use of the terms *horizontal vertigo* and *spatial psychasthenia* can be found in García (2015a: 69–70; 120).

2 'le fantastique est rupture de l'ordre reconnu, l'irruption de l'inadmissible au sein de l'inaltérable légalité quotidienne' (Caillois, 1965: 161).

3 'las preguntas de aquellos hombres, que no lograban entrar en la comprensión total del hecho, se perdían sin respuesta, como meros ademanes de una realidad ineficiente.' / 'Efectos ilógicos, al parecer, imprevisibles desde cualquier punto de vista exterior' (Chacel, 2008: 134). Translations from original texts in Spanish are mine.

4 This work also offers further theoretical insight on the differentiation of non-mimetic genres, an aspect that cannot be covered extensively in this chapter.

5 Elsewhere I have discussed in detail the difference between 'the fantastic as an event in space' (for example a house haunted by a ghost, such as E.T.A. Hoffmann's 'The deserted house') and 'the fantastic as an event of space' (a monster-house, such as *The Haunting of Hill House* by Shirley Jackson, a building with the power to induce madness in those who live in it). Whereas in the first category there is no ontological problem with the buildings as such – the problem is the creature/or power that haunts it, i.e., the ghost – in the second category the figure of the ghost who haunts space is absent and the agency is displaced from the ghost to the building (see García, 2015a: 19–47).

6 See Meta Mazaj's study (2019) for an extensive discussion on the migrant codes and transgressions in Abbasi's film, within the context of border aesthetics and European cinema.

7   'pour le bipède vertical que nous sommes, le sens de la chute et la pesanteur
    accompagne toutes nos premières tentatives autocinétiques et locomotrices'
    (Durand, 1992: 123).

8   Let us also remember in this respect that in ancient Greek philosophy the
    horizon (*jorismós*) was as much a physical as an ontological and epistemological
    boundary. What could be covered by the eye was the known. Nothing existed
    beyond that. The function of this *jorismós* was precisely to visually structure
    our world of the logos, that which is known to us. The Greek verb *horizein*
    means 'dividing', but also 'defining' in an ontological sense; to delimit so that
    things can exist.

9   'Hoy en día, México, Tokio, Calcuta, El Cairo o São Paulo carecen de confines.
    Sólo dentro de sus museos conservan el orden que una vez tuvo Ravena. Su informe
    vastedad se resiste a ser conocida por entero; [...]. Imposible entender las mentes
    que crearon esos abigarrados escenarios que sólo se detendrán cuando asfalten
    el horizonte. / En las primeras décadas del siglo XX, Alfred Döblin, Leopoldo
    Marechal, Andrei Biely y John Dos Passos escriben novelas cuyo protagonista es
    la urbe entera. Un populoso *casting*, una galería de voces simultáneas, pronuncia
    los nombres de Berlín, Buenos Aires, San Petersburgo y Manhattan. El retrato
    final es necesariamente fragmentario porque aspira a reproducir el caos. [...] A
    partir de la segunda mitad del siglo pasado, predomina una metáfora horizontal:
    la ciudad como océano, como infinita zona de traslado' (Villoro, 2003: 46–8).

10 The philosophical work by Ana Carrasco Conde, *Infierno Horizontal: sobre
    la destrucción del yo* (2012, 'Horizontal Hell: on the Destruction of the Self'),
    claims a new horizontal conception of the metaphor of hell starting in modernity.
    This contrasts with the traditional vertical geography of this trope. The modern
    idea of hell is located not underground but in our everyday environment. It is
    not external to the subject but arises from the subject itself.

11 'On pousse le condamné dans un interminable tunnel, entre les rails d'une voie
    ferrée [...]. Mirage, car le tunnel n'a pas de fin' (Sternberg, 1998a: 81). My
    translation.

12 'Quand, après deux jours et deux nuits, les voyageurs comprirent que le train
    n'était toujours pas sorti du tunnel, ils commencèrent à s'inquiéter' (Sternberg,
    1998b: 84). My translation.

13 What happens when the protective quality of the boundary is transgressed or
    subverted in these privatopias? This idea is explored in the Mexican film *La
    zona* (dir. Rodrigo Plá, 2007), a thriller on the break-in in an exclusive gated
    community in Mexico City.

14 For an insightful reconstruction on how psychasthenia has featured as a spatial
    pathology in postmodern socio-urban theory, see Theodore Michell's PhD thesis
    'The Psychasthenia of Deep Space: Evaluating the reassertion of space in critical
    social theory' (2002).

15 The titles translate into English as 'They witnessed it' and 'The asphalt' respectively.

16 'incomprensible, humanamente inadmisible' (Chacel, 2008: 129).

17 'Rodearon al hombre caído que ya no era un hombre caído: ya no era un
    hombre'; 'una masa espesa'; 'Pues el hombre, en suma, ya no era más que

esto: una masa sin contornos' (Chacel, 2008: 130); 'Ya no conservaba relieve alguno que correspondiese a la forma que había tenido'; 'su falta de densidad fue haciéndole irregular el contorno' (131).

18 '—¡Venga, por favor, venga! —Le hizo señas con la mano—; ¡estoy prisionero en el asfalto, ayúdeme a salir, por favor!' ('El asfalto', 1966).

19 '—¡Me encuentro solo ... solo! ... ¡Sáquenme, por favor! [...] Pero nadie pudo comprenderle, nadie se le acercaba. Y al día siguiente unos hombres quitaron las sillas y repararon el suelo, poniendo una nueva capa de asfalto' ('El asfalto', 1966).

20 'Todos se dispersaron por la ciudad y todos, menos éste, volvieron a sus vidas y faenas habituales, combatiendo unos el recuerdo hasta lograr lavarse de él, conservándole otros con gratitud y temor' (Chacel, 2008: 135).

21 'Sólo éste, el hombre que creyendo nada más ver gritó para despertarse, rompió su orden cotidiano, enajenó su vida al injertarla en la rama de aquella creencia en cuyo sentido, hostil a la mente, exento de toda ejemplaridad, se nutría una savia de locura' (Chacel, 2008: 135).

22 I have elsewhere analysed how narrative dynamics are generated in these limited and limiting 'one-man worlds' (García, 2015b).

References

Abbasi, A. (2018) *Gräns/Border*. 110 minutes film. Sweden.

Aguirre, M. (2017) 'Thick description and the poetics of the liminal in gothic tales', *Orbis Litterarum*, 72(4): 294–317.

Alfredson, T. (2008) *Låt den rätte komma in / Let the Right One In*. 115 minutes film. Sweden.

Bal, M. (2002) *Travelling Concepts in the Humanities: A Rough Guide*. Toronto: University of Toronto Press.

Ballard, J.G. (2006a) 'Having a wonderful time', in *The Complete Short Stories: Volume Two*. London: Harper, pp. 473–8.

Ballard, J.G. (2006b) 'Motel architecture', in *The Complete Short Stories: Volume Two*. London: Harper, pp. 502–6.

Ballard, J.G. (2006c) 'The enormous space', in *The Complete Short Stories: Volume Two*. London: Harper, pp. 697–9.

Bessière, I. (1974) *Le récit fantastique: La poétique de l'incertain*. Paris: Larousse Université.

Bollnow, O.F. (2011) *Human Space*. London: Hyphen.

Borges, J.L., and O. Ferrari (2005) *En Diálogo*. Vol. 2. Mexico: Siglo XXI.

Bozzetto, R. (2005) *Passages des fantastiques: des imaginaires à l'inimaginable*. Aix-en-Provence: Publications de l'Université de Provence.

Caillois, R. (1965) *Au cœur du fantastique*. Paris: Gallimard.

Caillois, R. (1984) 'Mimicry and legendary psychasthenia', *October*, 31: 16–32.

Campra, R. (2008) *Territorios de la ficción: Lo fantástico*. Seville: Renacimiento.

Carrasco Conde, A. (2012) *Infierno Horizontal: sobre la destrucción del yo*. Madrid: Plaza y Valdés.

Castex, P.-G. (1951) *Le conte fantastique en France de Nodier à Maupassant*. Paris: José Corti.

Chacel, R. (2008) 'Fueron testigos', in D. Roas and A. Casas (eds), *La realidad oculta: cuentos fantásticos españoles del siglo XX*. Palencia: Menoscuarto, pp. 127–36.

Clute, J., and J. Grant (eds) (1999) *The Encyclopedia of Fantasy*. London: Orbit.

Cohen, J.J. (1996) 'Monster culture (seven theses)', in J.J. Cohen (ed.), *Monster Theory: Reading Culture*. Minneapolis, MN: University of Minnesota Press, pp. 3–25.

Dejtiar, F. (2018) 'Horizontal Vertigo: Argentinian Pavilion at the Venice Biennale 2018', *ArchDaily*, www.archdaily.com/895249/horizontal-vertigo-argentinian-pavilion-at-thevenice-biennale-2018. Accessed 19 June 2019.

De Palma, B. (1976) *Carrie*. 98 minutes film. United States.

Durand, Gilbert (1992) *Les structures anthropologiques de l'imaginaire*. Paris: DUNOD.

Ford, R.T. (1993) 'Spaced out in L.A.: Race, real estate, and politics in the city of fallen angels', *Transition*, 61: 88–112.

Foucault, M. (1980) 'A preface to transgression', in D.F. Bouchard (ed.), *Language, Counter-Memory, Practice*. New York: Cornell University Press, pp. 29–52.

García, P. (2015a) *Space and the Postmodern Fantastic in Contemporary Literature: The Architectural Void*. New York: Routledge.

García, P. (2015b) 'J.G. Ballard's one-man worlds', *Reflexiones marginales: revista de saberes de frontera* (Blog), http://reflexionesmarginales.com/3.0/j-g-ballards-one-man-worlds/. Accessed 25 March 2020.

Hamon, P. (1992) *Expositions: Literature and Architecture in Nineteenth-Century France*. Berkeley: University of California Press.

Hansen, M.B.N. (2006) *Bodies in Code: Interfaces with Digital Media*. New York: Routledge.

Jackson, R. (2003) *Fantasy: The Literature of Subversion*. London: Methuen.

Mazaj, M. (2019) 'Border aesthetics and catachresis in Ali Abbasi's *Gräns/Border* (2018)', *Transnational Screens*. https://doi.org/10.1080/25785273.2019.1682229. Accessed 18 November 2019.

McKenzie, E. (1994) *Privatopia: Homeowner Associations and the Rise of Residential Private Government*. New Haven: Yale University Press.

Mendiondo, J., et al. (2018) 'ARGENTINA: Vértigo Horizontal / Vertigine Orizzontale / Horizontal Vertigo', *La Biennale di Venezia*, www.labiennale.org/en/architecture/2018/national-participations/argentina. Accessed 19 June 2019.

Michell, T. (2002) 'The psychasthenia of deep space: Evaluating the reassertion of space in critical social theory'. PhD dissertation, University College of London.

Olalquiaga, C. (1992) *Megalopolis: Contemporary Cultural Sensibilities*. Minneapolis: University of Minnesota Press.

Peñafiel, L. (1966) 'El asfalto', *Historias para no dormir*. 34 minutes TV episode (24 June). Spain.

Plá, R. (2007) *La zona*. 97 minutes film. Mexico / Spain.

Ransom, A. (1995) *The Feminine as Fantastic in the Conte Fantastique: Visions of the Other*. New York: Peter Lang.

Roas, D. (2018) *Behind the Frontiers of the Real: A Definition of the Fantastic*. Basingstoke: Palgrave.

Ruthner, C. (2012) 'Fantastic liminality: A theory sketch', in L. Schmeink and A. Böger (eds), *Collisions of Reality: Establishing Research on the Fantastic in Europe*. Berlin: De Gruyter, pp. 35–49.

Schimanski, J. (2006) 'Crossing and reading: Notes towards a theory and a method', *Nordlit*, 19: 41–63.

Schimanski, J. (2016) 'What is a border figure?', *Border Culture: The Blog of the EUBORDERSCAPES Project Research Group for Border Crossing and Cultural Production*, https://bordercult.hypotheses.org/92. Accessed 19 June 2019.

Sternberg, J. (1998a) 'La sanction', in *Contes glacés*. Brussels: Labor, p. 81.

Sternberg, J. (1998b) 'Le tunnel', in *Contes glacés*. Brussels: Labor, p. 84.

Todorov, T. (1975) *The Fantastic: A Structural Approach to a Literary Genre*. Ithaca: Cornell University Press.

Van Peursen, C.A. (1954) 'L'horizon', *Situation*, 1: 204–34.

Villoro, J. (2003) 'El vértigo horizonal: La ciudad de México como texto', in B. Muñoz and S. Spitta (eds), *Más allá de la ciudad letrada*. Pittsburgh: Biblioteca de América, pp. 45–58.

Welsch, W. (2003) 'Aesthetics beyond aesthetics', *Action, Criticism & Theory for Music Education*, 2(2): 1–26.

Part II

Living with the border (zones)

3

Capturing clouds: imagin(in)g the materiality of digital networks

Holger Pötzsch

Introduction

Titles such as the one above – capturing clouds – are ambiguous. Do clouds capture? Or are they themselves captured? Through this double meaning, the title enables a productive questioning of subject–object distinctions and therefore makes possible an interrogation of received notions of agency. In particular, when combining such ambivalences with issues of technology, a redrawing of arrows between a supposed subject and an assumed object entails interesting political consequences. This chapter conducts such a reframing in the context of contemporary digital networks, the power-laden dynamics of which are epitomised in the increasingly ubiquitous technology of cloud computing.

In the following, I interrogate how dynamics of capturing clouds in digital domains (in both possible meanings) interfere with borders and state power, and how they are resisted and rearticulated in and through contemporary works of art. Do digital networks and data clouds subvert state power and borders? Or do they, rather, reiterate and reinforce received structures of dominance by extending the 'capillary reach of the state' (Pugliese, 2013: 26) into every inch of a previously protected private sphere? To respond to such questions, this chapter will firstly revisit debates on the political implication of global networks. Highlighting the inherent materiality of digital technologies, I question and challenge discourses postulating liberating and empowering potentials of the Internet and argue for continuities rather than ruptures in transitions to contemporary network societies. Secondly, I use the example of cloud computing to relate this transition to issues of states, borders, power and territory, before, finally, directing attention to artistic responses to new forms of political management and control. This way, the

chapter explores a particular component of a global borderscape that is
investigated at a more local level by Chiara Brambilla in Chapter 4 below.

Where is the Internet? The political geographies of capturing clouds

I wish to begin this chapter with an anecdote from the early days of the
Internet. The 1980s and early 1990s saw the emergence and subsequent
popularisation of digital networking technologies, first and foremost the
transition from the military ARPA and DARPA nets, built with the objective
of sustaining communication in the case of a nuclear attack, to the contemporary Internet (see for instance Galloway, 2004; Abbate, 2000). The following
rapid technological developments engendered changes and new dynamics
also at societal, economic and eventually political levels that quickly attracted
activists, hackers and entrepreneurs.

John Perry Barlow was among the first to fathom the considerate potential
of digital networks for virtually all areas of life and work (see Lambert and
Poole, 2005: 8–14; Moberly, 2009). Coming from the countercultural
movements of the 1970s where he had experimented with mind-altering
drugs, Barlow quickly turned into a key figure in digital activism (he, among
other things, co-founded the Electronic Frontier Foundation) and became
instrumental to the formation of a new branch of the economy – the early
digital start-ups that eventually congregated at Silicon Valley. In 1996, Barlow
summarised the optimism of these first years in his *Declaration of Independence of Cyberspace* where he urged the 'weary giants of flesh and steel' of
the industrial era to leave the new generation and their open and inclusive
digital arenas 'of the mind' alone, stating that their time was over and that
they had 'no sovereignty where we gather' (n.p.).

Such optimism with regard to the potentials of technology to instigate a
better world, free from poverty, division and oppression, reverberate today
in beliefs in the advantages of digitisation for all areas of human life ranging
from education and politics, via health and well-being, to social networks,
individual love-lives, and human evolution (see, e.g., Diamandis and Kottler,
2015; Jenkins, 2006; Kurzweil, 2005; Schmidt and Cohen, 2013; Shirky,
2010). However, from the very beginning more critical voices have also
been heard, doubting assumptions regarding the glory of allegedly friction-free
new horizons and posing the critical question of what exactly has changed
and if such possible transformations have been solely positive or whether
certain downsides can be identified (Andrejevic, 2007; Chun, 2006; Fuchs,
2014; Galloway, 2004; Morozov, 2011). Similarly, the impact of global
flows and network technologies on border regimes and nation states has

been judged differently with positions ranging from early predictions of an imminent demise of borders in globalisation (Guehenno, 1995; Ohmae, 1999) to assertions of extensions and amplifications of state power in digital domains (Amoore, 2006, 2018; Bigo, 2007; Pötzsch, 2015).

Already some time before the publication of Barlow's manifesto, two New York-based hackers, known as Phyber Optik and Acid Phreak, set out to challenge the mantra that digital technology in itself heralds a new era of freedom, connection and inclusion – an immaterial realm that makes it possible to avoid the problems and inequalities of previous epochs (see Gupta, 2004: 223–6; Moberly, 2009: 145–7). In contrast to Barlow, Phyber Optik and Acid Phreak believed that there exist underlying continuities that intrinsically connect the digital with the preceding 'analogue' epochs and their peculiar power relations, inequalities and mechanisms of exploitation and oppression. For them, the postulated differences were merely semantic since at the level of everyday material practices virtually everything remained the same. They proved their point by hacking into the servers of the bank holding Barlow's digital credit card details and then forwarded him all relevant information in physical form. Through these acts, not only did they show that banks and other major corporations were at the forefront of the turn to the digital and that they were indeed the main beneficiaries of this transition, but they also reasserted the fundamental significance of the material world and its peculiar contradictions for allegedly autonomous digital domains.

This anecdote summarises what is at stake in the present chapter. As in the times of Barlow, Acid Phreak and Phyber Optik, today's enthusiasts of the virtual are juxtaposed with those who sourly point at continuities in wealth and power across an alleged digital–material divide. The often-asserted fundamental ambiguity of technology as pharmakon – both remedy and poison (Derrida, 1981: 70) – enjoys continued relevance in relation to new media ecologies, which today emerge as at the same time harbingers of genuine co-operation, liberation and free exchange, and as a site of massive surveillance, exploitation, commodification, inequality and environmental degradation (Andrejevic, 2007; Chun, 2006; Galloway, 2004; Morozov, 2011; Pötzsch, 2017). Awareness of this intrinsic double-nature and context-dependence of technology is key to an understanding of its possible effects and implications at collective and individual levels. As all technology, also the digital constantly oscillates between the opposing poles of 'freedom and control' (Chun, 2006), ultimately delegating the question of managing its various ramifications to politics. This is also relevant for the use of digital technologies by contemporary late-modern nation states and their increasingly globalised regimes of security and control that also extend into digital domains (Bigo, 2007; Martínez, 2018; Pötzsch, 2015).

When asking 'Where is the Internet?' this chapter points to the material inertia of apparently fluid and ephemeral digital networks. This inertia ties the allegedly novel to already established institutions and frames, and in doing so entails continuities in key aspects of society, politics, culture, the economy and personal lives that remain unaltered by merely technological change (Fuchs, 2014; Gehl, 2014; Pötzsch, 2017, 2018). In spite of Barlow's (1996) assertions that 'we declare our virtual selves immune to your sovereignty' and that 'cyberspace does not lie within your borders', it seems that state power and territory, as well as received political and economic positions of privilege, continue to enjoy salience for the time being. Indeed, they are key elements that interconnect the apparently old with the allegedly new.

In her article 'Cloud geographies', Louise Amoore (2018) addresses such dynamics through the increasingly important technology of cloud computing as a distributed form of online storage of data sets ranging from private files via corporate data to state documents. She introduces an important conceptual distinction that enhances our understanding of the data cloud as characterised by precisely the ambiguities that were highlighted in the section above. She defines cloud 1, 'a geography of cloud forms', as the concrete material arrangements of server parks, power plants and intercontinental fibre-optic cables where the actual data cloud is physically located, through which it is accessed and powered, and that are predominantly owned and administered by states and global corporations. Secondly, cloud 2, 'the geography of cloud analytic', describes the ephemeral practices and effects of working on and with the data flowing through this infrastructure. Amoore's use of the term *geography* enables a productive interrogation of the relations between power, knowledge and technology at the intersection between virtual domains and the material world. As such, cloud geography 1 enables an investigation into where, how and by whom clouds are captured, while cloud geography 2 makes possible interrogations of how, where and what clouds themselves capture. This division has implications for the continued salience of borders and (state) territory in the contemporary era of networks and makes cloud computing an essential component of contemporary borderscapes (Brambilla, 2015).

In border studies, such developments have led to a questioning of received understandings of borders as distinct dividing lines between territorially defined nation states, and they have also made palpable a need for new concepts capturing the shifting notion of borders and sovereignty in an era of globalisation and transnational networks and flows (Brambilla, 2015; Longo, 2017; Parker and Vaughan-Williams, 2009; Popescu, 2011; Pötzsch, 2015; Sidaway, 2011). Drawing upon the work by among others Rajaram and Grundy-Warr (2007), Brambilla (2015) has proposed the term *borderscapes* to account for such changes (see also Chiara Brambilla, Chapter 4 below), while I have addressed the role of networks, automation and human–machine assemblages in contemporary processes of bordering that, as I argue, crystallise in form of various distributed and personalised instances of an inherently constitutive iBorder (Pötzsch, 2015). Both approaches have salience for a better understanding of the implications of digital technologies such as cloud computing and capture for contemporary border regimes and processes of bordering.

Capturing clouds: borders, sovereigns and virtual geographies

The digital cloud is material. To operate, cloud computing is dependent upon physical devices, concrete locations, and sets of cables and machineries that power and interconnect them with each other (Amoore, 2018; Hogan, 2017; Johnson and Hogan, 2017; Parks, 2017; Pötzsch, 2017; Starosielski, 2015). As such, the apparently ephemeral world of data storage and dissemination also entails a spatial dimension that spreads across territory and makes Amoore's (2018) cloud 1 amenable to state power, interests and actions. She writes that 'understood as a spatial arrangement, materialized in and through data centres, the abstract deterritorialized cloud is thus reterritorialized as an intelligible and governable entity' (2018: 8). Now, how does this work?

According to Galloway (2004), global digital networks such as the Internet resemble at once a distributed, rhizomatic infrastructure composed of dispersed nodes (IP/TCP protocols, individual devices), as well as a hierarchical tree-like structure of control that channels all communication through certain pivotal hubs (DNS, key ISPs and material network infrastructure). As such, he asserts, 'the Internet is not simply open or closed but above all a form that is modulated … information does flow, but it does so in a highly regulated manner' (2004: xix). Today, both commercial and state actors exert significant influence on how and to what effect this modulation occurs (Fuchs, 2014; Gehl, 2014; Harcourt, 2015; Pötzsch, 2018; Zuboff, 2019).

The in-built ambiguity of contemporary network technology was exploited in the US National Security Agency's (NSA) and the British General Communications Headquarters' (GCHQ) various surveillance programmes that, according to the former NSA contractor Edward Snowden, successfully survey and mine global data streams and storage sites at an unprecedented scale. By homing in on the physical infrastructure of the Internet, these agencies extend the grasp of sovereign power into the allegedly unruly and immaterial environment of digital networks where, according to Barlow (1996), states should have 'no sovereignty'. Under the auspices of programmes such as PRISM, XKeyscore, Co-Traveller or TEMPORA, just to mention a few, the NSA and its allies have acquired access to key nodes of a global communication infrastructure such as the servers operated by commercial ISPs (such as Google, Facebook, Microsoft, Yahoo, Skype and others), mobile phone towers and the landing stations of intercontinental fibre-optic cables. What this means is that data are routinely intercepted at these bottlenecks and extracted for further analysis in specifically built server parks. Data gathering is routine and bulk, meaning both content and metadata are collected even without any concrete suspicion.[1]

The NSA surveillance scandal shows how sovereign power today is infused in digital networks and exploits physical infrastructure to submit apparently ephemeral global data flows to the purview of state agencies (Galloway and Thacker, 2007). In doing so, it increasingly enlists private actors and commercial enterprises in the surveillance effort. As such, rather than challenging and potentially subverting traditional forms of territory and state authority, new media technologies bring new practices and actors into the immediate proximity of sovereign power and enable new forms of management and control that are based on routine surveillance and assessment of massive sets of individual and aggregate data including, but by no means limited to, non-conscious somatic responses (Hayles, 2016). As a result, it seems that Barlow's fantasies about virtually boundless and borderless cyberspace need further refinement, since O'Dowd's (2010: 1031) assertion that even today state borders continue to be among the most important 'institutionalised dividers of world space' retains its validity also in an era of digital networks and increasingly ubiquitous connectivity on a planetary scale.

Today, states increasingly expand their borders and activities into digital domains (Longo, 2017; Popescu, 2011; Pötzsch, 2015). As Longo (2017) has shown, this leads to a gradual diffusion of state borders that resemble no longer clearly determined dividing lines, but multifaceted constructs that involve at least two sovereign units and that extend their technologically facilitated reach deep into the inside of nation states. Similarly, I have shown how contemporary states use networks and largely automated algorithmic assessments of sets of globally collected big data to at once expand states' bordering activities across the entire globe while at the same time attaching the border to individual bodies and digital profiles (Pötzsch, 2015). According to Amoore (2006: 348), this combination of digitisation, predictive algorithmic analysis and biometric techniques of identification makes the individual the 'carrier of the border' that emerges as almost invisible for normative subjectivities while becoming inherently uncrossable for individuals falling through the raster of the contemporary security state and its multiple databases.

As a result, cyberspace does not really challenge or undermine state and corporate sovereignty and power. It rather gives them new forms. Technologies that capture contemporary data clouds at the various material intersections and hubs of global networks are key components of this continued salience of centralised modern-era power structures and institutions. Rather than implying a rupture or break, the digital era is characterised by continuities with a past that is apparently not over. The digital 'smart' state is still a state, however with significantly enhanced abilities to assess, control and manage both specific individuals and abstracted population-level patterns of life.

Brambilla and Pötzsch (2015) have related such issues of inclusion and exclusion at the contemporary deterritorialised and increasingly boundless border to technologies behind the scopic regimes that determine the visibility and invisibility of particular subjectivities. Drawing upon Rancière's (2004) distribution and redistribution of the sensible, and reading this framework together with Arendt's (1958) politics of visibility, they argue for both liberating and oppressive potentials in the way new technologies hide and make visible certain forms of life at the border and beyond. Activating the concept of borderscape for their analysis (Brambilla, 2015; Rajaram and Grundy-Warr, 2007), they put technologically facilitated individual practices and representations of resistance up against state ambitions to total control and predictability (see also Chiara Brambilla's Chapter 4 below).

What becomes palpable in this context is a tension between a predominantly territorially defined form of sovereignty and the inherently global pretensions of an increasingly deterritorialised security apparatus. It seems that the emergence of Castells's (1996) network society has not led states out of their 'territorial trap' (Agnew, 1994). Rather, territorially defined states have extended their reach across classical fences and walls into the digital realms of global networks. It appears that the capacity to capture and process data clouds becomes key to a sustainability of national power and sovereignty in the contemporary era of networks. This also requires a continued close alignment between corporate and state power that overflows the boundaries of the modern nation state and creates inherently unlimited regimes of control over global space (Bigo, 2007).

What car and weapons manufacturers were to the industrial age are the new Silicon Valley-based media identity manufacturers to the contemporary era. Whilst Barlow's 'giants of flesh and steel' did indeed lose some of their significance, corporate power did not simply leave the 'realm of the mind'. Rather, this realm was quickly colonised by a new breed of neat and smart businesses that acquired comparable influence and power (Cheney-Lippold, 2017; Fuchs, 2014; Gehl, 2014; Pötzsch, 2018; Zuboff, 2019). The constant flow of data through global material networks not only fuelled their business models by enabling them to capture and commodify unprecedented amounts of data but it also strengthened the control apparatus of the late-modern globalised security state and its ability to capture the virtual clouds that increasingly define us as individuals and collectives. This has profound implications for politics and societies in democracies and adds new dimensions to reflections on the relation between borders and materiality (see, e.g., Green, 2019).

Artistic responses: white-boxing the dark geographies of capturing clouds

If one follows Amoore (2018), contemporary data clouds do not only rely upon a physical infrastructure prone to state intervention, access and control (cloud 1), but they also entail an epistemological dimension that brings more data under the purview of states than ever before (cloud 2). According to Pugliese (2013), the algorithm-driven and increasingly automated practices of cloud-computing, capture and analysis have created 'multiple mobile governmentalities' (2013: 21) that extend 'the capillary reach of state violence into the quotidian sites of civilian lives' (2013: 26). Virtually ubiquitous surveillance has transformed citizens into transparent entities that are easily aggregated into manageable and controllable groups of profiles (Cheney-Lippold, 2017; Gehl, 2014; Harcourt, 2015; Pötzsch, 2015, 2018). In these processes, fully fledged individuals are accompanied by data-doubles – series of profiles each one of which reflects back at them certain identity potentials emerging from various different contexts.

Extending from our driving or shopping habits, via movement patterns, networks of friends, colleagues or associations, browsing histories and preferences to our most intimate desires, fears or interests, the contemporary state-commercial digital infrastructure captures, processes, and ultimately instrumentalises data extracted from all of them. Governance, as such, becomes at once individuated (directed at particular subjectivities) and massifying (targeting abstracted aggregates and patterns of life). For Amoore (2018), cloud 2 circumscribes precisely such new epistemologies enabled by digital networking technologies and their political, societal, economic and cultural frames. They imply a peculiar new form of in/visibility – a specific distribution of the sensible in the sense of Rancière (2004) – that highlights certain and veils other subjectivities, lives and deaths.

How, then, are issues connected to technology, surveillance and control at and beyond state borders responded to and negotiated by artists and activists? How are the data-capturing clouds of late-modern security appa-ratuses themselves captured in artworks and political initiatives? Here, the work of the researcher, artist and activist Trevor Paglen, who has been mapping the 'dark geographies' of clandestinely operating branches of US military and intelligence for almost two decades, can show the way.

A geographer by training, Paglen has investigated the hidden dimensions of global US military and security practices.[2] Ranging from extraordinary rendition (Paglen and Thompson, 2006) via covert special operations and units (Paglen, 2008), secret sites (Paglen, 2009) and spy satellites (Paglen and Solnit, 2010) to the global surveillance disclosure (Paglen, 2014), he has mapped blank spots on the map of US military and secret service conduct across the globe. Paglen's (2014) visualisation of the physical and institutional infrastructure behind the NSA bulk surveillance of digital networks is of specific relevance to this chapter exploring critically the material aspects of cloud computing and capture and their relation to the state. In addition, Paglen's installation *Autonomy Cube* constitutes a critical comment on Internet-based mass surveillance and offers concrete steps towards efficient counter-measures.

Operating at the nexus of art and politics, Paglen's work invites a subversive redistribution of the sensible by making visible and palpable hidden material dimensions of contemporary hegemonic borderscapes and by pointing to alternative ways of organising political space. In his art, this happens both at the level of representation and through direct political implications of the works at a performative level.

According to Paglen and Gach (2003), every aesthetic work conveys an intended meaning or attitude by for instance deliberately commenting upon or raising awareness for specific political issues or challenges. This is the level usually perceived as important by both critics and artists. However, besides this more or less overt representational dimension, works of art always also do something – they entail concrete effects at a material level of everyday practice. As such, a work criticising capitalist commodification that is bought and sold in the art market runs into the danger of performatively reproducing the precise relations and conditions it overtly opposes at the level of its political attitude and message. Similarly, a huge installation that critically comments upon our inability to sufficiently tackle climate change somewhat undermines its political message when it is transported across the globe by aeroplane to be exhibited at the most important art fairs. In distinguishing between the attitudes and performance effects of artworks in this manner, Paglen and Gach (2003) do not imply that artists should stop selling or marketing their works. Rather, they demand general awareness for the relations of power within which works of art are positioned and call for a sensitivity for their concrete material impacts and effects in particular in cases where these are opposed to a work's critical message or political attitude. In their view, a positioned work of art is 'self-reflexive about the specific conditions of its own production and incorporates those conditions of production and reception into the form of the work itself' (Paglen and Gach, 2003).

In his own work, Paglen has sought to realise such ideas by combining research, political mobilisation and aesthetic production, thus consciously aligning attitude and performance effects of his interventions to form positioned works that recalibrate received understandings and frames. As Gustafsson puts it in relation to Paglen's project on black worlds of US special forces and clandestine operations, the artist's approach 'forms a hybrid of empirical science, investigative journalism, political activism and high-end art' (2013: 150). This awareness not only of what a work says but also of what it does in concrete contexts has predisposed Paglen's artistic responses to Snowden's revelations and the mass capture of global cloud data by commercial and state actors. In the section below, I will examine closer these two cases and focus on Paglen's visual documentation of physical surveillance and control infrastructure in the US and his museum installation *Autonomy Cube*.

In the aftermath of the Snowden revelations, Paglen (2014) noted 'a scarcity of images' that accompanied large amounts of written materials provided by the whistleblower to document the massive extent of clandestine surveillance operations conducted by key US and allied intelligence agencies on a global scale. In an attempt to 'expand the visual vocabulary we use to "see" the U.S. intelligence community', Paglen hired a helicopter and took pictures of the institutional infrastructure behind the world's most invasive surveillance and data gathering practices (Figure 3.1). He made the resulting series of pictures freely available in the public domain for anyone to use without restrictions (via *The Intercept*), as such ensuring their widest possible dissemination.[3] To explain his intervention, he writes that

> Although the organizing logic of our nation's surveillance apparatus is invisibility and secrecy, its operations occupy the physical world. Digital surveillance programs require concrete data centres; intelligence agencies are based in real buildings; surveillance systems ultimately consist of technologies, people, and the vast network of material resources that supports them. (Paglen, 2014)

Paglen's intervention targeted Amoore's (2018) cloud 1 – the physical underpinnings of contemporary digital media and cloud computing as key features of contemporary hegemonic borderscapes (Brambilla and Pötzsch, 2017) – and added attention to the institutional infrastructure required to implement the widespread surveillance and data extraction currently practised by the NSA and GCHQ. In redistributing the sensible in this manner, Paglen's work brings into view aspects of the scandal that had previously remained

3.1 Visualising the virtual cloud: Trevor Paglen's take on the materiality of NSA surveillance.

veiled, thus providing an important visual dimension to the abstract facts dominating the issue before.

After unveiling the institutional infrastructure of the global surveillance disclosure in this way, Paglen moved on to visualising the material choking points of global communication networks that afford such state-directed efforts of data gathering, analysis and appropriation. In an unnamed exhibition hosted by Metro Pictures in New York in 2015, Paglen displayed maps revealing the location of key landing stations of intercontinental fibre optic cables and showed photographs of secret NSA and GCHQ data centres and listening posts located in close proximity to these.[4] As if indirectly reiterating the points made by Phyber Optik and Acid Phreak in the early 1990s, Paglen's interventions undermine notions of the immateriality and fluidity of the digital and point to the palpable and visible concrete infrastructure behind apparently invisible state conduct. By visualising landing stations, cables, server centres and other physical features of state surveillance in the digital world, he makes palpable Amoore's (2018) cloud 1 and proves that Barlow's notion of an immaterial cyberspace free of sovereign power and state borders is wrong. In doing so, Paglen not only creates aesthetic objects that raise awareness for issues of state surveillance and control but also gathers and disseminates previously hidden information concerning the scale, location and administrative affiliation of these clandestine practices. In addition, he has assembled and disseminated important documentation facilitating further political measures aimed at countering unlimited state conduct. In this way his projects image and thereby make imaginable what was previously shrouded in secrecy, also fulfilling demands for combining political attitudes with an awareness of artworks' positions and performances in concrete sociopolitical contexts.

Such attention to the close nexus between aesthetic works, practices of imag(in)ing, and sociopolitical and economic ramifications is also characteristic of Paglen's installation *Autonomy Cube* (2014), which he built together with the programmer and activist Jakob Appelbaum. The cube consists of a rectangular white pedestal carrying a transparent glass box of 350 by 350 mm that contains a fully visible computer main frame. Through its aesthetic dimension, the work makes a clear point against black-boxed digital technologies, the various functions and modes of operation of which usually remain underneath the radar of average users. In addition to this critical attitude, however, the work also positions itself within the power vectors of contemporary tech-saturated societies and entails performance effects that not only enlighten spectators but directly facilitate political action.

Paglen's *Autonomy Cube* does more than open up normally sealed devices revealing what goes on inside, it also constitutes an open WiFi hot spot allowing any passer-by to connect to the Internet without registration. In addition, the provided connection defaults to the TOR network that makes anonymous communication possible by encrypting all traffic and hiding the IP addresses of connected devices. As such, the autonomy cube does not only make an argument about the necessity of transparency of digital technologies, but it becomes performative in that it ensures the anonymity and privacy of Internet-based communication. The installation also constitutes a TOR relay that facilitates the activities of other TOR users worldwide. The *Autonomy Cube* significantly complicates the data-gathering endeavours of the NSA, other state agencies and various commercial actors. In so doing, the work combines a critical message delivered through its aesthetic form with subversive performance effects based on the conscious positioning of the installation within the power-vectors of the contemporary security-state and techno-capitalism.

In other words, the *Autonomy Cube* highlights key aspects of politics in contemporary digital capitalism and offers immediate critical responses in order to facilitate resistance and mobilisation. It hinders attempts by states and major corporations to capture clouds of our data and provides the means and expertise necessary to devise adequate long-term responses by civil society and individual users. As such, it captures the essence of cloud-capturing technologies in an aesthetic work of art that combines a critical message with a political performance that matters.

Conclusion: a question of agency

So far, this chapter has established how contemporary digital networks make possible the capturing of data clouds by commercial and in particular state actors, and has highlighted how this facilitates a recalibration of global political space as a deterritorialised security regime that expands its activities, and thereby its borders, deep inside late-modern nation states. In addition, it has shown how Trevor Paglen attempts to capture such processes of capture in his works of art inviting a redistribution of the sensible that makes visible (and imag(in)able) the institutional and technical infrastructure behind these practices. The chapter has shown that an adequate understanding of the material and institutional dimensions of communication technologies, and especially the Internet, is a precondition for both state surveillance and economic profiling as well as for acts of resistance and (re)appropriation. Only expertise on how exactly technology operates in given socio-economic contexts enables the instrumentalisation of this technology for whatever purpose. Every technology, it seems, becomes what its contexts of application and use turn it into. This, it can be argued, retains its validity for the simplest hammer as well as for the most complex digital networks.

But is this true? Does technology passively bend to each whim and wish emanating from human users or institutions? Or do technical systems themselves predispose what we humans might do or even wish for? Do we have relations between subjects and objects where the former has agency to work upon the other instrumentalising it for a given purpose? Or do we see relations among series of subject-objects that continuously interact with each other and form one another in complex dynamics of mutual influence and formative feedback loops?

N. Katherine Hayles (2012, 2016), among others, has argued for the latter perspective. Using the concept of *technogenesis* (Hayles, 2012), she describes a gradual co-evolution of humans and technological objects where neither one nor the other is determinant, but both form and mould one another in complex processes of becoming. Regarding the distribution of power and agency in complex socio-technical networks, she proposes the term *cognitive assemblage* (Hayles, 2016) to fathom the increasingly dense interconnections between human users (their bodies, minds and institutions), physical networks and algorithms in contemporary digital domains. Expanding upon actor-network theory associated with Bruno Latour (2005) in particular, she argues for a notion of distributed agency that breaks up the concept into series of agential capacities potentially wielded by both human and machinic actors that become increasingly indistinguishable. In this perspective human and machinic agencies predispose and condition one another and cannot be adequately understood in isolation from one another.

In terms of Amoore's (2018) capturing clouds, this harks back at the initial question posed in this chapter. Do clouds actively capture and form human practices? Or are they captured by human users and institutions and simply put to use for given tasks? The complex learning and sorting algorithms conducting contemporary surveillance and profiling for state and commercial actors have access to unprecedented amounts of increasingly detailed information about users ranging from their vegetative states, non-conscious expressions of sentiments, subconscious fears, desires and urges, social networks, travel and consumption patterns, and political allegiances, to consciously expressed decisions or preferences (Gehl, 2014; Harcourt, 2015; Pötzsch, 2018). Giving states access to this type of data not only opens digital domains for sovereign power but extends the reach of states into the last uncolonised corners of human bodies and psyches.

Taken together these forms of data gathering and processing create a specific regime of the sensible that brings to the foreground certain subjectivities and practices, whilst tacitly hiding others from view. Through their increasingly boundless conduct, contemporary security states then extend the purview of these regimes across the entire globe creating deterritorialised zones of the exception that make borders impalpable for some and virtually uncrossable and limiting for others.

State actors, however, can be seen as being equally predisposed by complex algorithms that sort and profile vast data sets assembled by the massive surveillance of digital communication networks. Problematising agency in this context also implies problematising the agency of states on a global sphere where human regimes of knowledge, perception and action are to an ever-growing extent tacitly guided and predisposed by machines wielding agential powers in an increasing number of contexts. These examples make apparent that the capturing clouds of contemporary digital domains resemble complex assemblages in the sense proposed by Hayles (2016), rather than constituting networks that can neatly be divided into various state, human or machinic actors. The current regime of the sensible is distributed by machines and a proper redistribution requires both political awareness and technical expertise. Today, it seems, we are all part of the cloud since we both capture and are captured in varying contingent configurations of a globalised socio-technical borderscape.

Notes

1 Documentation about the 2013 Snowden revelations can be accessed via the websites of *The Guardian* newspaper (Macaskill and Dance, 2013), *WikiLeaks* (2019) and the American Civil Liberties Union (ACLU, 2019). For a concise overview and some background documentation and historical precedents, see *Wikipedia* (2019a, 2019b).
2 For an overview over his work, see Paglen (2019).
3 For the images, see Paglen (2014).
4 For documentation from the exhibition, see Metro Pictures (2015).

References

Abbate, J. (2000) *Inventing the Internet.* Cambridge, MA: The MIT Press.
ACLU (2019) 'NSA Documents', *ACLU.org*, www.aclu.org/nsa-documents-search. Accessed 29 September 2019.
Agnew, J. (1994) 'The territorial trap: The geographical assumptions of international relations theory', *Review of International Political Economy*, 1(1): 53–80.
Amoore, L. (2006) 'Biometric borders: Governing mobilities in the war on terror', *Political Geography*, 25(3): 336–51.
Amoore, L. (2018) 'Cloud geographies: Computing, data, sovereignty', *Progress in Human Geography*, 42(1): 4–24.
Andrejevic, M. (2007) *iSpy: Surveillance and Power in the Interactive Era.* Lawrence: University Press of Kansas.
Arendt, H. (1958) *The Human Condition.* Chicago: The University of Chicago Press.
Barlow, J.P. (1996) 'A declaration of the independence of cyberspace', *EFF.org* (8 February). www.eff.org/cyberspace-independence. Accessed 29 September 2019.
Bigo, D. (2007) 'Detention of foreigners, states of the exception, and the social practices of control of the banopticon', in P. Rajaram and C. Grundy-Warr (eds), *Borderscapes: Hidden Geographies and Politics at Territory's Edge.* Minneapolis: University of Minnesota Press, pp. 3–33.
Brambilla, C. (2015) 'Exploring the critical potential of the borderscapes concept', *Geopolitics*, 20(1): 14–34.
Brambilla, C., and H. Pötzsch (2017) 'In/visibility', in J. Schimanski and S.F. Wolfe (eds), *Border Aesthetics: Concepts and Intersections.* New York: Berghahn Books, pp. 68–89.
Castells, M. (1996) *The Rise of the Network Society.* Cambridge: Blackwell.
Cheney-Lippold, J. (2017) *We Are Data: Algorithms and the Making of Our Digital Selves.* New York: New York University Press.
Chun, W.H.K. (2006) *Control and Freedom: Power and Paranoia in the Age of Fiber Optics.* Cambridge, MA: MIT Press.
Derrida, J. (1981) *Dissemination.* Trans. B. Johnson. Chicago: The University of Chicago Press.
Diamandis, P.H., and S. Kotler (2015) *Abundance: The Future Is Better than You Think.* New York: Free Press.
Fuchs, C. (2014) *Social Media: A Critical Introduction.* London: Sage.
Galloway, A. (2004) *Protocol: How Control Exists after Decentralisation.* Cambridge, MA: MIT Press.

Galloway, A., and E. Thacker (2007) *The Exploit: A Theory of Networks*. Minneapolis: University of Minnesota Press.

Gehl, R.W. (2014) *Reverse-Engineering Social Media: Software, Culture, and Political Economy in New Media Capitalism*. Philadelphia: Temple University Press.

Green, S. (2019) 'Lines, traces, and tidemarks: Further reflections on forms of border', in O. Demetriou and R. Dimova (eds), *The Political Materialities of Borders: New Theoretical Directions*. Manchester: Manchester University Press, pp. 67–83.

Guehenno, J.-M. (1995) *End of the Nation State*. Minneapolis: University of Minnesota Press.

Gupta, S. (2004) *Hacking in the Computer World*. New Delhi: Mittal Publications.

Gustafsson, H. (2013) 'Foresight, hindsight and state secrecy in the American West: The geopolitical aesthetics of Trevor Paglen', *Journal of Visual Culture*, 12(1): 148–64.

Harcourt, B.E. (2015) *Exposed: Desire and Disobedience in the Digital Age*. Cambridge, MA: Harvard University Press.

Hayles, N.K. (2012) *How We Think: Digital Media and Contemporary Technogenesis*. Chicago: The University of Chicago Press.

Hayles, N.K. (2016) 'Cognitive assemblages: Technical agency and human interactions', *Critical Inquiry*, 43(1): 32–55.

Hogan, M. (2017) 'Servers', in I. Szeman, J. Wenzel and P. Yaeger (eds), *Fueling Culture: 101 Words for Energy and Environment*. New York: Fordham University Press, pp. 307–10.

Jenkins, H. (2006) *Fans, Bloggers, and Gamers: Exploring Participatory Culture*. New York: New York University Press.

Johnson, A., and M. Hogan (2017) 'Introducing location and dislocation: Global geographies of digital data', *Imaginations*, 8(2): 4–7.

Kurzweil, R. (2005) *The Singularity Is Near: When Humans Transcend Biology*. New York: Viking.

Lambert, L., and H.W. Poole (2005) *The Internet: A Historical Encyclopaedia – Biographies*. Santa Barbara: ABC Clio.

Latour, B. (2005) *Reassembling the Social: An Introduction to Actor–Network Theory*. Oxford: Oxford University Press.

Longo, M. (2017) *The Politics of Borders: Sovereignty, Security, and the Citizen After 9/11*. Cambridge: Cambridge University Press.

Macaskill, E., and G. Dance (2013) 'NSA files: decoded: What the revelations mean for you', *The Guardian* (online ed., 1 November), www.theguardian.com/world/interactive/2013/nov/01/snowden-nsa-files-surveillance-revelations-decoded. Accessed 29 September 2019.

Martínez, A.G. (2018) 'The end of data without borders', *Wired* (online ed., 2 January), www.wired.com/story/overseas-data-regulation/. Accessed 29 September 2019.

Metro Pictures (2015) 'Trevor Paglen: September 10–October 24, 2015', *Metro Pictures*. www.metropictures.com/exhibitions/trevor-paglen3. Accessed 30 September 2019.

Moberly, K. (2009) 'Codifying crime: A hacker's guide to computer culture', in J.R. Chaney, J.E. Ruggill and K.S. MacAllister (eds), *The Computer Culture Reader*. Newcastle: Cambridge Scholars Publishing, pp. 137–58.

Morozov, E. (2011) *The Net Delusion: How Not to Liberate the World*. London: Penguin.

O'Dowd, L. (2010) 'From a borderless world to a world of borders: Bringing history back in', *Environment & Planning D: Society & Space*, 28(2): 1031–50.

Ohmae, K. (1999) *The Borderless World: Power and Strategy in the Interlinked Economy*. New York: Harper Business.

Paglen, T. (2008) *I Could Tell You but Then You Would Have to Be Destroyed by Me: Emblems from the Pentagon's Black World*. New York: Melville House Publishing.

Paglen, T. (2009) *Blank Spots on the Map: The Dark Geography of the Pentagon's Secret World*. New York: Penguin.

Paglen, T. (2014) 'New photos of the NSA and other top intelligence agencies revealed for the first time', *The Intercept* (10 February), theintercept.com/2014/02/10/new-photos-of-nsa-and-others/. Accessed 29 September 2019.

Paglen, T. (2019) 'Work', *Trevor Paglen*, https://paglen.com/?l=work. Accessed 30 September 2019.

Paglen, T., and A. Gach (2003) 'Tactics without tears', *The Journal of Aesthetics and Protest*, 1(2), www.joaap.org/1/TacticsWithout/. Accessed 16 June 2020.

Paglen, T., and R. Solnit (2010) *Invisible: Covert Operations and Classified Landscapes*. New York: Aperture.

Paglen, T., and A.C. Thompson (2006) *Torture Taxi: On the Trail of the CIA's Rendition Flights*. New York: Melville House Publishing.

Parker, N., and N. Vaughan-Williams (2009) 'Lines in the sand: Towards an agenda for critical border studies', *Geopolitics*, 14(3): 582–7.

Parks, L. (2017) 'Networks', in I. Szeman, J. Wenzel and P. Yaeger (eds), *Fueling Culture: 101 Words for Energy and Environment*. New York: Fordham University Press, pp. 234–37.

Popescu, G. (2011) *Bordering and Ordering in the 21st Century: Understanding Borders*. New York: Rowman & Littlefield.

Pötzsch, H. (2015) 'The emergence of iBorder: Bordering bodies, networks, and machines', *Environment & Planning D: Society & Space*, 33(1): 101–18.

Pötzsch, H. (2017) 'Media matter', *TripleC*, 15(1): 148–70.

Pötzsch, H. (2018) 'Archives and identity in the context of social media and algorithmic analytics: Towards an understanding of iArchive and predictive retention', *New Media & Society*, 20(9): 3304–22.

Pugliese, J. (2013) *State Violence and the Execution of Law: Torture, Black Sites, Drones*. London: Routledge.

Rajaram, P.K., and C. Grundy-Warr (eds) (2007) *Borderscapes: Hidden Geographies and Politics at Territory's Edge*. Minneapolis: University of Minneapolis Press.

Rancière, J. (2004) *The Politics of Aesthetics: The Distribution of the Sensible*. Trans. G. Rockhill. London: Continuum.

Schmidt, E., and J. Cohen (2013) *The New Digital Age: Reshaping the Future of People, Nations, and Businesses*. New York: Random House.

Shirky, C. (2010) *Cognitive Surplus: Creativity and Generosity in a Connected Age*. New York: Penguin.

Sidaway, J. (2011) 'The return and eclipse of border studies? Charting agendas', *Geopolitics*, 16(4): 969–76.

Starosielski, N. (2015) *The Undersea Network*. Durham, NC: Duke University Press.

WikiLeaks (2019) 'The spy-files', *WikiLeaks*, https://wikileaks.org/the-spyfiles.html. Accessed 29 September 2019.

Wikipedia (2019a) 'Global surveillance disclosures (1970–2013)', *Wikipedia*, https://en.wikipedia.org/wiki/Global_surveillance_disclosures_(1970–2013). Accessed 30 September 2019.

Wikipedia (2019b) 'Global surveillance disclosures (2013– present)', *Wikipedia*, https://en.wikipedia.org/wiki/Global_surveillance_disclosures_(2013–present). Accessed 30 September 2019.

Zuboff, S. (2019) *The Age of Surveillance Capitalism: The Fight for a Human Future at the New Frontier of Power*. London: Profile Books.

4

In/visibilities beyond the spectacularisation: young people, subjectivity and revolutionary border imaginations in the Mediterranean borderscape

Chiara Brambilla

Moving beyond the spectacularisation of Mediterranean borders ...

The spectacularisation of Mediterranean borders assumes a crucial, often disquieting role in the dramatic staging of refugee crises and migrant deaths in the Mediterranean, and also in the discursive framing of terrorism, migration pressures and religious conflict. Focusing on the spectacularisation process enables a critical investigation of the complex relationship between border regimes and regimes of in/visibility. Through spectacularisation, the complexity of contemporary borderscapes is reduced to simple narratives and images. Complexity is made invisible: 'objects and subjectivities are given an aesthetic surface, which conceals b/orderings and the workings of power' (Schimanski and Wolfe, 2017: 157; see also Johan Schimanski, Chapter 10 below). The entangled tensions between visibility and invisibility take on a key role in the functioning of b/ordering regimes, and analysis of such regimes should thus include a wider focus on the multiple and shifting intersections of 'in/visibility and in/security in today's security-minded world' (Jusionyte and Goldstein, 2016: 3).

These considerations show the importance of devoting attention to the aesthetic dimension of b/ordering regimes and, especially, to the role of visual aesthetics in the politics of contemporary b/ordering and migration regimes. Diving into the manifold webs of b/ordering and in/visibility regimes reveals that simplistic yet dominant mass-media and political representations of what has been called 'the border spectacle' (De Genova, 2013) are not adequate for a productive understanding of the multifaceted and ambiguous nature of contemporary borderscapes. These representations are rich in border violence and undertake a crucial role in establishing the idea in the public opinion that such a violence is necessary and, thus, a fair and justifiable means with which to protect the citizens of the state against migration, which is understood as a dangerous threat to social peace and security. In this way, a politics of fear arises from – and is at the same time also the cause of – the enactment of a politics of exclusion based on the hardening and securitisation of borders that draws its legitimation from the politics of in/visibilities. This enactment figuratively produces (illegalised) migration and renders it visible through the border spectacle (Kasparek et al., 2015).

Since visibility and invisibility are central categories of border regimes, the border spectacle plays into what Marieke Borren has called a 'politics of in/visibility' (2008: 219), based on Hannah Arendt's conceptual investigation in her philosophical writings on politics (1958) of the intersections between 'public' and 'natural', and 'visibility' and 'invisibility'. Such a politics of in/visibility frames political subjects as either relevant or negligible through processes of making in/visible at the shifting threshold between what is worthy of being seen and what is not. Hence, border regimes and their scopic regimes, the latter defining 'an ensemble of practices and discourses that establish the truth claims ... and credibility of visual acts and objects and politically correct modes of seeing' (Feldman, 2000: 49), impact upon the lives and day-to-day practices of political subjects, bringing with them profound political, cultural and societal implications for subjectivities submitted to its peculiar gaze and regime. Due to the 'pathologies' of in/visibility (Borren, 2008: 224) that predispose the border spectacle, migrants and refugees, as well as civil society, groups and individuals inhabiting Mediterranean borderscapes suffer from what Arendt (1958) calls a 'public invisibility' that prevents them from actively participating in the public space, and deprives them of their political subjectivity and agency.

By embracing this perspective, what emerges is a more complex understanding of the border spectacle, one which makes us aware of the intertwined and ambiguous 'power-knowledge-networks that constitute the border regime and give rise to their public image' (Kasparek et al., 2015: 68). At the same time, this view productively fosters a rethinking of the relationship between b/ordering and in/visibility regimes, demonstrating that this relationship is politically ambivalent. On the one hand, it produces, and is traversed by, regimes of hegemonic in/visibility, which undertake a relevant role in the functioning of hegemonic borderscapes, in which the border is reduced to a mere tool for exercising and strengthening the violence of the state and its allegedly exclusive authority. On the other hand, the relationship between b/orderings and in/visibilities can be the basis for counter-hegemonic borderscaping. A form of performative resistance can potentially arise from the complex ambiguous relational space between b/ordering and in/visibility processes, through subversive forms of in/visibility and practices of in/visibilisation that feed into counterhegemonic frameworks, questioning and undermining naturalised social practices and discursive positions within a pre-established hierarchical social space (Brambilla and Pötzsch, 2017).

Such resistance encourages new conditions of possibility for agency beyond the media's spectacularisation of Mediterranean borderscapes, and in so doing induces a crisis in the concept of truth as a single, simplistic narrative, while returning historical and political agency to border crossers and inhabitants.

... through the borderscaping lens

In this section I will illustrate the potential of the borderscaping approach (Brambilla et al., 2015) for de-spectacularising and de-reducing images and narratives of Mediterranean borderscapes. The challenge associated with this research work is to displace monolithic and essentialised ideas of Mediterranean borderscapes that shape them as the southern external walls of fortress Europe, and rather foreground the historicity of the way in which border making is imagined and practised.

Specifically, this chapter highlights the relevant role of what I term the *politics–aesthetics nexus*, which is at the heart of the borderscaping formulation, where enquiry into the potentialities of the borderscaping approach for de-spectacularising images and narratives of Mediterranean borderscapes is concerned (Brambilla, 2018). Giving attention to the politics–aesthetics nexus enables me to critically examine another relevant argument that the borderscaping approach raises, which is the paramount importance of fostering a *political and performative method* in the study of borders.

The politics–aesthetics nexus and borderscaping as an inherently political and performative method

As has been documented elsewhere (Brambilla, 2015a) the double etymology of the borderscapes notion allows border representations and practices to be redirected through the very interactions between politics and aesthetics in which borderscapes originate, thus representing borders as complex socio-spatial processes that are symbolically and materially constructed. The ambivalence that characterises the etymological evolution of the borderscapes concept highlights the representation of borders as well as individual and collective practices of construction (bordering), deconstruction (de-bordering) and reconstruction (re-bordering) of borders. The concept thus allows us to recognise the complexity of border processes as constructed, lived and experienced by human beings (Rajaram and Grundy-Warr, 2007).

Navigating through the borderscapes lens is a way of bridging the *metaphorical-material border gap*, giving us an opportunity to rethink borders by overcoming modern oppositions between theories and narratives, and between representations and experiences, by highlighting instead how their interplay can produce new border knowledge. In contrast to the boundaries of nation-states, which were invented as lines on the flat and bi-dimensional surface of the map according to the modern territorialist geopolitical imaginary, borderscapes are multidimensional and mobile constructions inhabited by Michel de Certeau's 'spatial practices' (1984: 91–130). Such practices can reveal, at the intersection of experience and representation, the geographies of actions and stories taking place in the border place, as well as the itineraries of the mobile subjects that cross it (see also Strüver, 2005: 8–10). Following this, within the borderscape, different stories are represented and different practices are enacted.

This corresponds to what Jacques Rancière (2010: 139) calls 'politics as process', which 'occurs when there is a disruption of a hegemonic or dominant mapping of the sensible' (Aitken, 2014: 162), involving the constant inclusion of something new that ultimately prevents the emergence of a sedimented objectified political structure (see also Amilhat Szary, Chapter 7 below). Aesthetics takes on a crucial role in the functioning of politics as process; it is the expression of a political idea that is disruptive in the first instance, but then, in the second, elaborates the idea of another possible spatial and temporal distribution of the senses (what is done, seen, heard and thought, where, when and by whom) and another future (Rancière, 2005: 80). Political and aesthetic practices also involve the intertwining of several strategies that are intended to make the invisible visible or to question the self-evidence of the visible. Political and aesthetic discourses and practices 'introduce dissensus by hollowing out that "real" and multiplying it in a polemical way', as they re-articulate connections between signs and images and contribute to the emergence of plurivocal borderscapes that in Rancière's terms 'invent new trajectories between what can be seen, what can be said and what can be done' (2010: 149).

Drawing attention to bordering processes (Houtum and Naerssen, 2002) that involve a wide range of actors, with a focus on the everyday micro-practices, the concept of borderscapes liberates the border from the burden of state-centric 'territorial traps' (Agnew, 1994) and opens up new possibilities for interrogating the ordinary functioning of b/ordering processes and practices (Rumford, 2008). This implies that attention should also be devoted to subjective political experiences of b/ordering in the wider social context. Indeed, it is precisely in subjective experiences that one can trace the concurrent, dynamic and shifting processes of construction, deconstruction and reconstruction of borders, moving beyond the structure-versus-agency dichotomy. The borderscaping framework highlights 'the multi-vocal, mutually constitutive, shifting and contested meanings of contemporary bordering processes' (Yuval-Davis, 2013, quoted in Novak, 2017: 854). Borderscapes thus signify multifaceted spaces of interactions and intersections among 'a range of practices or "borderwork" in everyday life', which challenge monolithic hegemonic border regimes encompassing the 'differentially situated gazes' of borderlanders and border-crossers. These gazes contribute different 'contradictory, and, at times, conflictual' aspects of – as well as perspectives on – contemporary borders (Cassidy et al., 2018: 171).

In this light, the borderscape allows one to move beyond the often-criticised gap between practices and representations, by contributing to 'a shift from the *concept of the border* to the *notion of bordering practice*, and the adoption of the lens of *performance* through which bordering practices are produced and reproduced' (Parker and Vaughan-Williams, 2012: 729). Moreover, as Parker and Vaughan-Williams (2012: 729) have stated, 'practices of bordering and de-bordering are not just performed as theatrical spectacles but are also shown to be *performative* of particular socioeconomic and political realities and subject-positions'. In so doing, the borderscape approach favours a performative viewpoint on borders that also brings together the concept of performance and the notion of performativity. This last concept relates to performances, highlighting their political implications, and mainly connecting performance to a critical reflection on the exertion of power (Salter, 2011). Different performances of sovereignty co-produce the borderscape, where they can be found in a dynamic spatial and temporal relationship; at the same time, they are negotiated, resisted and countered by counter-hegemonic bordering practices acted out by a plurality of actors beyond the hegemonic nature of the sovereign state. Through the intersection of representations and practices, borderscapes also attend to the relationship between the visual and the material, contributing to exploring what kinds of new thinking on borders might emerge in that relationship. Practice is what humans do with things. Some of the effects of these doings is to make (or not make) things visible in specific ways. These considerations thus draw attention to the co-constitution of human subjectivities and the visual objects created by their practices. Following this, in my exploration of the potential of the borderscaping approach for de-spectacularising Mediterranean borders, I take aesthetics beyond its traditional focus on visual arts and representation, and towards the role of aesthetics in reproducing everyday life (Saito, 2007).

In the light of these considerations, I argue that borderscaping facilitates creative and innovative ways of making border-related individual experiences accessible in the public sphere by bringing the historicity of imaginations and practices of border-making to the foreground, while also reaffirming the importance of the political and performative method in border studies. Narratives and images are part of the borderscapes in which border-crossings and b/orderings take place, contributing to the negotiation of borders in the public sphere. The images and narratives of the border spectacle undertake a crucial role in depoliticising and naturalising political and social phenomena, in that they visibilise border inhabitants, border-crossers and social phenomena without showing subjects (migrants or civil society are visibilised, but not necessarily given subjectivity). However, by restoring subjectivity to the foreground as a crucial aspect of social and political life, the borderscaping approach might contribute to the de-essentialisation and repoliticisation of the border-migration nexus. It thus engages with a deeper reflection on the reconfiguration of political subjectivity in the midst of the 2010s so-called migration crisis in the Mediterranean, but at the same time sheds light on the urgency to return subjectivity to the foreground as a crucial aspect of social and political life.

Advancing an understanding of borders beyond their spectacularisation, reinterpretation through the borderscaping concept can be achieved only through attention to the *genealogical dimension* of the border-migration nexus. Only through this genealogical dimension is it possible to overcome the ahistorical bias that besets much of the political and mass-media discourse on the present political and sociocultural border-migration challenges (Donnan et al., 2017; see also Müller-Funk, Chapter 1 above). At the same time, such a historicisation of the border-migration nexus might make us able to resituate the relationship between states, local communities and individuals in the more concrete micro-history in which it originates. The ways in which borders are produced, but also how they function, act and are enacted – that is, how they are actualised in the day-to-day life (Green, 2010) – may thus be revealed.

Alternative forms of political subjectivity and agency in the Italian/Tunisian borderscape

Conceptual and methodological considerations in the previous section speak directly to my ethnographic research in the Italian/Tunisian borderland.[1] Adopting the borderscaping lens, this research provides a multi-sited analysis of the Italian/Tunisian borderland, zooming in on the urban space of Mazara del Vallo in Sicily (Cole, 2003), and its relations with the city of Mahdia in Tunisia (Cusumano, 1976).

Gazing into the history of the relationship between the urban borderscapes of Mazara and Mahdia tells us about a process that Naor Ben-Yehoyada (2011) has described as a progressive 'Mediterraneanisation' in the borderland in the Channel of Sicily. 'Mediterraneanisation' denotes the process by which a place becomes more intertwined in a network of connections and movements with other places in or around the Mediterranean. Embracing this viewpoint, significant emphasis is placed on the need to humanise the borderland by paying attention to the experiences of its inhabitants. As borders are not experienced in the same way by all people, my research was intended to describe how 'pluritopical' and 'pluriversal' experiences of borders (Rodman, 2003) often clash with the assumptions of geopolitical theory and dominant mass-media spectacularisation of Mediterranean borderscapes (see also Nyman, Chapter 9 below). I aimed to investigate how the rhetoric and policies of borders impact, conflict and exist in a dynamic relationship with everyday life, as well as how this rhetoric and policies are experienced, lived and interpreted by those who inhabit the Italian/Tunisian borderscape. This highlights the urgency of advancing a perspective that gives voice to a multiplicity of individual and group stances dealing with the Mediterranean neighbourhood as they are embedded in the realms of identities, perceptions, beliefs and emotions, whilst also examining practices and experiences of dealing with Euro/African Mediterranean interactions, both political and territorial, as well as symbolic and cultural. At the same time, a grounded diversity of perspectives and practices must relate back to the broader geopolitical shifts defining this region in order to better understand the dialogue between the various scales of action through which the Mediterranean is made and experienced beyond the spectacle.

Negotiating in/visibilities, or returning public visibility to young people

Among the different actors involved in this research, particular attention has been devoted to second-generation and third-generation young migrants whose families are originally from Tunisia (mainly from Mahdia), as well as to young people whose families are originally from Italy, all now living together in Mazara del Vallo.

Listening to youths' viewpoints on the borderscape where they live, and giving voice and visibility to their ideas, offer us the opportunity to make their agency emerge as a form of resistance capable of combating what Michel Foucault calls a 'microphysics of power' (1977: see especially 26–30), through which an essentialised, contemplative and passive idea of the Italian/Tunisian borderscape is externally imposed. These practices of resistance take place in young people's experiences of local places; they express what de Certeau describes as a counter-action of 'everyday practices' to Foucauldian 'microphysics of power' (1984: xiv–xxiv). These practices are enacted by young people, who inscribe them in the borderscape that they inhabit as a space of good life and liveability. They contest and challenge hegemonic configurations of the same borderscape as they are communicated by the mass-media spectacle of Mediterranean borders, whilst searching for novel and common configurations of the Italian/Tunisian borderland. Encouraging young people's active engagement represents the first important condition that must be met for new forms of political agency and subjectivity to happen in the Mediterranean. However, thanks to a research methodology capable of giving Arendtian 'public visibility' back to young people's experiences, this agency can be grasped, and we can thereby counterpoint what Borren eloquently terms the 'pathologies of in/visibility' (2008) on which the border spectacle in the Mediterranean is based. Fostering an active engagement of young people by making visible the lived complexity of their political subjectivities provides us with an opportunity to counterpoint these pathologies of in/visibility, and refocus the attention on the complex practices underpinning the diasporic public sphere, in which young migrants and Italian youths can become active agents and create a different image of migration across the Mediterranean.

In line with these considerations, my research with young people living in the Italian/Tunisian borderland has used an interdisciplinary qualitative methodology, bringing together social and human sciences. Adopting this methodological approach, we have organised educational workshop activities with young people whilst focusing on two topics: 'Landscape as an intercultural mediator' and 'Italian/Tunisian border: imaginations, imaginaries and images'. Young people's viewpoints were incorporated into a broader ethnographic work that involved different ethnographic methods (non-participant observation, field notes, narrative and semi-structured interviews, focus groups, photographs and short videos) and included also adults in the analysis, in order to make the genealogical complexity of the migrancy-borderscape nexus emerge (DeMaria Harney and Baldassar, 2007). These ethnographic observations have been useful for the interpretation of the young people's self-representations.

Mixed collaborative visual approaches have been used to outline possible tactics for negotiating regimes of in/visibility in an attempt to give public visibility back to young people. During the workshop activities, a great emphasis was put on to aesthetic narrative approaches, considering the relevant role of narratives and images – be they written texts, oral narrations or stories told by visual means – for expressing identity processes.[2] Specifically, narrative visual tools (including auto-photography, short videos, drawings, photo elicitation, participatory mapping, and counter-mapping) were used, as well as a variety of other qualitative research methods, including walking expeditions and shadowing, in order to encourage young people to tell their stories through aesthetic tools that bring their spatial imagination to the foreground (Brambilla, 2015b). What has proved to be particularly important to return public visibility to young people is a mixed methodological approach capable of using an innovative combination of narratives and images. Indeed, it is precisely by bringing narrative and visual methods together that we can gain a better insight into the functioning of the complex relational space between b/ordering and in/visibility processes and practices.

Special attention has been devoted to the videographic method. The research activities undertaken with young people in both Italy and Tunisia were filmed and included in the documentary *Houdoud al bahr | The Mediterranean frontiers: Mazara – Mahdia* (concept: Chiara Brambilla, direction: Chiara Brambilla and Sergio Visinoni, 2015). The documentary has been, in part, directly shot by the youths themselves. In this light, the videographic method and other visual methods have been adopted as an ethnographic practice and method for social research, understanding them as aesthetic, communicative and analytical tools. Such methods help us not only to describe visually social practices and discourses but also to understand how space is constructed, perceived, interpreted and represented by its inhabitants. The video medium and other visual aesthetic methods offer alternative ways through which we can reveal the constructed nature of information, allowing us to critically interrogate the tension between hegemonic images in the mass-media and counter-hegemonic descriptions. Such alternatives can co-produce the borderscape through the political presence of young people in the everyday.

Special attention has been given to people's perceptions, interpretations, experiences and representations of borders by adopting participatory and performative research approaches aimed to advance an act(or)-centred approach that fosters not only participation but also engagement of a broader spectrum of different and sometimes new actors (see also Horsti and Tucci, Chapter 11 below). Collaborative visual methods and media have been used to create routes through which young people, whose voices are not so often heard in public domains, can express their experiences and knowledge of the Italian/Tunisian borderscape. Following this, it is not necessarily simply the audiovisual products of the research that are important for de-spectacularising images and narratives of Mediterranean borderscapes, but also the performative dimension of the process through which they are made. The potential of the borderscaping approach for de-spectacularising images and narratives of Mediterranean borderscapes through the close connection between borderscaping, the politics–aesthetics nexus, and the application of a performative and political method is also enhanced by the ways in which the research results have been disseminated both at the academic and the non-academic level. In addition to the documentary film, an exhibition *Houdoud al bahr | I confini del mare* (*The borders of the sea*) has been conceived as a 'travelling' tool for disseminating research results from the EUBORDERSCAPES research project and for presenting our findings as training and educational tools. The majority of photographs, iconographic and different types of audio-visual materials in the exhibition come from the educational workshop activities undertaken with the young people living in Mazara del Vallo during the course of research (Brambilla, 2016).

In the light of this, both the topics and the methods of the educational workshop activities were intended to operationalise the politics-aesthetics nexus in which borderscapes originate by encouraging young people to problematise their political and aesthetic relationships with the borderland they inhabit. The activities also enable young people to conceptualise the border no longer as a divisive linear geometry but as a constructed, inhabited, and relational space – as a space where new political subjectivities and agency can be shaped, and therefore as a space of political opportunity.

Inhabiting the Italian/Tunisian borderscape: a Mediterranean-inspired citizenship

Both ethnographic research and the making of the film highlight a political agency of young people living in Mazara del Vallo that is a result of inhabiting the Italian/Tunisian borderscape in-between Mazara and Mahdia. Tunisian youths try to give meaning to their lives on both sides of the Sicilian Channel. Through their spatio-social trajectories of life, their multiple perceptions, experiences and imaginaries of the Mediterranean borderland, they refuse to be reduced to the choice between being Italian, Tunisian or global. These youths embody the borderscape and live in accordance with an identity that receives its form and flexibility from their inhabiting the Mediterranean constellation that has been developing in the Channel of Sicily over the centuries. In this context, the flux of transnational identities is reflected in multiple senses of belonging to place, describing emotional attachment rather than official citizenship. In view of this, Tunisian and Italian youths can probably be considered as the precursors and creators of new and original forms of citizenship: a Mediterranean-inspired citizenship that is fluid, relational and complexly interwoven with emotions and desires. It is a citizenship based on other forms of sociality, other political relations that are more complex than modern citizenship can allow or describe (Ben-Yehoyada, 2015).

This new form of citizenship was expressed by many of young Tunisians we met during the research.

> Each of us feels to be a bit Tunisian, a bit Italian, and a bit Mediterranean. For me, it is difficult to trap myself in an identity category that does not change and has rigid boundaries. I feel to belong in an equal way to my two countries … This multiplicity of belonging is, in my opinion, more representative of contemporary identities than a model based on fixed and unchanging belongings. (Interview with S.C., a sixteen-year-old Tunisian girl, by C. Brambilla, Mazara del Vallo, 7 May 2014, translation from Italian by C. Brambilla)

In the text accompanying her drawing of the Italian/Tunisian borderscape (see Figure 4.1), a sixteen-year-old Tunisian girl, M.B., living in Mazara, wrote that 'it would be great if the United States of the Mediterranean were founded' and added that 'Mazara is closer to Tunisia than it is to Milan or Bergamo' (from the text accompanying M.B.'s drawing, educational workshop at San Vito foundation's place, Mazara del Vallo, 5 May 2014, translation from Italian by C. Brambilla). Another sixteen-year-old Tunisian girl, S.C., wrote in her text that 'I feel like a girl who is half Italian and half Tunisian and who lives in the middle of the Mediterranean in-between Sicily and

4.1 Drawing and text by a sixteen-year-old Tunisian girl (M.B.), educational workshop at San Vito Foundation's place, Mazara del Vallo, 5 May 2014.

Tunisia' (from the text accompanying S.C.'s drawing, educational workshop at San Vito foundation's place, Mazara del Vallo, 5 May 2014, translation from Italian by C. Brambilla). A Tunisian guy aged eighteen years, B.Y.N., wrote that 'I feel attached to both Tunisia and Italy as my family lives in Tunis and my friends are in Mazara' (from the text accompanying B.Y.N.'s drawing, educational workshop at San Vito foundation's place, Mazara del Vallo, 5 May 2014, translation from Italian by C. Brambilla).

In this light, ethnographic research in the Italian/Tunisian borderland shows the urgency of rethinking Mediterranean border imaginaries from a situated perspective and capturing ways in which Mediterranean imaginaries are experienced and practised on the ground in multiple locations and by a diversity of actors. It is important to avoid a simple application of definitions and categorisations from the outside to a reality that instead requires a deeper understanding that takes into consideration the specificity of local experience. A situated approach also favours productive attempts to counterpoint unilateral or asymmetrical forms of political relations. Young people sketch a counter-image of the Italian/Tunisian borderscape through a resistance that is enacted not necessarily through organised movements but rather through a political presence in everyday Mediterranean contexts (Spyrou and Christou, 2014). It is a form of resistance that acts on the Italian/Tunisian borderscape through imagining, experiencing, and performing in the Mediterranean neighbourhood.

In this regard, it is worth referring to how the simplified presentation of the so-called Kasbah quarter in Mazara in dominant political and mass-media narratives and images conflicts with the complex image of the Kasbah as described by young people inhabiting the transnational urban space of Mazara in their day-to-day, multiple experiences. The Kasbah is a decayed quarter of the old town centre founded by the Arabs during their occupation of Sicily. Following the classical scheme of substitution, the presence of first migrants (above all Tunisians in the 1970s and later a vast group of Roma families preceding the Kosovo war in the 1990s) persuaded the Italian inhabitants of the historical centre to abandon their decayed houses, rather than spending money on restoring them, in order to move to recently built residential areas (Saitta, 2010). As a result, a new pattern of urban ethnic and social distribution came into the light and the Kasbah became a symbol of the foreign presence in Mazara, presented now by local and national media as well as by local authorities as a dangerous place. The presence of foreigners in the Kasbah has been associated with different forms of micro-criminality in the quarter and threatens the personal and social sense of security of the Italian inhabitants of the Sicilian town. Yet, it is worth considering the ways in which young people's narratives and images question this monolithic representation of the Kasbah. Although the dominant mass-media and political imaginary of the Kasbah influence young people's own ideas about the quarter, these youths are able to construct an alternative image of the Kasbah through their mundane experiences. Their ideas yield valuable insight into the complexity of the place, as well as offering people means for better understanding the places where they live, go to school, work, shop and socialise (Low, 2017: 1–10). In this regard, interesting examples can be drawn from the documentary film *Houdoud al Bahr* (Brambilla and Visinoni, 2015). In some scenes in the film, I asked questions about the Kasbah to an eleven-year-old Italian girl, N.M., attending first grade (I C, 2013/2014 school year) in the Paolo Borsellino junior high school in Mazara:

C.B.: What is the Kasbah?

N.M.: I don't actually ever go there, because I don't like it and it scares me, but I know that it's not that nice a place.

C.B.: Did your parents tell you that?

N.M.: Yes, my parents ... but almost everyone says that. I know that some time ago it was where all the Italians lived and it was the historical centre.

(Brambilla and Visinoni, 2015: 0:04:57)

C.B.: How do you imagine it [the Kasbah]?

N.M.: I don't know, where all the Muslims live.

(Brambilla and Visinoni, 2015: 0:16:06)

N.M.: My grandmother lived in Regina Square [in the Kasbah]. She left Regina Square because some Tunisians, who carried out some muggings, came to live there and my grandmother started to get worried and therefore she preferred to leave. I was told they keep it clean, but I've never been there again.

C.B.: Does your grandmother still have a house there?

N.M.: No, she doesn't ... When my grandmother lived there, people from Mazara still lived there. However, since my grandmother went away, when the Tunisians arrived, people from Mazara no longer live there.

(Brambilla and Visinoni, 2015: 0:16:16)

These parts of conversation drawn from the film help us understand that dominant narratives dealing with the Kasbah make the image of the quarter so stereotypical that real configurations of the neighbourhood are rendered invisible and absent in young people's imaginaries of the place. Indeed, although these youths go to school daily, attend after-school programmes, meet their friends, spend their free time outdoors and sometimes even live in buildings that are located within the Kasbah, they do not seem to be aware that they do so, and rather report that they have never been in the Kasbah and did not even know where it was. What young people know – they said – is that the Kasbah is a dangerous place where all the Muslims live. However, using mixed collaborative narrative visual approaches during the workshop activities offered us the opportunity to interrogate young people's perceptions, representations and experiences of the Kasbah quarter, showing complexity rather than simple and monolithic narratives.

During an education workshop on the topic 'Landscape as an intercultural mediator', carried out with a group of students attending the first grade (I C, 2013/2014 school year) in the Paolo Borsellino junior high school, we asked students to identify places which were very important for them and without which Mazara could no more be recognised as their town. Interestingly enough, most of the young people said that it was very important for them to keep the Kasbah. In this regard, it is worth quoting what the same Italian girl, N.M., whom I interviewed in the film, said during the workshop:

> I would like to keep the Kasbah in Mazara because my Tunisian friends live there and therefore I don't want to exclude it. If I exclude it, it would be as if they went away too, so I want to keep it. (Brambilla and Visinoni, 2015: 0:15:50)

A similar view of the Kasbah was expressed by young students attending the fourth/fifth grade (IV–V B, 2013/2014 and 2014/2015 school years) in the Daniele Ajello junior school in Mazara, who participated in other collaborative workshop activities on landscape as an intercultural mediator. Specifically, I would like to refer to some relevant examples taken from drawing and participatory mapping activities. In drawing their participatory map of Mazara – which they decided to entitle 'Mazara yesterday and today: the map made by young people living in town' both in Italian and Arabic – the youths gave a significant role to the Kasbah. In contrast to 'official' maps of the town, the participatory map made by Italian and Tunisian young people living together in Mazara shows the Kasbah as the historical and present heart of the town (see Figure 4.2). The most important places in the heart of the town (e.g., a Tunisian-house-style building coloured in white and blue, the Tunisian school, the Islamic Cultural Centre, a shop selling Tunisian ethnic items and products, Mahdia Square) are located there and give the town its peculiar Mediterranean urban identity in-between Italy and Tunisia. At the same time, these places in the Kasbah are identified as the most important ones in Mazara by the youth, who said several times

4.2 Participatory map of Mazara del Vallo drawn by young students attending the fourth/fifth grade (IV–V B) in the junior school Daniele Ajello in Mazara during collaborative workshop activities, 28–29 May 2015.

during the discussion that Mazara would have no more been their town, if there hadn't been those places.

These arguments show that the borderscaping approach is useful for advancing an understanding of borders that goes beyond their spectacularisation. Through a focus on performances, the borderscaping lens succeeds in reconnecting the level of the imaginary with that of experiences and practices that shed light on the plural tensions traversing the relational space between the two levels. In this way, the borderscaping perspective transcends the border spectacle (which describes borders as a powerfully evocative, highly condensed, singular symbol), as it follows the discursive and performative constructions of the border-migration nexus (which regard borders as a practice that has profound implications on imagination and turn away from absolutes) (Heyman and Symons, 2012). Borderscaping can be a potential form of performative resistance, which may lead to new imaginaries. In this sense, borderscaping can enable us to overcome the spectacle of the Mediterranean border–migration nexus whilst also favouring a new interpretation of this nexus based on a plurality of performances. Such performances call into question any neat definition of the Mediterranean border-migration nexus. They show that we should no more search for definitions and that more attention deserves to be given to ways in which this nexus is expressed in people's day-to-day actions and activities.

Seeking a better understanding of the events where subjects do not act within the modern idea of citizenship, and where political commitment to a certain kind of citizenship is either ambiguous or explicitly refused, William Walters (2008) suggests the idea of 'acts of demonstration'. Young people's imaginaries and experiences can be regarded as acts of demonstration. Indeed, young people suggest new constructive ways of obtaining knowledge and novel epistemologies of resistance via a process that involves the return of what was invisibilised to the zone of possible agency and historicity. At the intersection of individual and collective agency, young people's imaginaries and experiences challenge the tactical, pre-emptive invisibilisation that pervades hegemonic media narratives and political discourses of the spectacle. Hence, alternative political agencies of young people contribute to the understanding that Mediterranean borderscapes are constituted and traversed by acts that allow for a new conceptualisation of the spatiality of politics beyond the boundaries of the dominant institutional order. In this light, not only are the significant political implications of the borderscape reaffirmed, but they also re-establish the relevance of the performative approach that the borderscape enables.

There is a Mediterranean-inspired citizenship that criss-crosses Mediterranean space and expresses not only the geographical proximity but also a deep emotional closeness between Italy and Tunisia, between Europe and Africa. This particular feeling is expressed in a number of texts accompanying the drawings made by young people during educational workshops. Young people's narratives and images show that these youths do not perceive any distance in their daily lives between Italy and Tunisia. Regarding this, it is worth mentioning the text accompanying the drawing by an eleven-year-old boy, G.I., attending first grade (I C, 2013/2014 school year) in the Paolo Borsellino junior high school (see Figure 4.3). He wrote 'Border = history – people' and added, 'Tunisia and Sicily = two cultures that have been combined' (translation from Italian by C. Brambilla). In his drawing, G.I. represented the branch of sea between Sicily and Tunisia as a space traversed by a chain of people connecting the two shores.

Enacting this new form of Mediterranean-inspired citizenship through their daily presence in the Italian/Tunisian borderscape, young people become 'border subjects', that is to say 'border beings who have attained subjectivity, negotiating regimes of in/visibility so as to become sensible' (Schimanski and Wolfe, 2017: 153). As border subjects, young people can have the

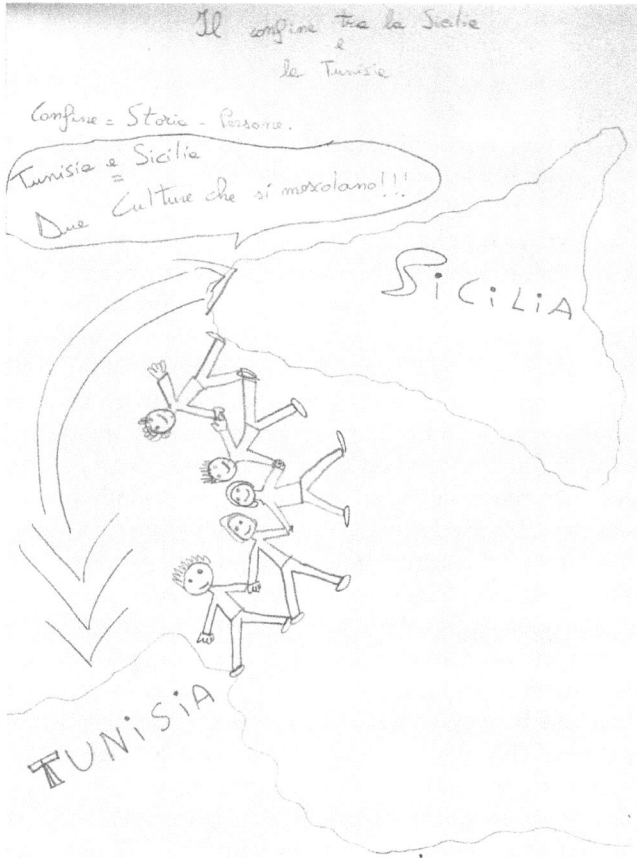

4.3 Drawing and text by an eleven-year-old boy (G.I.), attending the first grade (I C, 2013/2014 school year) in the Paolo Borsellino junior high school in Mazara, educational workshop, 7 May 2014.

potential to enact new strategies of in/visibility moving forward alternative and participatory forms of subjectivity that contribute to counter-hegemonic borderscapes. Future, emergent borders and subjectivities are in the state of becoming and counteract naturalised and traditional conceptions of borders and the communities inhabiting them as presented through the spectacularisation of Mediterranean borders. Counter-hegemonic borderscapes emerging from the work with young border inhabitants encourage the subversion of existing border regimes through tactics of in/visibility. Such subversion includes formerly excluded subjects, positions and articulations in the public discourse, potentially threatening the stability of pre-established hegemonic frameworks.

Revolutionary border imaginations towards an alternative horizon of hope

Borderscaping gives us the chance to de-spectacularise Mediterranean borders and the border-migration nexus by responding to the need to think outside the modern geopolitical imaginary to understand contemporary social and political change. Its aim is to promote the liberation of border imaginations from the straitjacket imposed by the pervasive methodological nationalism of the territorial trap, and ultimately to contribute to an understanding of new forms of belonging and becoming that are worth investigating.

Reimagining Mediterranean borderscapes around young people's imaginations and practices returns subjectivity to the foreground, and also favours new forms of performative participation in public political processes that make a conception of the border as a finite divisive geometry questionable and promote young people's 'revolutionary border imaginations' (Aitken et al., 2011). The opportunity of reconfiguring real and imagined borderscapes is revolutionary to the extent that it moves young people, regardless of whether the border seemingly (or actually) remains intact. In this sense, borderscaping can be a potential form of performative resistance leading to new imaginaries. This may be possible because the borderscape is concerned with bridging the metaphorical-material border gap, bringing together experiences and representations through the politics-aesthetics nexus, and allowing for new imaginaries based on a multidimensional understanding of borders. In this light, borderscaping allows for rereading of imaginaries as representations of socio-spatial conditions, contributing to highlight, as Arjun Appadurai (1996) pointed out, the fact that imagination should be regarded as a social practice and reinstated as the focus of social projects and sociocultural activities.

Thus, it is worth moving from a rendering of the Mediterranean as a space of crisis to a new outlook where it is regarded as a space of political creativity, as a space in which it may also be possible to cultivate a 'politics of hope' (Appadurai, 2013) – that is to say, a politics of possibilities to come. Embodying the Mediterranean borderscape where they live, Tunisian and Italian youths in-between Mazara and Mahdia give a relevant account of this politics of hope, expressed in the idea of Mediterranean-inspired citizenship. Taking up James Holston's concept (2009), this Mediterranean-inspired citizenship can be understood as a kind of 'insurgent citizenship'. Indeed, Holston locates forms of insurgent citizenship at the margins of the sociocultural and political space, which are, however, never really marginal. On the contrary, they are critical spaces where insurgent citizenship originates from the creativity of practices; through this the borderscape is imagined, perceived, experienced and inhabited daily.

In this light, Tunisian and Italian youths living together in-between Mazara and Mahdia are the creators of this new insurgent citizenship. While they do not explicitly challenge the modern categorisations of political belonging, they, however, do so through their day-to-day political presence in the borderscape. This does not mean that one must neglect the violence of the border regime and its impositions, or avoid the difficulties related to putting this new form of citizenship into practice. Rather, we inevitably need to look at spaces where new forms of political agency are shaped by revealing a *horizon of hope*, through which – as Aitken (2014) has described in his book on the ethnopoetics of space and the transformative potential of young people's agency – it will be possible to move towards a new productive understanding of borders and the border–migration nexus, one that will extend beyond the line and its anticipated future, beyond the contours of present political categories.

Notes

1 My conceptual and ethnographic research for this text has been conducted within the framework of the research project EUBORDERSCAPES (2012–2016) funded by European Commission FP7-SSH-2011-1 (290775). My reflection in this chapter is also closely related to my participation in the transdisciplinary Border Aesthetics research project (Norwegian Research Council 2010–2013).

2 In Mazara, we worked with four different age groups of youths: seven to nine years old, attending after-school programmes at the House of Hope Community's place; nine to ten years old, attending fourth/fifth grade (IV–V B) in the junior school Daniele Ajello; eleven to twelve years old, attending first grade (I C) in the junior high school Paolo Borsellino; sixteen to nineteen years old, attending the after-school programme Voices from the Mediterranean at the San Vito Foundation's place. This last group of Tunisian youths have also been involved in educational workshop activities on the same two topics in Mahdia in the summer, when they returned to Tunisia to visit their parents' families during the summer holidays.

References

Agnew, J. (1994) 'The territorial trap: The geographical assumptions of international relations theory', *Review of International Political Economy*, 1(1): 53–80.

Aitken, S. (2014) *The Ethnopoetics of Space and Transformation: Young People's Engagement, Activism and Aesthetics*. Farnham: Ashgate.

Aitken, S., K. Swanson, F.J. Bosco and T. Herman (eds) (2011) *Young People, Border Spaces and Revolutionary Imaginations*. London: Routledge.

Appadurai, A. (1996) *Modernity at Large: Cultural Dimensions of Globalisation*. Minneapolis: University of Minnesota Press.

Appadurai, A. (2013) *The Future as Cultural Fact: Essays on the Global Condition*. London: Verso.

Arendt, H. (1958) *The Human Condition*. Chicago: The University of Chicago Press.

Ben-Yehoyada, N. (2011) 'The moral perils of Mediterraneanism: Second-generation immigrants practicing personhood between Sicily and Tunisia', *Journal of Modern Italian Studies*, 16(3): 386–403.

Ben-Yehoyada, N. (2015) '"Follow me, and I will make you fishers of men": The moral and political scales of migration in the central Mediterranean', *Journal of the Royal Anthropological Institute*, 22: 183–202.

Borren, M. (2008) 'Towards an Arendtian politics of in/visibility: On stateless refugees and undocumented aliens', *Ethical Perspectives: Journal of the European Ethics Network*, 15(2): 213–37.

Brambilla, C. (2015a) 'Exploring the critical potential of the borderscapes concept', *Geopolitics*, 20(1): 14–34.

Brambilla, C. (2015b) 'Mobile Euro/African borderscapes: Migrant communities and shifting urban margins', in A.-L. Amilhat Szary and F. Giraut (eds), *Borderities and the Politics of the Contemporary Mobile Borders*. Basingstoke: Palgrave Macmillan, pp. 138–54.

Brambilla, C. (2016) 'Houdoud al Bahr: An exhibition about the Italo-Tunisian Border, Bergamo (Italy)', *Museums and Migration Blog*, https://museumsandmigration. wordpress.com/2016/06/30/houdoud-al-bahr-an-exhibition-about-the-italo-tunisian-border-in-bergamo-italy/. Accessed 26 June 2019.

Brambilla, C. (2018) 'Bordering or borderscapes? New migrant agencies', in J.W. Scott, C. Brambilla, F. Celata, R. Coletti, H.-J. Bürkner, X. Ferrer-Gallardo and L. Gabrielli, 'Between crises and borders: interventions on Mediterranean neighbourhood and the salience of spatial imaginaries', *Political Geography*, 63: 176–8.

Brambilla, C., and H. Pötzsch (2017) 'In/visibility', in J. Schimanski and S.F. Wolfe (eds), *Border Aesthetics: Concepts and Intersections*. New York: Berghahn, pp. 68–89.

Brambilla, C., J. Laine, J.W. Scott and G. Bocchi (eds) (2015) *Borderscaping: Imaginations and Practices of Border Making*. Farnham: Ashgate.

Brambilla, C., and S. Visinoni (2015) *Houdoud al bahr | The Mediterranean frontiers: Mazara – Mahdia*. 60 minutes film. Italy. www.alto-labs.com/download/DOC_ENG_mod.mp4. Accessed 27 June 2019.

Cassidy, K., N. Yuval-Davis and G. Wemyss (2018) 'Debordering and everyday (re) bordering in and of Dover: Postborderland borderscapes', *Political Geography*, 66: 171–9.

Cole, J.E. (2003) 'Borders past and present in Mazara del Vallo, Sicily', *European Studies: A Journal of European Culture, History and Politics*, 19: 195–216.

Cusumano, A. (1976) *Il ritorno infelice: I tunisini in Sicilia*. Palermo: Sellerio.

De Certeau, M. (1984) *The Practice of Everyday Life*. Trans. S.F. Rendall. Berkeley: University of California Press.

De Genova, N. (2013) 'Spectacles of migrant "illegality": The scene of exclusion, the obscene of inclusion', *Ethnic and Racial Studies*, 36(7): 1180–98.

DeMaria Harney, N., and L. Baldassar (2007) 'Tracking transnationalism: Migrancy and its futures', *Journal of Ethnic and Migration Studies*, 33(2): 189–98.

Donnan, H., M. Hurd and C. Leutloff-Grandits (eds) (2017) *Migrating Borders and Moving Times: Temporality and the Crossing of Borders in Europe*. Manchester: Manchester University Press.

Feldman, A. (2000) 'Violence and vision: The prosthetics and aesthetics of terror', in V. Das, A. Kleinman, M. Ramphele and P. Reynolds (eds), *Violence and Subjectivity*. Berkeley: University of California Press, pp. 46–78.

Foucault, M. (1977) *Discipline and Punish: The Birth of the Prison*. New York: Random House.

Green, S. (2010) 'Performing border in the Aegean: On relocating political, economic and social relations', *Journal of Cultural Economy*, 3(2): 261–78.

Heyman, J.M., and J. Symons (2012) 'Borders', in D. Fassin (ed.), *A Companion to Moral Anthropology*. Malden, MA: Wiley Blackwell, pp. 540–57.

Holston, J. (2009) *Insurgent Citizenship: Disjunctions of Democracy and Modernity in Brazil*. Princeton: Princeton University Press.

Houtum, H. van, and T. van Naerssen (2002) 'Bordering, ordering and othering', *Tijdschrift voor Economische en Sociale Geografie*, 93(2): 125–36.

Jusionyte, I., and D.M. Goldstein (2016) 'In/visible-in/secure: Optics of regulation and control', *Focaal: Journal of Global and Historical Anthropology*, 75(2): 3–13.

Kasparek, B., N. De Genova, and S. Hess (2015) 'Border spectacle', in M. Casas-Cortes, S. Cobarrubias, N. De Genova, G. Garelli, G. Grappi and C. Heller (eds), 'New keywords: Migration and borders', *Cultural Studies*, 29(1): 66–8.

Low, S. (2017) *Spatializing Culture: The Ethnography of Space and Place*. London: Routledge.

Novak, P. (2017) 'Back to borders', *Critical Sociology*, 43(6): 847–64.

Parker, N., and N. Vaughan-Williams (2012) 'Critical border studies: Broadening and deepening the "lines in the sand" agenda', *Geopolitics*, 17(4): 727–33.

Rajaram, P.K., and C. Grundy-Warr (eds) (2007) *Borderscapes: Hidden Geographies and Politics at Territory's Edge*. Minneapolis: University of Minnesota Press.

Rancière, J. (2005) 'From politics to aesthetics?', *Paragraph*, 28(1): 13–25.

Rancière, J. (2010) *Dissensus: On Politics and Aesthetics*. London: Continuum.

Rodman, M.C. (2003) 'Empowering place: Multilocality and multivocality', in S.M. Low and D. Lawrence-Zúñiga (eds), *The Anthropology of Space and Place: Locating Culture*. Malden, MA: Blackwell, pp. 204–23.

Rumford, C. (2008) *Citizens and Borderwork in Contemporary Europe*. London: Routledge.

Saito, Y. (2007) *Everyday Aesthetics*. Oxford: Oxford University Press.

Saitta, P. (2010) 'Immigrant Roma in Sicily: The role of the informal economy in producing social advancement', *Romani Studies*, 20(1): 17–45.

Salter, M. (2011) 'Places everyone! Studying the performativity of the border', in C. Johnson, R. Jones, A. Paasi, L. Amoore, A. Mountz, M. Salter and C. Rumford (eds), 'Interventions on rethinking "the border" in border studies', *Political Geography*, 30: 66–7.

Schimanski, J., and S.F. Wolfe (2017) 'Intersections: A conclusion in the form of a glossary', in J. Schimanski and S.F. Wolfe (eds), *Border Aesthetics: Concepts and Intersections*. New York: Berghahn, pp. 147–69.

Spyrou, S., and M. Christou (2014), 'Introduction', in S. Spyrou and M. Christou (eds), *Children and Borders*. Basingstoke: Palgrave Macmillan, pp. 1–23.

Strüver, A. (2005) *Stories of the 'Boring Border': The Dutch–German Borderscape in People's Minds*. Berlin: LIT Verlag.

Walters, W. (2008) 'Acts of demonstration: Mapping the territory of (non-)citizenship', in E.F. Isin and G.M. Nielsen (eds), *Acts of Citizenship*. London: Zed Books, pp. 182–206.

Yuval-Davis, N. (2013) 'A Situated Intersectional Everyday Approach to the Study of Bordering', *EUBORDERSCAPES* (Working Paper 2), www.euborderscapes.eu/fileadmin/user_upload/Working_Papers/EUBORDERSCAPES_Working_Paper_2_Yuval-Davis.pdf. Accessed 16 June 2020.

5

From heroism to grotesque: the invisibility of border-related trauma narratives in the Finnish–Russian borderlands

Tuulikki Kurki

Introduction

The turbulent history of the Finnish–Russian national borderland has been a source of various traumatic experiences for people moving across the national border and living in the borderlands. This chapter studies the visibility and invisibility of border- and mobility-related trauma narratives in the Finnish–Russian borderlands which are studied through literary works and their public reception from the 1920s until the 2000s. The traumatic experiences addressed by the literary works include experiencing and witnessing violence, oppression, shaming and otherising – or their severe threat. Such experiences destroy the worldview and identity of a person, forcefully interrupt their life course and thus create a pressing need to reformulate one's worldview and identity (see Sztompka, 2004: 158–62, 171–5).

The research material consists of Finnish-language literature that addresses the experiences of border-crossing people in Finland and Russian Karelia,[1] along with the criticism of these works. The memoirs and novels that were published in Finland are Boris Cederholm's *Punainen painajainen* (1929) (*In the Clutches of the Cheka*) and Kirsti Huurre's *Sirpin ja moukarin alla* (1942) (*Under Hammer and Sickle*), as well as Arvi Perttu's *Papaninin retkikunta* (2006) (*The Expedition of Papanin*) and *Kipu* (2014) (*Pain*). The novels published in Russian Karelia include Nikolai Jaakkola's *Selville vesille* (1968) (*Into the Clear Waters*) and Antti Timonen's *Me karjalaiset* (1971) (*We Karelians*). The selected works were produced in different political contexts during the twentieth and early twenty-first centuries. The analysis of these works and their reception makes visible the varying narrative strategies that the authors used to address traumatic experiences and reveal the different significances of the trauma narratives in each context.

The authors represent different groups who crossed the Finnish–Russian national border for various reasons: Finnish White army officers and businesspeople in the early twentieth century (Cederholm); Finnish working-class people and communists in the 1920s and 1930s (Huurre); Finnish-speaking Soviet Karelian writers who lived and worked in the borderland (Jaakkola and Timonen); and Finnish-speaking writers who moved from Russia to Finland during the post-Soviet era (Perttu).

The authors discuss border- and mobility-related traumas through different narrator positions and with different narrative strategies. Some of the studied works are based on the writer's own experiences that serve as witness to the trauma whilst others are regarded more as fiction. Whether these works rest on historical events or are purely fictional is not an essential question in this study. All these works are recognised as trauma literature, and as 'narratives, where an overwhelming and catastrophic experience' is transformed into 'a form of language' (Knuuttila, 2006: 22).

The main concepts used to discuss the traumatic experience and trauma narratives and their reception are visibility and invisibility. These concepts draw on two different situations. First, they refer to Hannah Arendt's (1958) concepts of invisibility and visibility in the political world. In Arendt's view, the political world is a space of appearances, where 'I' becomes visible to others, and others become visible to 'I' (Arendt, 1958: 198, 199; Borren, 2008: 214). According to Marieke Borren (2010: 163), in the space of appearances, individuals act, they are seen, they articulate opinions, tell stories, and become heard. Thus, visibility is about active, 'eloquent self-display'. Visibility is also about performance that would not exist without the receiving audience (Borren, 2010: 164). The politics of invisibility, on the other hand, refer to such concepts as silenced, erased or oppressed history (see also Brambilla, Chapter 4 above). Nevertheless, visibility is not automatically positive or empowering, but certain types of visibility may also appear as a burden to marginalised groups (Brambilla and Pötzsch, 2014).

In addition to Arendt's definition, invisibility and visibility refer to the difficulty of representing traumatic experiences. Based on Freud's trauma theories, Cathy Caruth (1991: 185) claims that traumas can never be approached directly, but can be represented only in another time and place. Furthermore, trauma representations are always fragmentary, partial and distorted. However, this does not mean that the history of traumatic events cannot exist. On the contrary, the traumatic events can be resituated in our understandings about the past. The history can become visible, although our understanding of the past events would be only partial (Caruth, 1991: 182). Literary works, including fiction, can function as instruments for processing traumas, and as instruments for secondary witnessing (LaCapra,

1999: 699) or for postmemory (Hirsch, 2008). Therefore, they have significance in processing and discussing collective and trans-generational traumas.

The traumatic events in the literary works are invisible to varying degrees because of different political reasons and the general difficulty of representing trauma. The literary works studied here demonstrate the narrative, societal and political invisibility and visibility of the traumas, and thus raise the following questions. When and how have Finnish–Russian border-related traumas and trauma narratives been able to become visible and acknowledged publicly? How could the various narrative strategies complement each other in representing border-related traumatic experiences? How could literary trauma narratives contribute to the construction of cultural memory that is based on traumatic experiences?

This chapter argues that, until the late twentieth century, the writers employed mostly a documentary style of narrating and eye-witnessing narratives when writing about traumatic experiences. Literature criticism also appreciated the documentary value of literary works. The emphatic documentary style tended to diminish or even hide the authors' attempt to address traumatic experiences. In the reception of these works, the emotional features of the narratives, often referring to underlying traumatic events, appeared as elements that reduced the credibility of the narrative. Furthermore, until the end of the Cold War, the reception of such works tended to diminish the trauma narratives of border-crossers. The border-crossers were seen as 'heroic survivors', and there was no space for a discussion about their traumas. The traumas were not regarded as being particularly significant in the context of the prevailing national order. Similar features characterise the reception of these border-related trauma narratives in Russian Karelia until the end of the Soviet era. However, during the post-Soviet era, the writers address the traumatic experiences of previous generations. Some writers have diverged from the documentary style of writing, and used various narrative strategies of fiction, such as hyper-naturalism and the grotesque, when addressing the traumatic events. With the narrative strategies of fiction, personal experiences, existing knowledge about the historical traumatic events together with the narrators' inner reflections have become visible in ways that were not previously possible.

Theoretical background

The theoretical framework of this chapter connects multidisciplinary border studies and trauma studies. In the field of multidisciplinary border studies, where the cultural point of view has increased its visibility during the past decade (Brunet-Jailly, 2005; Konrad and Nicol, 2011), the theoretical framework connects also with the so-called border 'perform-antics' research trend. Border perform-antics, which was introduced in cultural research on the USA–Mexico borderland, refers to the various performance activities for 'remaking the self through negotiating and shifting identities in situational and culturally specific ways' (Sandoval et al., 2012: 2). These performances serve to deconstruct and oppose the identity definitions that are imposed on these people from above or from outside perspectives. Overall, this chapter aims at discussing trauma narratives and trauma literature as a form of perform-antics and their role in defining the identities of border-crossing individuals.

The analysis of trauma narratives follows the recent trend in the multi-disciplinary trauma studies where the focus has moved away from the universal, psychological features of trauma, and refocused on the cultural and political contexts where traumas are expressed and discussed (Balaev, 2014: 2–6). Furthermore, the analysis focuses on the use of power that controls the narration and reception of trauma narratives.

The visibility of the border-crossers' traumatic experiences and trauma narratives appears in the context of the so-called 'national order'. The national order means mapping ideology to a certain geographical area when creating order (Cresswell, 1996). It supports the idea of the nation state and the groups in power. For example, in the context of the nation state, the national order prioritises certain values, opinions and concepts that the groups in power maintain, as well as the formation of such identities that connect with a certain geographical area and homeland. The national order also makes evident the need to control people and phenomena that seem 'out of place' or challenge the national order. The national order represents the 'naturalised' and 'normalised' order, and the idea of 'us' against the 'other' that does not belong to the national order or that challenges it (Cresswell, 1996; Malkki, 1995). In the context of the national order, the invisibility of the border-crossers' trauma narratives means that the border-crossers are the 'wrong' people in the 'wrong' places, and therefore their experiences remain unacknowledged and their narratives unrecognised. From a political point of view, this is connected with the question of whose trauma narratives can become parts of the collective and cultural memory, and visible in the public space.

The analysis of trauma narratives stresses the contexts of reception as well as examines the role of narratives as a strategy to address personally and societally challenging themes (De Fina and Georgakopoulou, 2015). The analysis focuses on the various narrative strategies, such as omissions, metaphors and images, in trauma narratives and pays attention to the trauma language as a language of 'erasure' (Caruth, 2013). Erasure means here that the trauma narrative tries to represent the traumatic events repeatedly, however, the narration simultaneously erases the traumatic experience. In addition, the narrative strategies of fiction are studied as instruments for constructing 'traumatic memory' in a situation where the narrator does not have personal experiences of the depicted events.

The first part of the analysis section studies the invisibility of traumatic experiences and trauma narratives in the context of national order in Finland and Russian Karelia. The latter part of the analysis examines the invisibility of traumatic experiences and trauma narratives in the context of the early twenty-first century, when the dominance of nation states and national ideologies as signifiers of borders and identities has been problematised.

Invisibility of traumas in the context of national orders

The 'White' national order was dominant in Finland from the early twentieth century until the Second World War. It was established after the 1918 war in Finland, where the Whites (bourgeois upper-class, right-wing) defeated the Reds (working-class, left-wing). According to Miika Siironen (2012: 62–6), the White national order defended the values of the middle and upper class, and aimed at defending the newly independent country against the communists and the Soviet Union. In the internal politics, the White national order aimed at preventing the outbreak of a new civil war. Consequently, those people belonging to left-wing and communist movements were made enemies of the state and seen as threats to the national order. The White national order forms the context for *In the Clutches of the Cheka* and *Under Hammer and Sickle*.

Cederholm was a former Finnish White officer who served in the Russian fleet before the 1917 Russian revolution. In the 1920s, he worked for a foreign commercial company in St Petersburg. In 1924, he was arrested on suspicion of smuggling and spying, and was sentenced to five years in prison. First he served in the prison of Cheka (later known as GPU, NKVD and KGB), and later in the notorious prison camp of Solovetsk. He served twenty months and was released in 1925. *In the Clutches of the Cheka* narrates the events leading up to his imprisonment, his life in prison and finally his release.

Kirsti Huurre (alias Kerttu Eurén), a young Finnish woman, left Finland for the Soviet Union, Leningrad and Petrozavodsk in 1932. Although she had a good life in Finland, she believed she could find something better in the Soviet Union. She married twice in the Soviet Union. Her first spouse was executed in Stalin's purges in the 1930s, and the second husband simply disappeared without a trace. Huurre herself lived under a continuous fear of violence and imprisonment. She returned to Finland in 1941 when the war between Finland and the Soviet Union broke out, and the Finnish army occupied the borderland area where she lived at the time. In 1942, she published *Under Hammer and Sickle* about her experiences in the Soviet Union.

In the early twentieth century, documentary writing about the Soviet Union was valued in Finland. Ordinary Finns did not necessarily have profound or exact information about the country, although revolutionary Bolshevist ideas had spread among the working-class population and left-wing ideologues. *In the Clutches of the Cheka* belonged to the first wave of literature about border-crossers' experiences in the Soviet Union (Vettenniemi, 2004: 54). It attracted significant public attention and was translated quickly into several European languages (*Helsingin Sanomat*, 1928). In the 1940s when *Under Hammer and Sickle* was published, more literature about the Soviet Union was available and thus it was regarded as quite ordinary. Nevertheless, *Under Hammer and Sickle* became popular and was reprinted several times (Haahtela, 1942). Finns, especially, were concerned about the fate of their relatives and friends in the Soviet Union because rumours about the cruel regime in Soviet prison camps had already begun to circulate. The war that broke out between Finland and the Soviet Union in 1941 increased the thirst for knowledge and concerns about the fate of Finns in the Soviet Union.

A restrained narrative of a White hero

Cederholm's narrative strategies strive for an accentuated documentary style. *In the Clutches of the Cheka* (1929) reports in detail the events Cederholm experienced, sometimes specified with dates and the time of day, and focuses on the narrative of survival. Regularly, Cederholm contextualises the narrated events with reports about Soviet economic and political life. The detailed descriptions, as well as contextualising interventions, increase his reliability as a narrator and the documentary value of his memoir. Throughout the book, Cederholm also describes the violent and traumatising events he witnessed. For example, Cederholm's narration includes his forced visit to a torture chamber and its graphic signs of torture, his witnessing regular lorry transportations of prisoners to a shooting range for execution (1929: 221), and his cell mate's suicide (226–7). When Cederholm reports on his own condition, he refers mostly to his physical habitus, his greying, long beard, dirty and ragged clothes, and the sensations caused by hunger and malnutrition. However, he narrates relatively little about his own emotions. He mentions his blackout due to mental overexertion (Cederholm, 1929: 227), his depression when hearing about his move to the Solovetsk prison camp (218); and his feelings of horror when he found out that the Finnish government could not offer him more help. He also conveys how remembering the violence towards the prisoners on death row sends a chill down his spine (Cederholm, 1929: 222).

In the documentary style of writing, the trauma of experiencing and witnessing extreme physical and mental violence, along with the horror of survival (the moment when one realises that he has narrowly missed death), are hidden under his detailed observations and objectifying verbalisation. The traumatised experiences he is subjected to are reduced to objects: rubber balls that are stuck into the mouths of men to stifle their screams, smells, sounds of violence, screams of gulls that fly over the prison camp yard, and details that show the decay in Cederholm's body. The narrative strategy simultaneously reveals the traces and signs of trauma, yet erases the trauma (Caruth, 2013). Attempts to verbalise and narrate the traumatic events in detail make the traumatic experience only partially and fragmentarily visible, whilst the rest of it remains invisible, hidden and unarticulated. In his work, as a narrator, Cederholm appears as a calm, rational and observant reporter without letting the turmoil disturb his observant eye or shake his peace of mind. He appears to remain as an outsider and distinct from the traumatic events that are taking place.

In addition to the documentary style, the author's silences render the traumatic experiences invisible. Cederholm's 'pen' is 'powerless' to describe the conditions in a cramped train carriage transporting prisoners to Solovetsk (1929: 240). He 'cannot describe the filth, sordidness, hunger, and cold where the prisoners live in the Solovetsk prison camp' (Cederholm, 1929: 269). In prison, when Cederholm hears about his release, he is 'happy and content' and returns in his room (1929: 307), and later, when he is finally released, he states that he 'does not have more to tell' (309).

The reviewers perceived the value of the book in the frame of Finland's White national order, and quickly Cederholm became a hero of White Finland. The public saw the book as a heroic narrative about Cederholm's ability to endure inhuman and horrible conditions, but this was also expected of him as a former soldier. The narrative of a strong, rational and intelligent hero did not have room for weaknesses. 'As a former soldier and a Finn with guts, the writer decided to bear it all [...] although he had lost even the rudimentary human-like features in his appearance' (O.A.K., 1929), but the celebrated hero-narrative that the public reception emphasised denied the possibility of addressing the author's traumatic experiences (*Helsingin Sanomat*, 1928; A.R., 1929; J.V., 1929).

Simultaneously, the reviews used Cederholm's book to highlight and criticise the weaknesses of the Soviet system and strike down the Finnish communists (O.A.K., 1929). The horrible events that Cederholm reported were seen as revelations and lessons for those who felt sympathy towards the Soviet Union: 'It [the book] is an evidence of the tyranny that prevails in the courtrooms in Soviet-Russia and is healthy reading, especially for those whose admiring gazes are directed towards the east.'[2] This politicised reading of *In the Clutches of the Cheka* fails to acknowledge Cederholm's traumatic experiences, and instead, the reviewers used Cederholm's narratives in order to support and strengthen the prevailing White national order, and to celebrate the heroes of White Finland.

An insignificant Red trauma?

Under Hammer and Sickle depicts life in Leningrad and Petrozavodsk, and the period of Stalin's terror in the 1930s. Huurre narrates in the person of her protagonist Kaarina about the turbulent era, various everyday events and her own experiences. Huurre uses narrative strategies that enable her to make visible the signs of trauma in Kaarina's observable body and in her actions. Huurre's strategy explicates Kaarina's powerful emotional upheavals, and simultaneously allows documentary narration and witnessing. Her strategy becomes visible when Kaarina narrates the events of disappearances, deaths and illnesses of her closest acquaintances.

> They have shot him, do you understand – shot him! That – that was straight talk. It was like a stab that does not kill, but still gives the pain. I remember that I stood up, and walked around mechanically; I was like unconscious and moved somewhere else. I stopped in the front of a mirror, my hand rose up to mimic a familiar move. I arranged my hair without understanding what I was doing. They said that I stood there for quite a while, and when I moved, I saw my aunt's frightened eyes. She told me later that she was afraid that I was going insane.[3]

> My sleep was just some kind of a drowse into which I sank from time to time, but it wasn't real sleep. Many times, I screamed and flinched awake without remembering anything [...] I could not avoid thinking about suicide, and that thought preyed on my mind continuously [...] my thoughts circulated on the same track, day and night.[4]

Huurre's narrative strategy makes visible the simultaneous appearance of trauma in her body, mind and behaviour. Similar traumatic experience is repeated again when Kaarina marries Aarne, a Finnish Red officer who is also arrested and disappears. Aarne's arrest is something that Kaarina cannot describe: 'I cannot explain what ran through my mind. I watched that procedure like an outsider, from aside or in a nightmare. Iron armour squeezed my heart and hindered my breathing.'[5]

Huurre strives to verbalise the traumatic experience narrating Kaarina's reactions that mimic a traumatic experience. Mimicking can be seen as one artistic strategy of trauma narration, especially in trauma fiction (Whitehead, 2004). In using mimicking, Huurre uses metaphors such as 'paralyses', 'circulating thoughts', 'mechanical walking', 'being unconscious' and 'iron armour' that squeezes her heart. In these narrative strategies, the traumatic experiences being discussed become partially visible through Kaarina's inner reflections, and they materialise in her own observable body and in her peculiar actions. The second strategy that Huurre uses is to distance Kaarina from everyday reality in a state where she acts almost unconsciously or autonomously like a machine. In addition, Kaarina objectifies her trauma in the form of an external object that presses her body and signals her pain.

Huurre's strategy to make trauma partially visible is different from Cederholm's narrative strategies. While Cederholm focuses on external realities and events around him, Huurre gazes into Kaarina's inner world. Furthermore, Kaarina appears as a sensitive person, who feels horror and agony, and even becomes suicidal. She survives, but she does not appear as a stoic, heroic survivor, such as featured in Cederholm's narrative.

Huurre's trauma narrative, unlike Cederholm's heroic account, was diminished in the public reception of the novel. The literature critics read *Under Hammer and Sickle* first and foremost in the context of the White national order in Finland. The reception silenced Huurre's traumatic experiences in three different ways. First, the reception stressed the documentary value of the book and the information about the Soviet Union that it used to slander the Soviet Union and strengthen White unity in Finland (Haahtela, 1942; Heimomme tuhooja, 1942). This was very understandable because the war between Finland and the Soviet Union had just broken out. Furthermore, the public reception ignored Huurre's traumatic experiences by interpreting her novel as a survival narrative of the Finns as a nation, rather than an individual survival story (Heimomme tuhooja, 1942). The critics attempted to show that Finland was a brave and heroic nation that fought together with other small nations against the vast Soviet Union.

The second strategy for silencing Huurre's trauma was to belittle her experiences. The reviews often did not regard her traumas as significant or worth telling in detail, although generally her life story was considered 'a lively piece of literature' (Haahtela, 1942; U.V., 1942). For example, one of the reviewers stated that Huurre exposed 'a little too much' about her 'personal worries', and narrd 'in unnecessarily detailed ways' issues that are 'so private' that 'they should not be told in public' (U.V., 1942). The critic also stated that these particular descriptions were of hardly any interest to the readers. Instead, the reviewer assumes that descriptions of Soviet people's everyday life would be more interesting. Another critic states that

Huurre does not present anything new, and does not always address the 'crucial issues' regarding her husbands' fates (V.P., 1942). By 'crucial issues', the critic meant the reasons that led to their destruction.

Third, trauma is diminished by holding Red border-crossers responsible for their own traumas. Red border-crossers were condemned as threats to the White national order. They were not considered obedient citizens, nor were they equal to 'normal' or sensible citizens, because Bolshevism had managed to fool them (H., 1942). In these reviews, Huurre was found as guilty for her own traumas in the Soviet Union. One critic even wished similar experiences to all who still dreamed of Bolshevism ('Kirsti Huurre', 1942).

For the critics, the significance of Huurre's trauma narrative was to function as a warning (U.V., 1942). *Under Hammer and Sickle* provided an example of what could happen if a person was not an obedient and dutiful citizen, or did not address Bolshevism with criticism. Huurre was therefore seen as a person who had managed to be 'cured' from the illness of Bolshevism, and who 'confessed' her mistakes (T.S., 1942). Therefore, in the end, she was able to return to the White national order.

The examples show that the reception of these texts fails to recognise the trauma and the need to process it, nor does the reception regard the trauma as important enough in the context of the national order. Additionally, the reception simply denies any seriousness of the Red border crossers' traumas. Because of this, Red border-crossers' traumas were excluded from the great national narrative of White Finland as they did not form a significant element in the narrative of White Finland's shared past. Instead of emphasising the unity of Finland, the exposed trauma narratives would have shown still unresolved societal problems and challenges, such as the division of the population into Whites and Reds, the political oppression of the Reds, unemployment, inequality and poverty, and also their tragic consequences. Acknowledging the traumas of the Red border-crossers would have made visible various reasons that had led to the 1918 civil war and Finns' mass migration to the Soviet Union. Instead of having their traumas acknowledged, the communists and Reds became targets of aggression and hatred in the public discussion, and especially in the extreme right-wing discourse (Paastela, 2003: 78–9; Siironen, 2012).

After the Second World War, a period of 'Finlandisation' began. Finlandisation meant an extremely cautious public discussion about the Soviet Union and even self-censorship of the Finnish media (CIA, 1972). It naturally affected the reception of books about the Soviet Union. From 1944 – when the war ended – until 1958, some of the books written by communists and Red border-crossers were blacklisted. Books which described the Soviet Union and its political system too critically or negatively were censored and removed from the libraries and book stores (Ekholm, 2000: 59, 68). *Under Hammer and Sickle* became such a book. After 1958 when the relationship between Finland and the Soviet Union became less tense, these books were released from the blacklist, but any public discussion of their reliability and significance remained controversial until the 1970s (Ekholm, 2000: 59).

Trauma in the context of the Bolshevist national order

Since the 1960s, in Soviet Karelia, few novels have addressed border-crossing individuals and their traumatic experiences of violence, or experiences of in-betweenness, homelessness and ideological uncertainty (Jaakkola, 1968; Timonen, 1961, 1971). The well-known Soviet Karelian writer Antti Timonen (1915–90) addressed these themes in his historical novel *We Karelians*. The novel depicts the civil war in Soviet Karelia in the 1920s, when the Karelian population was divided into the Reds and the Whites. Timonen describes the main phases of the war, but also problematises the identities and idea of belonging of Karelians. One of the novel's main characters, a Karelian man named Vasselei, vacillates between his Red and White allegiances. Every time he crosses national or ideological borders, he contemplates his loyalties to ideological and national orders, along with his relationship with 'we' and 'them'. Along with these various border-crossings, he gradually becomes an enemy to his own home country and a stranger to himself. He realises that he is like his enemies and other murderers, whom he has previously despised (Timonen, 1971: 338–9).

Vasselei finds himself in a situation where he does not know where he should belong, and he just wishes to be able to live in peace. Finally, he is murdered by a Karelian man, similar to himself, on the Soviet Union–Finnish national border. Even at the moment of his death, Vasselei is unsure of where to fall and where to belong (Timonen, 1971: 442–3). A similar character appears in Nikolai Jaakkola's novel *Into the Clear Waters*. One of its main characters is a Karelian man named Pulikka-Puavila, who does not reveal his ideological allegiances with the Reds and Whites because he does not regard it as important. Because of his ambiguity however, other Karelians shoot him dead as a potential enemy (Jaakkola, 1968: 232). A key point in his narrative is that Pulikka-Puavila does not recognise that his 'otherness' causes his destruction.

Both novels received positive reviews from contemporary critics (Rugojev, 1969; Summanen, 1973). Since the late 1960s and early 1970s, the ambiguity and relativity of identities was briefly made visible, although the dogma of Socialist Realism aimed at silencing ambiguous and hesitant expressions of identities in literature. The critics interpreted the novels primarily as representations of the tragic history of Karelia as a national borderland, but the ambiguity of individual identities was not an aspect that was visibly emphasised. Nevertheless, some reviewers appreciated that there were no strong, black and white contradictions between the protagonists representing the different sides of the war, as was commonly found in Soviet literature discussing war and revolutionary themes (Rugojev, 1969; Summanen, 1973).

Ambiguous and hesitant identities appeared as ideologically wrong, and often the fate of these protagonists was to die or vanish, unless they were able to return to the prevailing national order (Kurki, 2018: 365). The function of Socialist Realism was to raise exemplary and patriotic Soviet citizens who were strongly connected with the ideological centre of Moscow, and the values and ideals it represented. Thus, any connection across the national and ideological border was seen problematic (Chandler, 1998: 76; Statiev, 2013: 4). The ideal characters were portrayed morally and physically strong, optimistic and resilient. They were embodiments of the national order and its values (Kaganovsky, 2008), and the lives of these exemplary Soviet heroes were narrated in canonical novels such as Nikolai Ostrovski's *Kak zakaljas stal* (1934) (*How Steel Was Tempered*)), and Boris Polevoi's *Povest a nastojaštšem tšeloveke* (1947) (*Story of a Real Man*).

The national order in both Finland and the Soviet Union directed the narrating and reception of the border- and mobility-related trauma narratives in literature, and also defined the public significance of these trauma narratives. Often in the context of the national order, trauma was discussed in connection with heroism, with the hero being able to live through the trauma, process it and return home, and become a functional part of the prevailing national order. However, this also meant that such meanings of trauma that potentially questioned the prevailing national order remained invisible. Consequently, those trauma narratives where the border-crosser is unable to return into the prevailing national order, to recover and become a 'model citizen' remained invisible.

Trauma would also remain invisible when the narrator could not become an active citizen in the public space (see Borren, 2010: 163–4). Published literary works can therefore be understood as attempts to create an identity performance that is based on a traumatic experience. However, the performance does not materialise because the contemporary audience refuses to see the performance in the same way that the performer intended. In terms of a performance, Red border-crossers in Finland and Soviet citizens with their ambiguous and hesitant identities became invisible. To contextualise this point, in Finland over four thousand communists were imprisoned between the First and Second World Wars. They were regarded as politically unreliable (Paastela, 2003: 76–7), and they could not function in the White national order because their active citizenship was denied. Starkly, in Soviet

Karelian writing, the fate of ambiguous border-crossers was simply to die or vanish.

Traumas increase visibility: using the grotesque as an instrument for traumatic memory

In the Soviet Union during Perestroika, novels addressing the traumas of Soviet history started to flood into the publishing houses and editorial boards of literary journals. The new demand for openness both allowed and created the conditions where past traumas could be addressed and reassessed in a critical way. Many literary works published during Perestroika made visible themes that were labelled as social and mental abscesses, such as revealing previously suppressed information about Stalin's terror and the Second World War (Scherrer, 2010). Publishing previously forbidden literature was an indicator of a history that existed parallel to the official history, and it was now becoming visible (Marsh, 1995: 189–99). After Perestroika, the world gradually moved towards a situation where the significance of nationalistic discourses as signifiers of borders and identities was problematised due to the strengthened global flows of mobilities and migration. These changes have influenced the visibility of border- and mobility-related traumas, and their public reception.

Currently, the best-known Finnish-speaking writer originating from Russian Karelia and discussing the historical and contemporary traumas of the Finnish–Russian borderlands is Arvi Perttu (born 1961). Born in the Soviet Union, Perttu has created a literary career as a representative of minority-language literature in the Soviet Union and Russia in the 1980s and 1990s. At the turn of the twenty-first century, Perttu moved to Finland. In his recent novels, Perttu discusses the lives and fates of individuals in the Finnish–Russian borderlands, interaction across the border and various border-related conflicts. His novel *The Expedition of Papanin* addresses Stalin's terror from the perspective of Finnish migrants and border-crossers. His novel *Pain* addresses the civil war in the Russian Karelia in the 1920s, from the perspective of a Finnish border-crossing woman, Riikka.

In the novels, the victim and perpetrator are two sides of the same coin, and thus inseparable. Perttu provides a novel perspective into the traumatising historical events that had not been widely discussed in the contexts of national order in Finland or in Russian Karelia. In his novels, the narratives named neither heroes nor enemies, and therefore allow a more multifaceted discussion about traumatic events.

The Expedition of Papanin and *Pain* address the violence and oppression as well as trauma of the victim and the perpetrator from the point of view of a border-crosser. *The Expedition of Papanin* focuses on the fates of emigrated Finns in Soviet Karelia in the 1930s. The main protagonist is an American-Finnish writer, Jaakko Pettersson. Pettersson becomes both a victim of the Stalinist oppression but also a perpetrator, which aids him in surviving the terror. Realising his own capacity to do evil is a traumatising experience for Pettersson. He realises that his slandering and careless talk about his colleagues have led to their arrests and their ultimate destruction. Despite this cruel realisation, Pettersson is convinced that exposing others is the only way to survive in the illogical and mad game of terror. Pettersson parallels exposing his colleagues and family members to the amputation of a limb: it is something extremely unpleasant but something that he is forced to do to survive. 'I was in the game already, but now I had to follow the rules. They were cruel, and the purpose of the game was merciless: to survive. It was like an amputation, an amputation of necrosis: it horrifies, it hurts, but there is no other way to maintain the other parts of the body healthily.'[6]

Using power over others pleases Pettersson, but recognising his own evilness causes him agony. Perttu explicates Pettersson's perpetrator trauma by using grotesque and sadomasochistic fantasies. In these fantasies, Pettersson is the one who uses power, but, simultaneously, he is also the victim. This double role reflects Pettersson's simultaneous roles as a victim of the terror and as the cruel informer who uses power to expose his friends to the secret police and thus throw them into the machinery of the Red terror.

In the novel *Pain*, a Finnish woman, Riikka (Fredrika Eriksson), participates in the civil war in the Soviet Karelia on the side of the White Finns. A traumatising moment for her is to realise that she is a murderer and acts with mindless violence, although, at the same time, she is also a victim of cruel violence. Although she had entered the war as an advocate of the White 'Greater Finland' ideology,[7] she soon realises that this ideology cannot justify the violence of the Finnish troops. However, the ideological intoxication that had created unity and enthusiasm among the White soldiers soon evaporated in the midst of the war. In the mayhem of killing and mutilated bodies, Riikka realises the absurdity of the war, and that her only task is to kill others and survive. Realising this is a traumatising experience for Riikka that causes her both internal agony and even physical pain. She realises that she has been betrayed by the ideology and that she is a perpetrator, and that no exalted ideology can justify her actions: 'This was the war, you could not follow any rules, and the war could not have any logic. Riikka felt that the feeling of emptiness that now filled her, killed her hopes of curing her internal pain. From now on, there was just new pain that would not erase the old one – pain just piled up.'[8]

When describing Pettersson's and Riikka's traumas, Perttu uses a narrative strategy that exceeds the limits of a realistic world. The characters move in a world of intoxication, hallucination and finally in the world of art. As an additional effect, Perttu uses grotesque and even pornographic narrative elements that belong in the narrative strategies of hyper-naturalistic prose. Hyper-natural prose was introduced in Russian postmodernism in the 1990s, and 'depicts the everyday cruelty, the horrors of prisons and corporeality of people in ways that are often despised' (Lipovetsky, 2011: 179). According to Lipovetsky (2011: 179–80), the purpose of hyper-natural prose is to open past traumas for discussion by introducing shocking and sometimes repulsive depictions.

When Pettersson ponders his own evilness as an informer he simultaneously fears for his own fate; he has nightmares. In one of them, the town of Petrozavodsk becomes a stage of infernal destruction: houses collapse, and blackened and swollen bodies and stinking mire emerge from the cellars and sewers and float on the flooding streets. Jaakko himself enters a claustrophobic metro tunnel filled with water. In the tunnel, the mire and floating bodies corner him. In the end, a beautiful, detached woman's head approaches Pettersson. Pettersson realises that he has fallen in love with the head, but the head takes his last gasp (Perttu, 2006: 325–7).

Riikka also moves in a world that is beyond everyday reality, when she mulls over the madness of the war and her unbearable role as a perpetrator. The trauma and betrayal (Caruth, 2008; Freyd, 1998) show themselves in the feelings of emptiness, culminating in physical pain and mental agony. Like other soldiers, Riikka tries to numb and control the agony with self-inflected sadomasochistic pain, including whipping, bondage, drugs and sex (Perttu, 2014: 239).

Furthermore, in the midst of the violence, Riikka feels as if she is moving into Kazimir Malevich's painting the *Tshornyi kvadrat* (ca. 1923) or *Black Square*. *Black Square*, signifying eternity, emptiness and depth (Esanu, 2013: 84–5), symbolises Riikka's experiences in the war and her existence in a world that has become unrecognisable. In her experiences, the war had changed the world entirely and profoundly, and therefore the world could no longer be depicted through traditional art forms (Perttu, 2014: 14). Only abstract art could provide instruments for depicting this new, changed world, and the new world appears to Riikka as a place where previous forms of harmony and balance have disappeared:

> She felt that she was on the shore, on the edge of an abyss, ready to fall into the emptiness, to death, an eternity that would not give her oblivion but eternal pain. In St Petersburg, almost three years ago, she had stood in front of Malevich's Black Square for a long time, and did not understand it. Now she knew that the war had changed the world entirely, and it could not be described

with the traditional means of art, because the world had contracted or expanded into a black square.[9]

'Black Square' represents the world where Riikka acts and orients herself. In her mind, the geometrical shapes and blackness of the painting parallel the world around her, and this becomes one of the few ways she has to cope in traumatising, violent situations. As a result, the young men whom she is about to execute seem like cardboard pictures and inanimate targets; shooting them does not disturb her conscience:

> She felt that she was inside Malevich's painting, the world around her was like even, bright surfaces: red, black, squares, circles and sharp lines piercing them. The former harmony had disappeared, it could not exist anymore.[10]

> These young men were only cardboard figures, maybe targets. She tried to look inside them, but she saw through them like a bullet.[11]

Perttu's narrative strategies reflect a traumatised person's move outside the coherent experience of place and time. The narrative strategy makes the traumatic experience visible in ways that are not possible in documentary writing, where the experience exceeds a person's cognitive capacity and disrupts the flow of the everyday reality. This is typical when processing traumatic experiences where distinctions between the past and present may become blurred (LaCapra, 1999: 699). Traumatic events 'defy comprehension and cannot be overcome or integrated meaningfully within ordinary cognitive structure through simple recollection' (Schweiger, 2015: 347). Whitehead (2004: 83–4) even claims that, in some cases, unusual and alienated viewpoints are the only possible means for addressing traumatic experiences. Moving outside the boundaries of realistic narration is possible for Perttu because he does not have the burden of documentary writing or a requirement for writing only about historical events. Furthermore, the grotesque, repulsive and shocking elements function as a narrative strategy intended to create confusion. In this way, the trauma representations epitomise the multifaceted and complex nature of traumas that is never simple or clear, but deeply disturbing and confusing.

Applying Kerstin Bergman's (2008: 148) concept of trauma representation, this chapter claims that Perttu's narrative strategies create his own personal literary 'theory' for representing trauma. Furthermore, this chapter proposes that grotesque and hyper-natural narrative strategies provide 'theories' or 'languages' for remembering and representing individual, collective and cultural traumas occurring at the Finnish–Russian borderlands. Perttu's hyper-naturalist and grotesque narrative strategies may also function as an artistic traumatic memory of traumatic events that he has not experienced himself. This follows Walter Benjamin's idea of a traumatic, involuntary memory that is something that a person remembers but yet the person does not have any real memory trace of the remembered event (Knuuttila, 2006: 26). However, by way of his works, Perttu participates in constructing a collective, cultural memory of traumatic events which occurred at the Finnish-Russian borderlands.

Furthermore, Perttu narrates the traumatic experiences of the borderland people in a way that their narratives and identity definitions are based on traumatic experiences, and how they do not necessarily fit into the national framework of interpretations. Instead, Perttu forces us to see these border-crossing and borderland people in new ways: not exclusively as victims or perpetrators, heroes or enemies, but as all these roles simultaneously. For example, Perttu's grotesque and hyper-naturalist narration criticises the traditionalising and nationalising gazes that are directed at the borderland people and their culture, from both Russia and Finland. Thus, protagonists such as Riikka and Pettersson appear as counter-images of the heroes created in earlier Russian Karelian literature. Being self-destructive and grotesque questions the idea of an ideal and heroic citizen in many ways. Personal and corporeal motives, hedonism and a wish to escape reality guide their actions, and any noble ideologies remain in the background. So, in Perttu's works, the borderland people become visible, and they are seen and heard in the cultural and artistic space of the literary works.

Conclusions

In Finnish and Russian contexts, border- and mobility-related trauma narratives have been received in controversial ways, and partly the narratives and experiences they seek to represent have remained invisible. In the twentieth century, trauma narratives were often written and received in ways that supported the prevailing national order and dominant history narratives. Whilst the national interpretation of such trauma narratives was stressed, individual experiences and impacts of the trauma narratives that potentially challenged or subverted the ideological values of the prevailing national order were overlooked.

The trauma narratives that could potentially challenge the prevailing national order were the narratives written by political migrants. On the Finnish side of the border, these groups were the Reds, the Communists, and the supporters of Bolshevism who moved from Finland to the Soviet Union and Russia for political and ideological reasons. On the Russian side of the border, individuals who were unsure about their ideological or national identities, allegiances or ideas of belonging, or were hesitant about their identities, appeared as dangerous or dubious in the context of the national order. During the past decades, the role of national discourses as signifiers of identities and borders have diminished due to the strengthening of global migrant flows, the revaluation of the grand national narratives. These changes have increased the visibility of various groups living in the various borderlands.

As a whole, literature that addresses border- and mobility-related traumas can function as an instrument for making visible the identities of borderland people. Narrative strategies of literature such as confusing metaphors and surreal narrative worlds can reveal various identity articulations and experiences of the borderland people that have not been visible before. The literature addressing the border and mobility-relate traumas also creates a 'theatre of the oppressed' and facilitates border perform-antics (Sandoval et al., 2012). For centuries, the people living in the Finnish–Russian borderlands have been subject to the use of power and to intellectual colonialism. The representations and identity definitions of these people have mostly been created through outside perspectives, from Russia and Finland. In these definitions, the borderland people have been positioned between two dominating national cultures, or they have simply remained invisible. Literature that addresses border-related traumatic experiences, and the identities and histories of border-crossers and border people can become visible and audible in ways that are not possible in unifying, national-history narratives (see also Konrad and Hu, Chapter 6 below).

So, what is the additional meaning that aesthetic strategies may bring to border related trauma narratives? Literary narrative strategies can serve to complement documentary narrative strategies. Literature, together with other arts, can supersede the limitations of the realistic world, and offer such possibilities for narration that can make traumas visible in other ways than documentary narration or narration that aims purely at witnessing. Literature and art can utilise various different codes simultaneously for representing traumatic experiences. These multilayered representations provide 'moral, political, and aesthetic ways of understanding trauma, these understandings are not simple, flat, and formulaic' (Winn, 2008: 7). Traumas are complex, and they need complex, even confusing ways of representation, and these can be provided by artistic means of representation. At best, literature and art can deepen and widen our understandings about border- and mobility-related traumatic experiences, as well as traumatic history.

Vera Nünning (2008: 123–5, 137) suggests that the traditional definition of 'witness' may be too narrow when applied to trauma fiction or artistic works representing traumatic events, and also suggests that works of popular culture that are not based on eyewitness narratives can still impact significantly on the remembering and processing of collective traumas. According to Nünning, the representations provided and repeated in popular culture can strengthen the role and significance of some trauma representations as part of the collective and cultural memory. Literary works and art can also transform a personal trauma into a collective or cultural trauma. So, artworks based on individual narratives could provide a basis for discussing the making visible of the larger traumas that may connect groups of people in various borderlands worldwide.

Thus, it may be that perhaps trauma representations always require deviant ways of narration, in order to make the complex and confusing nature of trauma even remotely visible and comprehensible.

Acknowledgements

This chapter was written as part of the research project *Traumatised Borders: Reviving subversive narratives of B/Order, and Other* (Academy of Finland, SA 297533).

Notes

1 Russian Karelia refers to the Republic of Russian Karelia established in 1991. Soviet Karelia refers to the following administrative regions: the Workers' Commune of Karelia (1920–23), Autonomous Socialist Soviet Republic of Karelia (1923–39), Karelian Finnish Socialist Soviet Republic (1940–55), and Autonomous Karelian Socialist Soviet Republic (1956–91).

2 'Se on yhtenä todistuksena siitä hirmuvallasta, joka Neuvosto-Venäjällä vallitsee oikeudenkäytön alalla ja sellaisen terveellistä lukemista ennen kaikkea niille, joiden ihannoivat katseet ovat suuntautuneet itään' (A.R., 1929). My translations from texts in Finnish.

3 'Ovat ampuneet hänet, ymmärrätkös, – ampuneet! Se – se oli jo selvää puhetta. Se tuli kuin viiltävä isku, joka ei tapa, vaan tuo kivun. Muistan nousseeni koneellisesti kävelemään, kuin tajuttomana siirryin jonnekin. Seisahduin peilin eteen, käsi kohosi tuttuun liikkeeseen, järjestelin hiuksiani käsittämättä mitä tein. Seisoin kuulemma siinä kauan, ja kun vihdoin liikahdin, näin tädin kauhistuneet silmät edessäni. Hän pelkäsi minun tulevan hulluksi, kertoi hän myöhemmin' (Huurre, 1942: 64).

4 'Uneni oli vain jotain horrosta, johon saatoin aika ajoittain vaipua, oikeata unta se ei ollut. Kiljahtaen ja säpsähtäen saatoin öisin havahtua, muistamatta mitään [...] En saanut mielestäni itsemurha-ajatusta, joka ilkeänä päähänpinttymänä vaivasi minua lakkaamatta [...] ajatukseni kiersivät aina samaa rataa, eivätkä yksin päivällä, vaan myöskin yöllä' (Huurre, 1942: 66).

5 'En osaa tarkalleen eritellä, mitä mielessäni liikkui. Katselin kuin vieraana, sivulta tai pahassa unessa tuota tarkastusta. Sydän tuntui saavan ympärilleen lujan rautaisen panssarin, joka tukahdutti hengitystäkin' (Huurre, 1942: 106).

6 'Olin jo pelissä mukana, nyt oli pakko noudattaa sääntöjä. Ne olivat julmia, mutta pelin tarkoituskin oli armoton, hengissä selviytyminen. Se oli kuin leikkaus, kuolion amputaatio: hirvittää ja sattuu, mutta ei ole muuta keinoa säilyttää muu ruumis terveenä' (Perttu, 2006: 297).

7 The Greater Finland ideology developed in the nineteenth century and aimed at unifying all Finno-Ugric peoples living in Finland and elsewhere (Niinistö, 2001: 80–3). It laid the ideological foundation for the idea that Finnish troops could occupy those areas in Soviet Karelia where the Finno-Ugric population lived.

8 'Tällaista sota oli, ei siinä mitään sääntöjä voinut noudattaa, eikä siinä voinut olla mitään mieltä. Riikka tunsi tyhjyyden imaisevan hänestä viimeisen toivon päästä kivustaan. Nyt edessä oli vain uutta kipua, joka ei poistaisi vanhaa vaan ainoastaan kasautuisi sen päälle' (Perttu, 2014: 60).

9 'Hän tunsi olevansa siinä rannalla kuin kuilun reunalla, valmiina putoamaan tyhjyyteen, kuolemaan, ikuisuuteen, joka ei silti antaisi unohdusta vaan iänkaikkisen kivun. Pietarissa, melkein kolme vuotta sitten, hän seisoi pitkään Malevitšin Mustan neliön edessä eikä ymmärtänyt. Nyt hän tiesi, että sodan myötä maailma oli muuttunut kokonaan, sitä ei voinut enää kuvata perinteisin keinoin, koska maailma oli supistunut tai laajentunut mustaksi neliöksi' (Perttu, 2014: 12).

10 'Hän tunsi olevansa Malevitšin maalauksen sisällä, maailma oli ympärillä tasaisia kirkkaita pintoja: punaista, mustaa, neliöitä ja ympyröitä ja niitä puhkovia teräviä viivoja. Entistä harmoniaa ei enää ollut, ei voinut olla' (Perttu, 2014: 50).

11 'Nämä nuorukaisetkin olivat vain pahvisia kuvia, ehkä maaleja. Hän yritti nähdä niiden sisään, mutta näki läpi, kuin luoti' (Perttu, 2014: 50).

References

A.R. (1929) 'Punainen painajainen', *Kaleva* (2 March 1929).

Arendt, H. (1958) *The Human Condition*. Chicago: The University of Chicago Press.

Balaev, M. (2014) 'Literary trauma theory reconsidered', in M. Balaev (ed.), *Contemporary Approaches in Literary Trauma Theory*. Basingstoke: Palgrave Macmillan E-book, Chapter 1.

Bergman, K (2008) 'The amnesiac flashback: Theories, fiction, and trauma', in U. Ekman and F. Tygstrup (eds), *Witness: Memory, Representation, and the Media in Question*. Copenhagen: Museum Tusculanum Press, pp. 143–9.

Borren, M. (2008) 'Towards an Arendtian politics of in/visibility: On stateless refugees and undocumented aliens', *Ethical Perspectives: Journal of the European Ethnic Network*, 15(2): 213–37.

Borren, M. (2010) *Amore Mundi: Hannah Arendt's Political Phenomenology of World*. Amsterdam: F. & N. Eigen Beheer.

Brambilla, C., and H. Pötzsch (2014) 'In/visibility', in J. Schimanski and S.F. Wolfe (eds), *Border Aesthetics: Concepts and Intersections*. New York: Berghahn, pp. 68–89.

Brunet-Jailly, E. (2005) 'Theorizing borders: An interdisciplinary perspective', *Geopolitics*, 10(4): 633–49.

Caruth, C. (1991) 'Unclaimed experience: Trauma and the possibility of history', *Yale French Studies*, 79: 181–92.

Caruth, C. (2008) 'History as false witness: Trauma, politics, and war', in U. Ekman and F. Tygstrup (eds), *Witness: Memory, Representation, and the Media in Question*. Copenhagen: Museum Tusculanum Press, pp. 150–73.

Caruth, C. (2013) *Literature in the Ashes of History*. Baltimore: Johns Hopkins University Press.

Cederholm, B. (1929) *Punainen painajainen*. Helsinki: WSOY. [Translation from original *I Tjekans klor: Upplevelser i Sovjets fängelser* (Helsinki: WSOY, 1929)].

Chandler, A. (1998) *Institutions of Isolation: Border Controls in the Soviet Union and its Successor States 1917–1993*. Montreal: McGill-Queen's University Press.

CIA (1972) '"Finlandisation" in action: Helsinki's experience with Moscow', Central Intelligence Agency (Intelligence Report RSS No. 0059/72), www.foia.cia.gov/sites/default/files/document_conversions/14/esau-55.pdf. Accessed 22 April 2012.

Cresswell, T. (1996) *In Place / Out of Place: Geography, Ideology, and Transgression*. Minneapolis: University of Minnesota Press.

De Fina, A., and A. Georgakopoulou (2015) 'Introduction', in A. De Fina and A. Georgakopoulou (eds), *Handbook of Narrative Analysis*. Oxford: Wiley, pp. 1–17.

Ekholm, K. (2000) *Kielletyt kirjat 1944–1946: Yleisten kirjastojen kirjapoistot vuosina 1944–1946*. Oulu: Oulun yliopisto.

Esanu, O. (2013) *Transition in Post-Soviet Art: The Collective Actions Group before and after 1989*. Budapest: Central European University Press.

Freyd, J.J. (1998) *Betrayal Trauma: The Logic of Forgetting Childhood Abuse*. Cambridge, MA: Harvard University Press.

H. (1942) 'Totuutta neuvosto-komennosta', *Viitasaaren seutu* (30 July 1942).

Haahtela, S. (1942) 'Neuvosto-Elämän tämänpäiväiset kasvot', *Aamulehti* (19 July 1942).

Helsingin Sanomat (1928) 'Suomalaisen kirjailijan teos saavuttanut menestyksen Ranskassa', *Helsingin Sanomat* (12 December 1928).

Hirsch, M. (2008) 'The generation of postmemory', *Poetics Today*, 29(1): 103–28.

'Heimomme tuhooja' (1942) 'Heimomme tuhooja', *Uusi Suomi* (9 July 1942).

Huurre, K. (1942) *Sirpin ja moukarin alla: Yhdeksän vuotta Neuvostoliitossa*. Helsinki: WSOY.

Jaakkola, N. (1968) *Selville vesille*. Petroskoi: Karjala-kustantamo.

J.V. (1929) 'Kuvaus Neuvosto-Venäjän vankiloista', *Kymenlaakson sanomat* (18 April 1929).

Kaganovsky, L. (2008) *How the Soviet Man was Unmade: Fantasy and Male Subjectivity under Stalin*. Pittsburgh: University of Pittsburgh Press.

'Kirsti Huurre' (1942) 'Kirsti Huurre: Sirpin ja moukarin alla', *Salmetar* (30 July 1942).

Knuuttila, S. (2006) 'Kriisistä sanataiteeksi: Traumakertomusten estetiikkaa', *Avain: Kirjallisuudentutkimuksen aikakauslehti*, 3(4): 22–42.

Konrad, V., and H.N. Nicol (2011) 'Border culture, the boundary between Canada and the United States of America, and the advancement of borderland theory', *Geopolitics*, 16(1): 70–90.

Kurki, T. (2018) *Rajan kirjailijat: Venäjän Karjalan suomenkieliset kirjailijat tilan ja identiteetin kirjoittajina*. Helsinki: Suomalaisen Kirjallisuuden Seura.

LaCapra, D. (1999) 'Trauma, absence, loss', *Critical Inquiry*, 25(4): 696–727.

Lipovetsky, M. (2011) 'Post-Soviet literature between realism and postmodernism', in E. Dobrenko and M. Balina (eds), *The Cambridge Companion to Twentieth-Century Russian Literature*. Cambridge: Cambridge University Press, pp. 175–94.

Malkki, L. (1995) 'Refugees and exile: From "refugee studies" to the national order of things', *Annual Review of Anthropology*, 24: 495–523.

Marsh, R. (1995) *History and Literature in Contemporary Russia*. Oxford: Macmillan & St Antony's College.

Niinistö, J. (2001) *Bobi Sivén Karjalan puolesta*. Helsinki: Suomalaisen Kirjallisuuden Seura.

Nünning, V. (2008) 'Witness, collective memory, and British national identity', in U. Ekman and F. Tygstrup (eds), *Witness: Memory, Representation, and the Media in Question*. Copenhagen: Museum Tusculanum Press, pp. 123–39.

O.A.K. (1929), 'Kirja bolshevikkien vankiloista', *Aamulehti* (22 February 1929).

Paastela, J. (2003) *Finnish Communism under Soviet Totalitarianism*. Helsinki: Aleksanteri Institute.

Perttu, A. (2006) *Papaninin retkikunta*. Helsinki: Minerva.

Perttu, A. (2014) *Kipu*. Helsinki: Myllylahti.

Rugojev, J. (1969) 'Eräitä näkymiä Karjalan kirjallisuudesta eletyn ja nykypäivän valossa', *Punalippu*, 1969(6): 90–7.

Sandoval, C., A.J. Aldama and P.J. García (2012) 'Toward a de-colonial performatics of the US Latina and Latino Borderlands', in A. Aldama, C. Sandoval and P. García (eds), *Performing the US Latina and Latino Borderlands*. Bloomington: Indiana University Press, pp. 1–27.

Scherrer, J. (2010) 'Perestroika in retrospective: Historical consciousness and responsibility', in M. Kangaspuro, J. Nikula and I. Stodolsky (eds), *Perestroika: Process and Consequences*. Helsinki: Suomalaisen Kirjallisuuden Seura, pp. 37–58.

Schweiger, I. (2015) 'From representing trauma to traumatised representation: Experiential and reflective modes of narrating the past', *Frontiers of Literary Studies in China*, 9(3): 345–68.

Siironen, M. (2012) *Valkoiset: Vapaussodan perintö*. Tampere: Vastapaino.

Statiev, A. (2013) *The Soviet Counterinsurgency in the Western Borderlands*. Cambridge: Cambridge University Press.

Summanen, T. (1973) 'Ristiaallokosta selville vesille', *Punalippu*, 5: 114–21.

Sztompka, P. (2004) 'The trauma of social change: A case of postcommunist societies', in J.C. Alexander, R. Eyerman and B. Giesen (eds), *Cultural Trauma and Collective Identity*. Berkeley: University of California Press, pp. 155–95.

Timonen, A. (1961) *Pieni valkosiipi*. Petroskoi: Karjala-kustantamo.

Timonen, A. (1971) *Me karjalaiset*. Petroskoi: Karjala-kustantamo.

T.S. (1942) 'Yhdeksän vuotta Neuvostoliitossa', *Hämeen kansa* (23 July 1942).

U.V. (1942) 'Sirpin ja moukarin alla: Kirsti Huurteen muistelmateos', *Turun Sanomat* (2 August 1942).

Vettenniemi, E. (2004) *Punaisen terrorin todistajat: Neuvostoliitto suomalaisten leirivankien muistelmissa*. Helsinki: Suomalaisen Kirjallisuuden Seura.

V.P. (1942) 'Neuvostoliiton kuvausta', *Eteenpäin* (17 July 1942).

Whitehead, A. (2004) *Trauma Fiction*. Edinburgh: Edinburgh University Press.

Winn, J.A. (2008) *Poetry of War*. Cambridge: Cambridge University Press.

6

Expanded border imaginaries and aligned border narratives: ethnic minorities and localities in China's border encounters with Myanmar, Laos and Vietnam

Victor Konrad and Zhiding Hu

Introduction

Most traffic between northern Vietnam and Yunnan Province, China, now uses the highway bridge between Hekou and Lao Cai, where inspection is rapid and thorough, with scanners and computerised identity checks (see Figure 6.1). Scaled down from this facility and crossing process is the traditional crossing between the centres of Hekou and Lao Cai across the Red River. The local crossing is now restricted to pedestrian traffic although substantial trade still occurs here. Before the highway bridge was completed, a massive rush of thousands of Vietnamese crossed daily in an assortment of vehicles and on foot. Today, the crossing ritual still begins precisely at 8 am but film records confirm it is more subdued and managed than previously. Queues for people with and without goods form in Lao Cai before the bridge barrier is lifted. The quickest Vietnamese across the border are assured of more rapid access to begin the day of domestic work, vending or other sanctioned activity in Hekou. After immigration and customs clearance, waiting taxis and motorbikes take the Vietnamese to workplaces. Vendors move carts and bicycles to their spots around the city. Most entrants carry local identity documents that are not machine-readable, and consequently may not be used to leave the Hekou security zone. One of the domestic workers interviewed showed us her 'passport' which contained multiple pages of entry and exit stamps, each recording a day spent working in a Chinese home in Hekou. Daily registration takes place in a newly renovated and air-conditioned facility that also boasts a large duty-free shop which caters mainly to the returning Chinese. Chinese who do not cross the border are not barred from making purchases, thus calling into question the concept of duty-free purchase. As one local informant put it, 'What happens in Hekou stays in Hekou'. Yet, Hekou is now a place increasingly connected

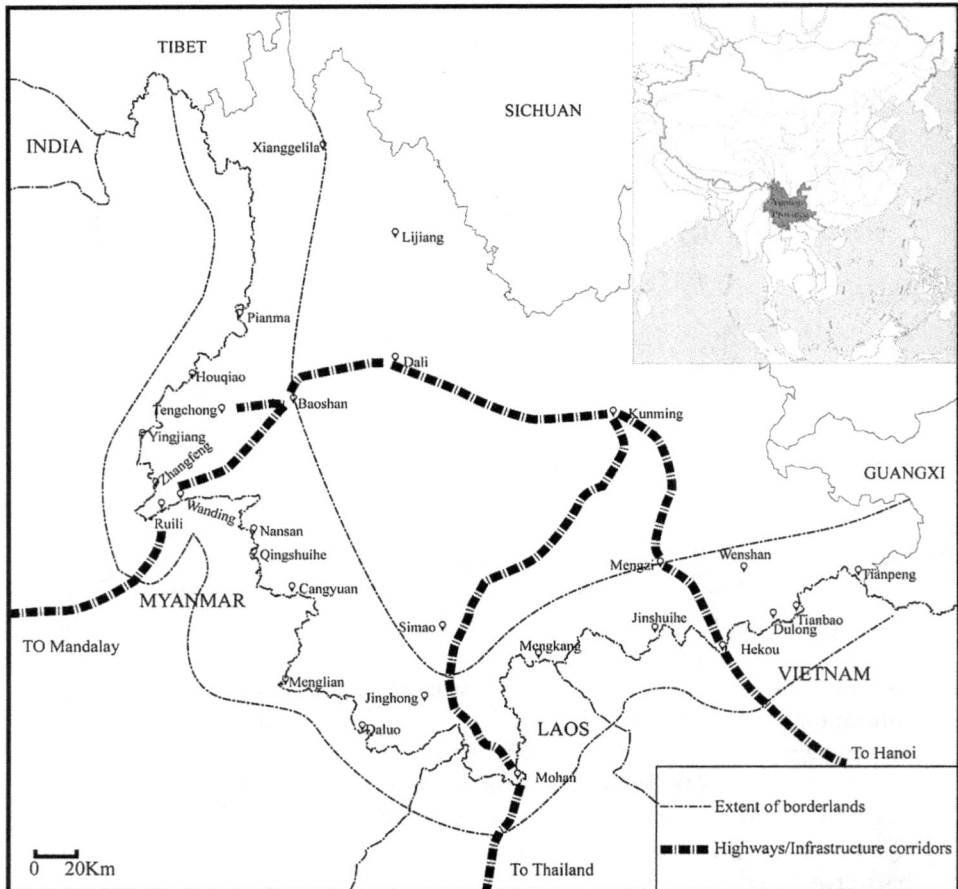

6.1 Emerging borderlands of China and South East Asia.

with other places in China and Vietnam as homeowners rent their houses to Vietnamese and Chinese business representatives while they live elsewhere in the community or work in eastern China. Across the border, Lao Cai serves in part as a dormitory community for the workforce that migrates daily to Hekou. Lao Cai features a growing number of gambling facilities and clubs now outlawed in adjacent China. Also evident are services catering to cross-border traffic of local and long-distance nature, including auto repair, brokerage, accommodation and restaurants.

Lao Cai and Hekou perform the border ritual daily to sustain the imaginary of significance of locality in a rapidly rescaling border context, where both cities are experiencing changes brought about by enhancement of the flow-through corridor between Hanoi and Kunming. Local people and visitors congregate to watch and record the event, which now has a massive following on the Internet. The performance pieces of the aesthetic spectacle – line-up for the border, rush to cross to China, show 'passports', competition for favoured vending locations, gaze of the Chinese authorities – all comprise parts of visual consumption as well as a local script that remains consistent in an otherwise rapidly expanding border context. More than a daily destination, Hekou is also the border city of the day where local Vietnamese work, meet and mix with local Chinese. Lao Cai, on the other hand, is the city of the night where Vietnamese go to sleep and Chinese go to gamble and seek other pleasures. The message of the narrative is that continuity is important in sustaining the border relationship, particularly at the local level. The daily enactment at the border punctuates the significance and heritage of border locality. The performance situates inhabitants of both Hekou and Lao Cai in border space and time although an increasing number of border-crossers between Kunming and Hanoi now bypass the traditional port, and governments of both China and Vietnam are separating informal, local and international crossings and discourses. The government of China is actively scaling the border between Vietnam and China by separating the national and the local, designating national and local goods and services, and differentiating national and provincial crossings in the region. Significantly, national crossings are also elevated to international level with use of English signs. Yet, Hekou and Lao Cai are encouraging plurality in the border space where Vietnamese fruit merchants on bicycles ply their trade next to shops selling Apple communication devices. Border performance and ritual punctuates both locality and multiscalarity.

For three decades, China has accelerated trade and interaction across its boundaries. The 'Belt and Road' initiative (BRI) emphasises that China's territorial vision has moved beyond the historical metaphor of the 'wall' to define edges and limits, yet articulate borderlands creation that combines cross-border engagement with territorial integrity (Sidaway and Woon, 2017). In these new borderlands, extensive infrastructure enhancement, economic development, cultural viability and political positioning all play roles in rescaling and rearticulation of border space, and shaping coexistent spaces of exception and integration (Hu and Konrad, 2018). New spaces of exception and integration allow and enable substantially greater cross-border interaction and enhanced mobility across borders with Myanmar, Laos and Vietnam, and build on the Greater Mekong Subregion initiative of the 1990s (Su, 2012). The Belt and Road narrative of cross-border expansion, extension into foreign and challenging territory, engagement with non-Han peoples, economic and cultural growth, Chinese hegemony and the narrative's revisions and renewals during the last decade are all steeped in Silk Road history and tradition. In this way, the Sino-centric global vision links to an extensive and inclusive master narrative, which in turn is translated into local and regional borderlands imaginaries and narratives. These regional and local imaginaries and narratives may align with the national, or, more commonly, they may adjust imaginaries and narratives to express ethnic identity and local prerogative. The evolved imaginaries and narratives are used by actors connected to the Chinese state as well as provincial and local authorities, ethnic minorities and other constituencies to negotiate border-crossing and enable bordering (Lagerqvist, 2013).

This chapter examines emerging borderlands between Yunnan Province in China and adjacent Vietnam, Laos and Myanmar, and aims to convey a fuller understanding of how borderlands evolve as synchronic spaces of both exception and integration (see Figure 6.1). Specifically, the chapter explores how narratives and imaginaries of border-crossings and processes contribute to border negotiation in the public sphere, and, particularly, how these aesthetic forms deliver a range of 'top-down' and 'bottom-up' discourses among national interests and a richly intertwined tapestry of minorities in this mountainous region. Aligned with Chapter 4 (Brambilla), Chapter 5 (Kurki) above, and Chapter 7 (Amilhat Szary) below, and informed by explorations of shifting space-time of borders in previous publications in this series (Donnan et al., 2017; Demetriou and Dimova, 2019), this chapter addresses, from a geographical perspective, the prevailing yet constantly evolving in-betweenness of borders. Consistently with the aims of this volume, the chapter addresses, in the South-East Asian context, the issues of form, medium and genre of aesthetical strategies in 'borderscapes' (geopolitical and epistemic multidimensionality of the border enabling understanding of borders in globalisation (Brambilla, 2015)) transformation, how these forms, genres and discourses cross into the public sphere, and what making visible and giving voice to border perceptions does to empower both national interests and local minority constituencies.

A prominent illustration is found in the 'Tea Road' narrative that speaks of ancient, well-worn trading routes for tea and other commodities originating in the heart of Yunnan and extending across the formidable Himalayan massif (see Figure 6.2). The 'Tea Road' narrative, a derivative, parallel and variant of the 'Silk Road' narrative, has been co-opted by Yunnan Province to situate the south-western region of China at the apex of time-honoured border-crossing routes (Zhou, 2012). Yet, the narrative also serves Chinese national interest, defining and substantiating the historical roots and legitimacy of the BRI. Furthermore, the narrative resonates globally because the story of Chinese 'roads' beyond the famously isolated dynastic kingdom are legend. Also, the narrative works exceptionally well to infuse recognition and external

6.2 The 'Tea Road Narrative'.

connection into localised, high-quality tea production by ethnic minorities in Yunnan.

The chapter is arranged as follows. It begins with a conceptualisation of the border discourse cycle and theoretical grounding associated with this concept. Then, the role of minorities is addressed in order to situate border people as border keepers and border-crossers, so that the reader may comprehend more fully the aesthetical strategies in borderscapes transformation that operate between China and South-East Asia. A brief discussion of scaling minority appropriation is followed by case studies from borderland locales along China's borders with Myanmar, Laos and Vietnam. The outcomes of the analysis suggest four recurring themes of *empowerment, contestation, borderation* (a term we use for engaging border constituencies) and *negotiation*.

Concept, theory and approach

Underlying narratives and imaginaries derived from crossing borders, evolving bordering practices and creating borderscapes are inevitably impacted by top-down and bottom-up forces, and negotiated to produce forms in media.

We suggest this process may be identified as the *border discourse cycle*, the circulation and revision of written and visual discourse about a border in the public sphere. Imaginaries and narratives merge, link, collude and reinforce border discourse. Top-down narratives and imaginaries negotiate border space with bottom-up narratives and imaginaries. These, in turn, reinforce, modify or adjust border-crossing, bordering practices and borderscapes. If the top-down and bottom-up narratives and imaginaries collide and clash, new ones may be originated, or the process may become stalled. Yet, with any cross-border interaction, aesthetical strategies are evident for coexistence and empowerment in border-crossing, bordering and the creation of borderscapes. The border discourse cycle of repeated and revised processes may then manifest in a sequence of empowerment, contestation, borderation and negotiation.

The theoretical grounding that informs this conceptualisation draws from thinking about the interface of borders, politics and culture in both the humanities and the social sciences, and predominantly among scholars who identify as cross-disciplinary border studies specialists. Although some of this work is considered classical border thinking in geography and anthropology, a substantial breakthrough is evident as well in cross-disciplinary exploration of border concepts. The concept of the border discourse cycle is rooted in different but aligned ideas of liminality (Turner, 1969) and in/visibility (Arendt, 2013 [1958]), both linked to fundamentals of transition in duality. The concept of the border discourse cycle acknowledges reshuffling and realignment of spatialities and temporalities in globalisation (Sassen, 2000; Donnan et al., 2017). Unanchored from territory (Agnew, 1994), borders and borderlands are now recognised as spaces of exception, and beyond nation states rather than just between them (Agamben, 2005; Gregory, 2004). Borders are in motion (Konrad, 2015; Urry, 2012), and this mobility and fluidity enlarges spaces of exception and time-space constructs of borders. Multi-scalar production of borders ensues (Laine, 2016) and an enmeshing of material and non-material mediations of borders emerges (Demetriou and Dimova, 2019). Here borderscapes (Brambilla, 2015; Brambilla et al., 2015; Rajaram and Grundy-Warr, 2007) are created by actors at various scales and in multiple spatial and temporal contexts. In this expanding yet integral 'borderworld', dissensus vies with consensus to characterise the conceptualisation and materialisation of borders (Rancière, 2015; Rodney, 2017). With a growing participation of actors in borderlands and bordering, a broader range and complexity of cultural production of borders is evident (Schimanski and Wolfe, 2010). Also, the aperture for expression of border aesthetics is enlarged, and the concomitant richness and complexity of cultural production of borders invites greater research and understanding (Schimanski, 2015; Schimanski and Wolfe, 2017).

As other contributions to this volume confirm, particularly Chapter 4 (Brambilla), Chapter 5 (Kurki) above, and Chapter 7 (Amilhat Szary) below, confirm, aesthetical strategies in borderscapes as mobile, relational and contested sites are expressed in the form, medium and genre of cultural expression related to borders. In the interest of brevity, we will not provide an extensive discussion of the literature but direct the reader to the theoretical underpinnings of this work in the Introduction to the volume, as well as theoretical discussions linked to work in anthropology and geography discussed in Chapters 4 and 5 above. In the current chapter, form, medium and genre are viewed as aligned with the traditional cultural traits of minorities in the border region of Yunnan Province and adjacent borderlands of Myanmar, Laos and Vietnam. There is an alignment of national spaces with minority identity, and empowerment of both the local and the national. Furthermore, we argue that these strategies are making space for the global.

Exploring evolving borderlands has led us to examine the length and breadth of Yunnan border regions and venture into adjacent parts of Vietnam, Laos and Myanmar. This empirical work, conducted over the past five years, includes detailed observation and documentation of regional infrastructure, processes and places, and interviews with hundreds of local residents, ethnic minorities, business people, government representatives at local, regional and national levels, military and cross-border migrants. The information gathered has been assessed and analysed for several research projects, but it has become evident that the data collected, and the extensive record of exploration in the cross-border region, also yield substantiation of a massive shift in border region geography, and, significantly, the narratives and imaginaries contributing to evolving borderlands.

The role of minorities in the China-South-East Asia borderlands

Ethnic minorities are more numerous and evident along the border between Yunnan Province, China, and Myanmar, Laos and Vietnam than they are in the heartlands of these states. Characteristically, minority territories and cultural presence extend across the boundary throughout the region although strong national identities are also expressed at the border. Cross-border extent of ethnic minority territories is evident, particularly among Dai (Tai), Hmong (Miao, Zhuang), Shan and Kachin (Lisu). Ethnic group names may differ across the border but most aspects of culture extend across the boundary. Even the Han Chinese majority in Yunnan is represented as a cross-border ethnic presence in Myanmar's Kokang 'autonomous territory' (Hu and Konrad, 2018). Our research has shown that 'border people' have evolved specific roles that link with their location, cultural traditions, business interests and ethnic identities. In the mountainous north-western borderlands, Lisu are gatekeepers of mountain trails and passes. In the major gateway between Myanmar and China, Jingpo traders play a prominent role as intermediaries. Dai also operate in this region but they are more prominent as business leaders and agriculturalists in the upper Mekong region where Myanmar, Laos and China converge. Where the Shan states meet Yunnan, Wa control cross-border trade, both legal and illicit, through small, isolated border-crossings in the uplands. East of the Mekong Valley, Hani tea traders occupy the borderlands. The Hmong in the eastern portion of the border-lands manage cross-border agricultural trade ranging from spices to water buffalo.

Our fieldwork confirms that the role of minorities is essentially to anchor the border while facilitating 'borderwork' or everyday and ordinary construction, shifting and dismantling of borders (Rumford, 2012). Due to the remote nature of the borderlands, far from Kunming and central Yunnan, and also far from the populated parts of Myanmar, Laos and Vietnam, central governments in all of the countries depend on decentralised border control. This control is assured to a degree by national military presence in borderlands but it depends also on ethnic-minority participation in border security management. The approach used in Myanmar has been to invest ethnic minorities with autonomy to manage and control their territories, but this has led to conflicts between central and provincial (state) authorities, when authorities are not aligned, and when regimes change. China has evolved an approach to engage ethnic minorities in localised border control, and compromise national control to enable traditional trade and interaction patterns. Upscale trade is facilitated through special trading zones at major crossings. The goals are to facilitate increasing cross-border flows and to manage the border more efficiently. The ethnic minority role is to link formal and informal borders, and to align opposing forces of mobility and indigeneity.

Our research shows that ethnic minorities have evolved from border keepers to border managers throughout the borderlands. Armed border keepers in the Shan and Wa states, for example, have shifted from being stewards of the drug trade to a greater engagement in a combination of illicit and legal trade, while they develop the economies of their territories and enhance the well-being of local inhabitants. In some parts of the Myanmar–China borderlands, where hostilities linger between central government forces and Kachin and Kokang minorities, the fortified border allows rebels to hide in China. In major crossing corridors, however, labour migration, extensive trade and growing collaboration prevail, all facilitated by ethnic-minority linkages across the border.

Renewing locality and scaling minority appropriation in emerging borderlands

In Yunnan's border regions shared with Vietnam, Laos and Myanmar, interplay of increased cross-border interactions, at various scales and in specific locales, has set the stage for borderlands emergence (Sturgeon, 2013). Cross-border co-operation has become intertwined with region-making in rescaled and multi-scalar regional development (Chen, 2006, 2018; Su, 2012, 2014). Territorial entitlement and sense of ownership across the border prevail, particularly among Chinese occupants of borderlands who recognise historical evidence of Chinese construction in Lao Cai, Vietnam, for example, or claim kinship with Han residents of Kokang, now in adjacent Myanmar (Hu and Konrad, 2018). The border has never closed completely, and it is difficult for governments on both sides to close the border to informal exchanges. China has recognised the growth potential of cross-boundary exchange, and offsets from this trade may help to increase the standard of living for residents in Yunnan borderlands. Sanctioned movement of goods and people across borders now epitomises a new order in border relations on China's perimeter (Summers, 2013; Zhao, 1996).

China's borderlands with Myanmar, Laos and Vietnam have been, until recently, remote and removed from multi-scalar cross-border connections and flows. Change has been rapid, and resulted in development of specific border constructs and visible and measurable evolution of a borderlands regime. Forces and constructs are evident, and their inter-relationship and sequencing illustrate components of evolving borderlands. In a China–South East Asian context, top-down influences and articulation by central governments, and particularly by Beijing, are catalysts for borderland development. Yet, whereas central governments often define and form borderlands and establish controls, local and provincial governments and powerful local agents lead change in borderlands (Baird and Li, 2017). Then, bottom-up initiative, resistance and compliance, mainly by ethnic minorities, shape evolving borderlands. There are multiple Chinas, rather than a monolith, at work in fashioning the borderlands (Ptak, 2017).

Situating ethnic minorities occupying borderlands into this multi-scalar, dynamic border zone is not a simple matter of placing them as local actors at the base of the continuum – from local to regional to national to supra-national – in which their roles are limited. In the China–South-East Asia borderlands, lodging the national at the border also involves attaching and assuring the local, and increasingly linking the supra-national. Consequently, so-called 'national crossings' are scaled to serve concurrently as local, regional, national and supra-national crossings, thus elevating and expanding the role of ethnic minorities at these locations. There is competition among ethnic minorities, and between majority Han, Lao, Vietnamese and Burmese and the ethnic minorities at these major crossings, to control and manage cross-border activity because here stakes are high and profits lucrative. At smaller, binational crossings, some almost adjacent to major corridors, identity politics are rarely displayed and crossing space is not contested, even by national interests. This scaling of minority appropriation is evident throughout the borderlands of China and South-East Asia. The neatly defined and stacked local and minority, regional, and national borderlands narratives and imaginaries have been rearranged as local through global borderscapes, and minority appropriation of these borderscapes as sites of both belonging and becoming (Brambilla, 2015) extend through multi-scalar border space in motion and engage with national narratives and imaginaries. These conceptualisations are substantiated in the following discussions situated in border contexts along the extensive and diverse boundary. The example from Hekou, presented in the introduction, illustrates how a border narrative punctuates locality and multi-scalarity.

Making China and recapturing an ethnic homeland

In the upper Mekong River valley, where the Chinese prefecture of Xishuangbanna links to adjacent Laos and Mynamar, the Dai minority has emerged as a dominant force in cross-border activity. Dai are supportive of Chinese government initiatives to make China in Laos and Myanmar, and simultaneously to recapture their identity within the upper Mekong border region. After centuries of colonisation, separation and national and provincial control, Dai have become empowered in their ancestral homeland. The Dai, one of the largest minorities in Yunnan Province, have turned population strength, extensive land ownership and increasing wealth into cross-border clout in the region. Also, Dai have made effective use of aesthetic images to convey identity and presence in architecture, design and symbolic markers in the landscape. 'Thai style' permeates the region and is evident in rural and urban places throughout Xishuangbanna and into adjacent Laos and Myanmar. The Dai narrative is recounted in stories of ethnic origin, celebrated in the water festival, and displayed in museum villages and tourist attractions throughout traditional Dai territory as well as other localities appropriated in the borderlands.

The upper Mekong border region narrative promoted by the government of China speaks of national imperatives of trade with South-East Asia and national control in the borderlands. Our research confirms that this narrative is represented by national monuments, state buildings, infrastructure and posters throughout the region. Also, it is evident at Mohan, the main crossing point from China to Laos and subsequently to Thailand. Current infrastructure development on both sides of the border is expanding and driven by Chinese interests. Officials confirm that the Laotian government has rented space at Boten to Chinese business interests for 99 years. By locating on the Laotian side, Chinese businessmen exclude Chinese diplomatic and military interests (and controls) at the border. Accordingly, many Chinese companies are investing in this new approach to cross-border integration. Astride this border, the grey stone of the Chinese facility contrasts in architectural style and colour with the golden Laotian portal which resembles a Buddhist temple. Yet, this contrast is deceptive because the symbolic differentiation at the boundary masks the crossing in a border region with considerable cultural continuity and economic integration.

Jinghong, the centre of Dai culture in Xishuangbanna, a sprawling urban area of over one million inhabitants, serves as service centre for Yunnan Province and the cross-border region. The city is home to other ethnic minority groups originating nearby, and attracts Han Chinese and ethnic minorities from other parts of Yunnan and China. The airport provides not only regular scheduled service to Kunming but also international service to Thailand and other locations in South-East Asia. Jinhong is linked directly to several land border-crossings, and is the terminus of cross-border boat traffic on the Mekong. Throughout Jinghong, visible evidence of cross-border economy, society and culture abound in architecture, symbolic statuary, street decoration and Buddhist religious sites. Jinghong is reminiscent of a Thai city, and it is where national and regional ethnic-minority narratives meet and mesh.

Balancing official zones and informal crossings: narrative validation and everyday compromise

In agricultural borderlands that stretch from Tengchong near the foothills of the Himalaya south to mountainous Kokang (see Figure 6.1), Han as well as ethnic Dai and Jingpo work farms or, increasingly, are occupied in trade, manufacturing and service sectors. Wanding Border Port Culture Park celebrates the interface of China and Myanmar and displays borderscapes of ethnic minorities who occupy the borderlands. Nearby, Ruili is the main gateway to Myanmar and centre of the jade and hardwood trade. The region has long been occupied by Han Chinese at the mountainous frontier of Chinese expansion and trade. One new highway and infrastructure corridor, completed in 2017, leads to Dehong, and its Jingpo and Dai minorities engaged in cross-border trade. The high-speed railway, and other aspects of infrastructure are nearing completion. Adjacent to the north is rural

Longchuan County where Han farmers and entrepreneurs from other parts of China engage in small business including cross-border trade. Tengchong, junction of Han civilisation and the Lisu mountain tribe frontier, was a south-western hub of the Silk Road established in 206 BCE. The small yet rapidly expanding city gained an airport at Tuofeng in 2009 and was connected to Baoshan by expressway in 2016. The mix and often clash of progressive and traditional narratives is palpable in road signs, architecture, artistic expression and landscape alteration in the city and surrounding borderlands.

Near Tengchong, Hou Qiao Port was opened to Myanmar in 2003. In 2017, despite limited cross-border traffic, an international market and duty-free facility were completed, reflecting China's 'build it and they will come' policy of border-crossing development. Here, members of the Lisu minority, which constitutes 98 per cent of the local population, find themselves astride an emerging global pathway (Kunming to Calcutta) central to the BRI national narrative. Border-crossers without papers do not use this national/global crossing. They use seven small, local crossings, and, beyond these, informal crossings where people feel confident in merely jumping the border at will. This is tolerated by both Chinese and Myanmar officials because interior checkpoints seal the immediate borderlands. About 50 km into China from the 'Tengchong border' lies the frontier checkpoint at Feng Ping. Like other interior checkpoints, this military post secures movement in the borderlands. Coexisting border discourses of traditional and informal interaction of Lisu, and emerging Sino-centric global trade, prevail in one border space, yet, as predicted by the local Lisu headman in an interview, there is an inevitable collision of these narratives as the pathway widens and gains more traffic.

Ruili is a modern, sprawling and affluent city with wide boulevards and substantial suburban expansion fuelled by growing trade with Myanmar. The focal point is the special trade zone of Jiegao. Here is an entry and exit checkpoint before one actually arrives at the pedestrian and vehicular crossings to Myanmar at Ruili/Muse. The special trade zone is dominated by Chinese merchants engaged in the jade trade whereas other cross-border trade, particularly hardwood, is found both in the zone and beyond it in the burgeoning city. In the trade zone, the jade section hugs the border and conducts a brisk and competitive trade, mainly to Chinese from other parts of the country. Also here, low-order goods like cigarettes, candy and other consumer goods and high-order goods like drugs are sold 'through the fence'. According to informants, the murky border 'where Burma dissolves into China' is found in the trade zone as well as in more remote rural areas nearby. In Ruili, at the Tengchong border and in other border contexts researched, everyday compromise and everyday bordering and de-bordering

(Yuval-Davis et al., 2018), shift sites of traditional belonging to sites of transitional becoming, and potentially into new sites of belonging.

Changing place and trading space

Dalou is gateway to Myanmar in the Wa region, and northern apex of the infamous 'Golden Triangle' of illicit trade. Once a busy border town, Dalou boasted a mix of legitimate and illicit businesses and tourist attractions, but, due to Chinese government crackdown on illegal practices, Dalou lost most of its border business to adjacent Mongla in Myanmar. In effect, Mongla has become Dalou as Chinese-controlled businesses have moved across the boundary to avoid government scrutiny, particularly of activities now listed as illegal by China. In addition to the long-established trade in narcotics, this list now includes gambling and endangered species trade. Once visible borderscapes of drug trade are now being made invisible through government crackdowns in both Dalou and Mongla. In Dalou, the authorities combat drugs with numerous military checkpoints and aggressive measures designed to stop the trade. In Mongla, the combined Chinese, Burmese and international effort is more subdued and relies on signs urging 'LET US ALL PARTICIPATE IN REALISING THE DRUG FREE ZONE' and selective enforcement by police. The illicit trade in live animals and parts of endangered species is, however, rampant, and made more visible in street-front shops and by vendors throughout Mongla. The border narrative is simple juxtaposition of space and place.

Laugai, in the Myanmar territory of Kokang, and its counterpart Nansan town in China, are also juxtaposed in space and place. In this instance, due to recent hostilities in Kokang between central Myanmar government forces and Kokang rebels, residents of Laugai moved businesses and a large part of the population to Nansan and the surrounding countryside in China (Hu and Konrad, 2018). Laugai is a space of exception within Kokang due to its close affiliation with China; Kokang is a space of exception in Myanmar due to its Han Chinese legacy and its strident political autonomy (Kyu, 2012). Kokang, the First Special Region of Myanmar, a borderland settled centuries ago by the Yang clan with hereditary rights granted in the Qing dynasty, both identifies with China and is a Han transition between China and Myanmar. Also, Kokang is a metaphor and vantage point for understanding border dynamics in the space between exception and integration in removed and unfamiliar places. Kokang has become a zone of co-dependence where powerful agents employ the border as a resource. It is both deterritorialised and reterritorialised. Border security is multifaceted and multiscaled in a region where national, regional and local security interests all converge. Kokang border culture operates as a formidable, effective force in borderland construction and sustainability. The remoteness of Kokang is chimerical in globalisation: remote border regions are at once isolated and increasingly part of global geopolitics and geopolitical repositioning.

The people of Kokang and their counterparts in adjacent China are accomplished borderlanders who negotiate boundaries across space and time. More than 60 per cent of over four hundred Chinese and Kokang interviewed indicated at least occasional associations across the border, and 30 per cent of Kokang respondents and 20 per cent of Chinese respondents reported substantial and frequent crossings (Hu and Konrad, 2018). Yet, cross-border culture is not blended but rather expressed in multiple imaginaries and narratives at different scales and advocated by different interests.

Prominent among the Kokang narratives are three perspectives. Local interests view Kokang in a space between Shan state and Yunnan Province, and they differentiate themselves from Shan and align with Yunnanese. Another narrative describes Kokang as nested with other ethnic minorities, and, as such, allied against the central government of Myanmar. A third narrative confirms Kokang as a separate ethnic-minority region between China and Myanmar, but related to China. These narratives have each been promoted by media aligned with geopolitical positions of national, regional and local interests, and they, collectively, describe the space between exception and integration. Exception and integration coexist to define a place that remains in between and a state (both condition and territory) that remains becoming. Geopolitical narratives thrive and multiply in this space. The border is interpreted as between definitive and permeable as long as the location of the border is not in question. This space in between has emerged to at once mediate and facilitate cross-border imagination and interaction. The space between exception and integration transcends the border yet it contains a culture evolved over centuries in these borderlands.

From edges to crossings: narratives of the changing role of places and spaces

The story of Kokang also illustrates the changing role of place as transformation of edge places into crossing places in a hierarchy of enhanced border-crossings (Fox, 2009). Some edge places, the vanguard border cities, have changed most dramatically in size, with an increase and alteration of functions, crossing facilitation and overall settlement viability (Teng et al., 2017). Edge places further down the hierarchy of border-crossings have experienced less change. For example, whereas Hekou and Jin Shui He are both 'national' crossings between China and Vietnam, the former has seen extensive transformation whereas the latter remains a relatively unaltered crossing point where transfer of a load of bananas appears as a highlight of border activity. At Jin Shui He and other remote places on the China–Vietnam border, 'upland trading-scapes' of ethnic minorities still prevail (Turner et al., 2015). In some border places, Han Chinese emulate the cross-border business success of minorities and appropriate the minority narratives. In Heshun, the cross-border business culture is linked to 'Rushang', a dynamic Confucian entrepreneurship to reinforce flourishing cross-border activities, thus transforming wealth into reputation (I-chieh, 2010).

Coincident with the growing complexity and diversity of edge places is transformation of border administrative spaces, particularly counties, into focal areas for development of border trade (Baird and Li, 2017; Zhao, 1996). This model of decentralised development originated early in the establishment of formalised cross-border trade and prevails to alter border territory as well as specific border places. Each county in the borderlands has established narratives to promote local and ethnic minority features such as hot springs and Dai culture in Delong County.

National narratives identify favoured crossings for enhancement and development. Primary crossings, in particular, stand to become even more significant places in the emerging border-crossing system. Here are found expanding special border economic zones. Hekou, Mohan and Ruili all exhibit such developments, and these facilities are also projected at Hou Qaio near Tengchong. As cross-border traffic increases, and the border-crossing system becomes more established, special economic zones and facilities such as duty-free shops and 'international' markets are likely to grow. Already evident at Hekou, Ruili and Jinghong, cities designated and evolved as gateways are becoming destinations for Chinese from across the country, both as tourists and as residents. International tourism remains limited but is increasing (Li and Wall, 2014). Connections among places at the top of the crossing hierarchy are national and increasingly binational and global, whereas smaller localities in the borderlands remain isolated.

Situating and sustaining borderlands through empowerment, contestation, 'borderation' and negotiation

As established earlier in this chapter, ethnic minorities predominate along the border to define segmented border territories extending across the border. In these territories, ethnic minorities sustain cross-border linkages now sanctioned and encouraged by authorities (Wang et al., 2013). Linkages are accomplished in part through cross-border periodic markets in the Yunnan–Vietnam border area (Masaru and Badenoch, 2013). In Ruili and surrounding

Dehong County, Jingpo and Dai, in co-operation with Han, are active in operating the growing cross-border trade in hardwoods and jade. Some Dai pedlars in Dehong dress in traditional Thai clothing to destabilise their lower-status position in Han-dominated society in the region (Siriphon, 2007). Together, the minority and majority ethnic groups in the region are directing China's largest trade centre for natural resources, and products emerging from these valuable commodities (Bie et al., 2014). Co-operative working arrangements are similar in other cross-border territories where minorities predominate. In some remote areas, Lisu territory for example, cross-border interaction is emerging more slowly, but this region may see considerably heightened trade in hardwoods as resources are depleted in areas closer to Ruili, and if endemic conflict in far northern Myanmar winds down. According to a Lisu headman in the village adjacent to Hou Qaio, normalisation in adjoining Myanmar may result in accelerated cross-border interaction and greater manifestation of cross-border linkages. In Kokang, Han ethnic continuity and co-operation across the border has been a major factor in expansion of cross-border sugar cane production. The patterns are consistent. Cross-border connections, sustained even in times of closed borders, flourish when borders are loosened. Yet, more instructive than this predictable result are the patterns of collaboration among ethnic minorities, and between ethnic minorities and the Han majority as borders are opened. 'Border strategies' of trade mobility among Dai (Tai Lue) on the China–Laos frontier rely on sustained connection and adherence with Han authority and approach as 'part of a long-applied governing pattern of "experimentation under hierarchy" on the Sino-Lao frontier' (Diana, 2013: 25).

Borderlands then appear to be regions in which traditional ethnic identities are both enhanced and celebrated, but also spaces in which greater interaction and perhaps even integration between minorities, and between minorities and Han Chinese, are evident (He, 2008). In some prefectures, several minorities are present whereas in others a clear dominance of one group appears. With increased Han migration into Yunnan, and minority mobility from traditional territories to Kunming and growth centres in and beyond the province, there is growing integration of ethnic minorities and Han. Also apparent is that some minorities maintain greater integrity than others in the face of urbanisation, migration and ultimately integration. In borderlands, both integration and minority integrity and persistence are operating. Evidence from informants suggests that Dai, Lisu and Lahu minorities are more resilient than other minorities in the borderlands.

One finding evident across all borderlands is an established local nature of border scale pervading cross-border regions. Even larger primary crossing settlements sustain a sense of locality and identification of inhabitants with this locality. This is in part connected to ethnic-minority lineage of place and space. One village of Dai in Long Choan County was resettled from its former locale before a dam flooded its lands. The manifestations of Dai culture in the new village are extensive and designed to underscore their identity verification (Baird and Li, 2017). Beyond identification with locality, primary border-crossing places display regional, national and often global symbols of identity. These include regional expressions of Dai culture, for example in the extensive Xishuangbanna area where elephant statuary, Thai structural decoration and other visible elements of material culture are on display. These are found alongside symbols of the Chinese national state on government buildings, banks and other institutions in Jinghong. Also, in the city are found emerging signs of international economic and cultural connections. Near the border, and particularly in Boten Economic Zone, signs in English as well as Mandarin proclaim emerging global connections and 'multilingualism of the borderscape' (Gorter, 2006).

Borderlands are situated and sustained because ethnic minorities have been made visible and given voice through narratives acknowledged by others, and particularly by the national government. In Yunnan, governments at all levels respond to minority voices, and this empowers ethnic minorities. Border policy aligns national and minority interests and displays them together when they coincide, but separates them spatially when they do not, as illustrated in the adjacent formal and informal crossings evident all along the border. Minority symbols of cultural identity – dress, rituals, monuments – are both allowed in the borderlands space and appropriated by the national government for display in the 'national' space within the borderlands. Throughout the borderlands, and particularly at crossings where multiple narratives of territorial control are evident – Dalou, Ruili, Jinhong – the national government sanctions borderlands culture parks to celebrate and align minority identities with the national. In this way ethnic minorities 'know their place' politically as well as culturally.

Contestation may occur without necessarily eclipsing the national voice. The national voice prevails in the 'reserved space' of national crossings. These national crossings have strict rules and conventions of behaviour that must be adhered to by all border-crossers. Invariably, these rules are posted in several languages including English, and rules are enforced by the military. The crossings are formidable and messages of compliance are clear and reinforced by media presentations. Yet, there is extensive and precipitous localisation that occurs just beyond the national crossing space. Everyone knows where to cross easily; contestation is the simple act of crossing elsewhere than at the national crossing.

The engagement of local and minority constituencies so that border and local and minority culture are aligned may be termed 'borderation', and viewed as an example of becoming in the borderscape. The ethnic minority identifies with and utilises the border as part of cultural expression, and this border identity and culture is branded in tourism and other economic ventures. Dai exemplify this 'borderation' and, owing to their success in marketing their border identity, they have expanded their cultural entrepreneurship into other parts of the borderlands beyond their traditional homeland. Our research confirms that new Dai places and spaces have emerged in other culture areas, particularly where development opportunities exist.

Culturally diverse border space is evident in areas of rapid borderland transformation. Fences are typically a last resort to divide interests, people and flows where change is too rapid and authority needs to be exercised. The Ruili–Muse interface is an example. More typically border space is negotiated and people know where to cross. Most local border-crossing is informal until thresholds of employment, sale of higher-order goods and services, and legality are crossed. Through negotiation and compromise, both local minority constituencies and national interests remain empowered during borderland transformation.

Conclusions

This study offers compelling evidence that borderlands culture is integral to developing and sustaining borderlands emergence and evolution. In emerging borderlands of China and South-East Asia, ethnic minorities have been associated with borderlands since borders were drawn between and through their territories. For many ethnic minorities, borders have helped establish their identities and enabled their livelihoods. Even closed borders did not stop cross-border interaction. The emergence of sanctioned borderlands of cross-border trade and migration has renewed and validated the role of ethnic minorities in cross-border engagement and interaction. Borderlands culture also flourishes locally where it is nourished by tradition, identity and attachment to place and space. Both locality and ethnicity, then, help to create borderscapes and imaginaries of borders and borderlands, and to anchor the narratives associated with these imaginaries.

The national interests of China, and its neighbours Vietnam, Laos and Myanmar, are ostensibly aligned to craft border imaginaries and narratives of cross-border development, economic expansion and global connection, although, in South-East Asia, China dominates the imaginary, and the BRI narrative prevails. Yet, media forms of imaginary and narrative both combine and diverge in borderlands where they are appropriated by minorities and charged with new stories to support identity verification and political and economic gain. Hybrid forms result to weave a rich tapestry of borderland interaction and display. When this tapestry is examined carefully, different levels of discourse are evident. Also evident is the fact that border space allows these diverse discourses to coexist, and even to flourish and grow. Significantly, borderlands accommodate a diversity and plurality of cultural memories and expressions, and the imaginaries and narratives that are created. Borderlands are not only 'third space' but plural space as well, and the 'in-betweenness' enlarges transactional space of human political, economic, cultural and other interests.

Making visible and giving voice through border imaginaries and narratives are strong acts of empowerment for minority and local constituencies as long as local and minority imaginaries and narratives do not eclipse the national discourse. Among the strategies to ensure that this incursion does not occur is the simple act of apportioning space. National border space is assigned, identified and fortified, yet it is also limited to the national border-crossings. Whereas national authority prevails along the entire boundary, it is exercised strategically at and near national crossings. This leaves ample border space for contestation, ameliorating trauma associated with bordering, the revitalisation of visibility, and the expression of local and ethnic minority identity. Moderation of the national and the local, and particularly engagement of minority constituencies, have evolved a 'borderation' effect wherein the border is the catalyst for mediation and merging of multi-scalar border narratives. This 'borderation' works at multiple scales and also at the same scale where some ethnic minorities are joining with others to operate more effectively in border space. Diverse border space is then negotiable between and within scales. In this negotiable and diverse border space, border images and narratives help to ease a rapid borderland transformation, and to make sense of border spaces that have changed substantially in the experience of people inhabiting them.

Opening borders and emerging borderlands engage governments, people – in the majority and the minority – in expansive alteration of space and place, massive investment, substantial construction and potentially irreversible environmental impact. These processes need to be better understood so that measures may be undertaken to assure that impacts on valued cultures, landscapes and lifeways are mitigated. Creation of 'third space' among nation states, and in globalisation, carries with it a responsibility of stewardship and sustainability.

References

Agamben, G. (2005) *State of Exception*. Trans. K. Attell. Chicago: The University of Chicago Press.

Agnew, J. (1994) 'The territorial trap: The geographical assumptions of international relations theory', *Review of International Political Economy*, 1(1): 53–80.

Arendt, H. (2013 [1958]) *The Human Condition*. Chicago: The University of Chicago Press.

Baird, I.G., and C. Li (2017) 'Variegated borderlands governance: Examples from Dehong Dai-Jingpo Autonomous Prefecture along the China–Myanmar border', *Geoforum*, 85: 214–24.

Bie, Q.L., C.S. Li and S.Y. Zhoa (2014) 'Evaluation of the effectiveness of border policies in Dehong Prefecture of Yunnan, China', *Sustainability*, 6(8): 5284–99.

Brambilla, C. (2015) 'Exploring the critical potential of the borderscapes concept', *Geopolitics*, 20(1): 14–34.

Brambilla, C., J. Laine, J.W. Scott and G. Bocchi (eds) (2015) *Borderscaping: Imaginations and Practices of Border Making*. Farnham: Ashgate.

Chen, X. (2006). 'Beyond the reach of globalization: China's border regions and cities in transition', in F. Wu (ed.), *Globalization and the Chinese City*. New York: Routledge, pp. 21–46.

Chen, X. (2018) 'Rethinking cross-border regional cooperation: A comparison of the China–Myanmar and China–Laos borderlands', in E. Nadalutti and O. Kallscheuer (eds), *Region-Making and Cross-Border Cooperation: New Evidence from Four Continents*. Abingdon: Routledge, pp. 81–105.

Demetriou, O., and R. Dimova (eds) (2019) *The Political Materialities of Borders: New Theoretical Directions*. Manchester: Manchester University Press.

Diana, A. (2013) 'The experimental governing of mobility and trade on the China–Laos frontier: The Tai Lue case', *Singapore Journal of Tropical Geography*, 34(1): 25–39.

Donnan, H., M. Hurd and C. Leutloff-Grandits (eds) (2017) *Migrating Borders and Moving Times: Temporality and the Crossing of Borders in Europe*. Manchester: Manchester University Press.

Fox, J. (2009) 'Crossing borders, changing landscapes: Land use dynamics in the golden triangle', *Asia Pacific Issues*, 92: 1–8.

Gorter, D. (2006) *Linguistic Landscape: A New Approach to Multilingualism*. Toronto: Multilingual Matters.

Gregory, D. (2004) *The Colonial Present*. Oxford: Blackwell.

He, Y. (2008) 'Cross-border ethnicalism in the border region of southwest China', *Journal of Yunnan Nationalities University*, 25(1): 11–16.

Hu, Z., and V. Konrad. (2018) 'In the space between exception and integration: The Kokang borderlands on the periphery of China and Myanmar', *Geopolitics*, 23(1): 147–79.

I-chieh, F. (2010) '"Talking landscape": The culture dynamics of Rushang (Confucian entrepreneurs) in a peripheral migrant hometown in Yunnan', *Asia Pacific Journal of Anthropology*, 11(2): 191–204.

Konrad, V. (2015). 'Toward a theory of borders in motion', *Journal of Borderlands Studies*, 30(1): 1–18.

Kyu, M.M. (2012) 'The rise of the Chinese minority – The new neo-liberal state?' in W. Tantikanangkul and A. Prichard (eds), *Politics of Autonomy and Sustainability in Myanmar*. Singapore: Springer, pp. 13–35.

Lagerqvist, Y.F. (2013) 'Imagining the borderlands: Contending stories of a resource frontier in Muang Sing', *Singapore Journal of Tropical Geography*, 34(1): 57–69.

Laine, J. (2016) 'The multiscalar production of borders', *Geopolitics*, 21(3): 465–82.

Li, Y., and G. Wall (2014). *Planning for Ethnic Tourism*. Burlington, VT: Ashgate.

Masaru, N., and N. Badenoch (2013) 'Why periodic markets are held: Considering products, people, and place in the Yunnan–Vietnam border area', *Southeast Asian Studies*, 2(1): 171–92.

Ptak, T. (2017) 'Considering multiple Chinas in the shifting regional geopolitics of Mekong river dams', *Political Geography*, 58: 136–8.

Rajaram, P.K., and C. Grundy-Warr (eds) (2007) *Borderscapes: Hidden Geographies and Politics at Territory's Edge*. Minneapolis: University of Minnesota Press.

Rancière, J. (2015) *Dissensus: On Politics and Aesthetics*. London: Bloomsbury.

Rodney, L. (2017) *Looking Beyond Borderlines: North America's Frontier Imagination*. New York: Routledge.

Rumford, C. (2012) 'Towards a multiperspectival study of borders', *Geopolitics*, 17(4): 887–902.

Sassen, S. (2000) 'Spatialities and temporalities of the global: Elements for theorization', *Public Culture*, 12(1): 215–32.

Schimanski, J. (2015) 'Border aesthetics and cultural distancing in the Norwegian–Russian borderscape', *Geopolitics*, 20(1): 35–55.

Schimanski, J., and S.F. Wolfe (2010) 'Cultural production and negotiation of borders: Introduction to the dossier', *Journal of Borderlands Studies*, 25(1): 38–49.

Schimanski, J., and S.F. Wolfe (eds) (2017) *Border Aesthetics: Concepts and Intersections*. New York: Berghahn.

Sidaway, J.D., and C.Y. Woon (2017) 'Chinese narratives on "One Belt, One Road" in geopolitical and imperial contexts', *The Professional Geographer*, 69(4): 591–603.

Siriphon, A. (2007) 'Dress and cultural strategy: Tai peddlers in transnational trade along the Burma–Yunnan frontier', *Asian Ethnicity*, 8(3): 219–34.

Sturgeon, J.C. (2013) 'Introduction – Regionalization at the margins: Ethnic minority cross-border dynamics in the greater Mekong subregion', *Singapore Journal of Tropical Geography*, 34(1): 3–8.

Su, X. (2012) 'Rescaling the Chinese state and regionalization in the greater Mekong subregion', *Review of International Political Economy*, 19(3): 501–27.

Su, X. (2014) 'Multi-scalar regionalization, network connections and the development of Yunnan province, China', *Regional Studies*, 48(1): 91–104.

Summers, T. (2013) *Yunnan – A Chinese Bridgehead to Asia: A Case Study of China's Political and Economic Relations*. Cambridge: Chandos-Elsevier.

Teng, L., Z. Zhang, Q. Du and Y. Ma (2017) 'Regional customs collaboration development strategy in the background of the Belt and Road Initiative', in W. Li and J.E. Mueller (eds), *Proceedings of the 2017 World Conference of Management Science and Human Social Development*. Paris: Atlantis Press, pp. 394–9.

Turner, S., C. Bonnin and J. Michaud (2015) *Frontier Livelihoods: Hmong in the Sino-Vietnamese Borderlands*. Seattle: University of Washington Press.

Turner, V. (1969) *The Ritual Process: Structure and Anti-Structure*. Chicago: Aldine.

Urry, J. (2012) *Sociology Beyond Societies: Mobilities for the 21st Century*. London: Routledge.

Wang, Y.X., K. Kusakabe, R. Lund, S. Mishra Panda and Q. Zhao (2013) 'Mobile livelihoods among ethnic minorities in China: Insights from Yunnan', *Norwegian Journal of Geography*, 67(4): 187–99.

Yuval-Davis, N., G. Wemyss and K. Cassidy (2018) 'Everyday bordering, belonging and the re-orientation of British immigration legislation', *Sociology*, 52(2): 228–44.

Zhao, G. (1996) 'A model of decentralized development: Border trade and economic development in Yunnan', *Issues and Studies*, 32(10): 85–108.

Zhou, C. (2012) 'From Yiwu to Menghai: Yunnan border town on the ancient Tea Travel Road', *Urban China*, 55: 54–5.

Part III

Crossing the border (migrations)

7

Borders: the topos of/for a post-politics of images?

Anne-Laure Amilhat Szary

Introduction

In 2014, the artist Adrien Missika flew a small drone across the border connecting the United States to – and separating it from – Mexico. By editing together the footage he had collected, the artist produced a video entitled *As the Coyote Flies* (Missika, 2014b, see Figure 7.1), the central element of an installation entitled *Amexica* presented at the Swiss Cultural Centre in Paris in 2014 (Missika, 2014a). 'Coyote' is both the desert fox in Spanish and the name that is given to the smugglers on the illegal border crossings of that region. By putting himself in the position of a surveillance officer, and using the types of images that are typically associated with controlling flows (of migrants and the smuggling of illegal goods), Missika appeared to offer the viewers of his video unprecedented means of action, as if counter-visualisation could be a way of engaging into politics (cf. Monahan, 2006).

In recent years, an increasing number of visual artworks at borders have explored different issues relating to the possible politics of the image. These interventions have come in response to the spectacle of control that is now admitted as a characteristic aspect of the border system (Brown, 2010; Amoore and Hall, 2010). What is made visible at places where international boundaries are performed can be considered a sovereign exercise of power. When in 2018 border fence prototypes, whose ultimate goal would be to reinforce the USA–Mexico border wall were erected at the behest of Donald Trump, the artist Christoph Büchel went so far as to question their possible qualification under the label of 'works of art'. In an act of derision, he launched a petition to support the Trump project and began organising

7.1 A still image from Adrien Missika's video *As the Coyote Flies*.

visits to the US government's trial site, until it was razed in the spring of 2019 (Yi, 2018).

The act of building a wall serves as a landscape weapon (Amilhat Szary, 2012). Because of the budget and political investment required, once the barrier has been erected, it functions as a self-fulfilling prophecy: if so many resources were needed to build it, this has to mean that the threat it is supposed to protect against is real. In these conditions, we can ask whether producing visual interventions at borders is to participate in a 'war of images' that are themselves the 'vehicles of all powers and all resistances' (Gruzinski, 1990: 15, author's translation). Without delving too deeply into the debate on what a work of art is (or what differentiates an image created with an aesthetic intention from a more traditional media image), I propose examining the confrontation between two types of pictorial proliferations: those originating with public actors pushing for a new demarcation of the border, and those produced by people who appear to attach politically resistant meaning to their visual interventions (Kester, 1998). Such an approach helps us to compare images that, although created in opposing political contexts, are made according to aesthetic criteria that are in many respects similar. My method of analysis combines a consideration of the context in which the image is produced with the aesthetic power of visual production. Grasping it requires two further axes of study: first, a hermeneutic investigation questioning the representations and imaginaries that underlie its emergence, and second, an appreciation of the materiality of what is at work. These contextual, hermeneutic and material perspectives allow me to work on what can be summarised as the performativity or the 'agency' (Bredekamp, 2018) of images. These images interact with and impact on our imaginaries. According to Bredekamp, the 'image act' is defined as the power 'by which the latent capacity of the image may be stirred into impacting upon the feelings, thoughts and motivation of engaged observers' (Bredekamp, 2018: 35, quoted by Huetz et al., 2019: §2).

Despite the considerable heterogeneity of the forms and media of artistic productions at borders that have surged since the 1980s, and especially after the fall of the Berlin Wall, the relationship such productions have with the border space brings them together, forcing us to relate works that may not have aesthetic links given the huge diversity of their authorship. Beyond the classic figurative/non-figurative duality, this sense of multiplication opens up a possibility of thinking about works that have been created and relate to – or are situated on – the lines of geopolitical structuring formed by international boundaries in a global perspective. It is their intense proliferation that suggests the possibility of seeking a comprehensive overview of works composed around borders that are closing – especially the most visible (and, paradoxically, the most aesthetic) ones, namely the new walls. But this approach is also valid for the other types of borders, those that are opening up, and for which artistic intervention is often a way of transforming artefacts of passage and control into cultural heritage. Therefore, the link between art and politics can be analysed within the framework of the 'hyper-territorialisation' of contemporary borders; in a world marked by incessant processes of deterritorialisation and reterritorialisation suggesting a lability of landscapes, we paradoxically witness an increased use of material artefacts in the structuration of place making. This is why, in a world of flows, this approach adds new value to border materiality in all its diversity. Even though the operations of controlling and sorting flows extend far beyond the international limits of individual countries, a new staging of power is at stake at borders: an art of turning games of domination into images, which draws much of its power from the type of place in which it is rooted. The present book explores the narrative power of images: What does a visual product tell us? How does it generate and/or produce a discourse that may or may not have a political nature? In their Introduction above, Schimanski and Nyman ask us whether 'images negotiate borders, borderlands, and border-crossings in a different way from narratives'. Our objective here is to investigate the political discourse that a visual product is likely to generate in so far as its creator links it to a space as specific as a border.

Border art informs recent analyses of the geopolitical dimension of contemporary aesthetic production. The international boundary is a space that is made public through the direct control of the state whilst simultaneously pulling back from an everyday use. As a complex place of both negotiation and conflict the boundary offers an original perspective to artists who wish to engage in activist work, or at least to integrate their work into a political dimension. Following Rosalyn Deutsche (1992), who showed how intervening in a public space can influence both the aesthetic and the political sphere, we can imagine how the re-enactment of the link between the local and the global which takes place at the border makes it an attractive space for a growing number of artists.

Finally, before considering the geopolitical power of images produced by artists at contemporary borders, it seems crucial to examine the extent of these images' critical potential. Can an image do anything in so far as it obeys the 'aesthetical strategies' (see Schimanski and Nyman in the Introduction) that would lay the ground for image politics? Under what conditions can these artistic creations effectively respond to the existing visual order by providing emancipatory visibility? What does 'making visible' mean? Does border art reveal otherwise hidden power relations or mimic official border elements (i.e., by revealing the surveillance apparatus that is supposed to give images taken of us to official agents)? By comparing the analysis of political anthropology with an aesthetic reading of the works, can we move forward and reformulate the relationship between art and politics? Would border art allow us to affirm that we have moved from a 'critical or resistance perspective, one that claims without being able to prove that a performative dynamic of artistic activism or "artivism"' (Holmes, 2009)? Does it really answer a 'real need to break with the existing order' (Helias and Jouffroy, 1990, quoted by Jimenez, 2005: 276)? At the border, might art no longer speak out by representing a socio-political situation of domination, but by highlighting the aesthetic forces of geopolitical mechanisms and, in so doing, subverting them?

In this chapter, I will first present how contemporary works at borders have increased in number and, in so doing, demonstrate how these places are a locus, that is, the anchor point of a multidimensional message. The second part of the text will highlight the links between the different aesthetic productions at the borders, a performative 'inter-visualisation' that would constitute a type of 'global art' (Belting, 2009) of the border. Finally, this overview will allow me to lay the foundations for a renewed reflection on the relationship between aesthetics and politics as mediated by the space.

In a post-political approach to images, i.e., one that reveals the conceit of the quest of consensus, who is subverting what? A post-political analysis is the opposite of searching for consensus in a democracy where, after an election, power is exercised on behalf of the entire community. In the post-political context, artistic intervention is considered powerful because the presence of the work makes it possible to renew the presence of contradiction within the political arena. Whilst nearing Jacques Rancière's notion of 'dissensus' (2008), Chantal Mouffe goes further, insisting on the fact that art could be 'agonistic' inasmuch as, beyond stemming debate, it also implies the impossibility of a 'final reconciliation' (2007: 3).[1] The form/figure dialectic and its link to the medium imply that, both from an aesthetic and a political point of view, we should shift our understanding of representation, from the old figurative/non-figurative opposition to questioning the notion of democratic representativeness.

From place to topos: Geopolitical and artistic proliferation

The art–borders link produces images whose aesthetics interferes with the geopolitical positioning caused by the location on the edge of the nation state. The first disruptive element of the art–borders link is indeed the recent proliferation of these images, which transforms it into a commonplace or an artistic locus. The uptick in the number of works, installations and exhibitions whose intention involves the border issue raises concerns that go beyond the formal content of these creations. On the one hand, it links artistic intention to the setting and the context; on the other hand, it requires us to consider as a whole visual products whose artistic status is, in fact, very heterogeneous. Looking at this increased artistic production through the lens of border sites allows me to bring together more or less successful creative works, by more or less famous artists on the international scene, without any necessary correlation between these two criteria.

The 'world's first artistic border' – at least, according to the news website SWI swissinfo.ch – is part of the border between Switzerland and Germany, where 'the 280-metre fence marking the border between Konstanz (Germany) and Kreuzlingen (Switzerland) [has] been replaced by 22 sculptures' (SWI swissinfo.ch, 2006, author's translation).[2] However, this did not mean an absolute end to local border controls, as cameras were added to Johannes Dörflinger's installation of sculptures in the form of tarot cards on this open border. They form part of this work contemporary with the inauguration of the intra-European, free-movement Schengen area.

It is however more common to date the advent of 'border art' to 1984, with the establishment of a collective at the international dyad that is simultaneously the most contradictory, most closed and most integrated or crossed in the world: the line between the United States and Mexico.[3] Based between San Diego and Tijuana, this collective was the group of artists calling itself the Border Art Workshop / Taller de Arte Fronterizo and better known by its double acronym, BAW/TAF – a grouping of letters that reflects the collective's intrinsically cross-border and bilingual character.

The group, which brings with it a renewed hybrid cultural expression, has followed the border-related political struggles for several decades – from the rights of immigrant workers and Chicanx activism claims in the fight against security policies that have affected the region since 2001. Its members have changed their artistic practices from interventions on the landscape to an increasing questioning of the body. Guillermo Gómez-Peña embodied this performance art better than anyone else by helping it spread quickly and well beyond the border line itself. Distancing himself from the BAW/TAF in 1990, he broke with the local contradictions between the signing of NAFTA (and the integrationist dream) and the first effective measures to fortify the border (Operation Gatekeeper). For him, and also for the poet Gloria Anzaldúa (1987), the border is his body; he carries it within him and does not have to be in that very same place to perform it. By condemning, as early as 1991, the fact that 'instead of transforming the margins into the centre, [border art] has brought the centre to the margins', he tried to escape the tension inherent in the works produced on the USA–Mexico limit in the 1990s, which were inspired by the border, to divert focus away from it and renew border imaginaries in a non-site-specific manner.

If we take a step back from the place itself and try to escape the pull of the USA–Mexico border, which continues to play a structuring role in how art forms are configured at political borders, we can go back in time to re-establish other connections in the art–borders link. Artists' fascination with geopolitical places is due not only to their social value but also to their form and aesthetic appeal. Therefore, I hypothesise that border art owes a great deal to conceptual art and its work on the line and, more specifically, to the land artists' work in the outdoors.

The first artist to approach the materiality of territorial boundaries was probably Dennis Oppenheim with his interventions in 1968 at the USA–Canada border (*Boundary Split* and *Time Line* in 1968; the latter short film was remade as *Time Track: Following the Border Between USA and Canada* in 1969). In these filmed performances, using a snowmobile and a chainsaw, he cut lines in the ice uniting the two shores of the Saint John River in the winter and seasonally connecting Fort Kent, Maine (USA), and Clair, New Brunswick (Canada), and drew lines a few miles long where the time zones change, as well as segments perpendicular to it. He played on the multidimensionality that the line reveals, particularly how it works with both time and space: the temporality of seasons, which makes the landscape more or less labile; and the duration of the performance (exactly one hour). *Time Pocket*, his third intervention at the same location, plays on the fact that the line he traces is interrupted when, half-way, it hits an island that is one mile long and creates a 'pocket' whose temporal status is uncertain because of the topographical arrangement of the land and the water. In this regard, Dennis Oppenheim worked as much with the rigidity of human conventions of spatial and temporal grids (change of country, time and/or date on either side of a line) as with the poetic potential of an arbitrarily drawn line and the aesthetic strength of a straight line.

The thread connecting these works and the places where their presence brings about a language 'topos', beyond the diversity of forms of expression used in the service of border art, is complex but no less obvious! In an early work on the links between geography and visual aesthetic production, Irit Rogoff (2000) identified the border as one of the four recurring motifs of this relationship. She highlighted the border's power to express processes of deterritorialisation or reterritorialisation – in particular, its ability to underscore the complexity of the relationship between bodies and places. She concluded by writing that 'we have no choice but to attack [borders]' (Rogoff, 2000: 143). The ambiguity of the second part of the sentence leaves open the question of the political impact of such works. When art is placed at the border, is it there to express a geopolitical situation and, where appropriate, call out its injustice or to actively contribute to developing political awareness and agency?

We can rework Kant's statement in the *Critique of Pure Reason* that '[t]houghts without content are empty, intuitions without concepts are blind' (1998 [1781]: A51/B75) and his development of the notions of understanding and sensibility by stating that '[t]houghts without images are empty, images without discourse are blind'.[4] Nevertheless, the status of the image in politics has traditionally been more on the side of strengthening order, such as the use of propaganda images by authoritarian regimes in the 1930s. Historical analysis tends to emphasise the power of an image to ensure social stability, and the political geographer Jean Gottmann links this phenomenon to the power of religious icons, demonstrating how, in the political domain, 'iconography in geography becomes a bastion of resistance to movement' (1952: 214). If a political image has traditionally been a hegemonic anchor, (how) can we give it its power back? Is it enough to give voice to another reading of the image by virtue of an aesthetic sensibility that is expressed in a different way? Can art anticipate a political explosion as a canary detects gas in the coal mine and warns the miners of the firedamp before it is too late (Didi-Huberman, 2014)?

However, Missika's installation, on which I have based my analysis above, pushes this reasoning further because of his use of the drone. It is often claimed that it is enough to re-turn one's gaze to transform the political potential of an image. However, the technological dimension of the distant image radically displaces our framing of the question: how can an image produced by an electronic eye be subverted, and by what kind of transformation of which gaze? How does the human/non-human interaction challenge our understanding of the links and resonances that artworks create between them?

From site to location: 'inter-visualisation' in deeds

'The image itself and by itself does not prove anything [...] Conversely, not everything is discursive, and one cannot make images say anything, because materially, physically, concretely, and under certain verifiable and cross-verifiable conditions they present, say or attest to something that cannot be reduced to discourse' (Lageira, 2017: 11). This position relates mainly to the content of a visual work to show that, in a work of analogical or metaphorical representation or transposition, the figural thinks beyond the symbol. Its composition involves elements in a non-rational way, as well as the relationship.

However, there are two reasons for the intensity of the image: on the one hand, its aesthetic charge, that is, its ability to set a feeling in motion; on the other hand, its materiality, to the extent that the work that is produced is tied to places – both the place where it is produced and the place(s) where it is exhibited. These two dimensions are undergoing a profound transformation due to the circulation of images online but also at a deeper level because of the nature of digital images themselves. The latter transform the nature of the image, which becomes the product of a calculation and a constant reconfiguration of pixels. Images' electronic dimension goes beyond the importance of the medium and the impact of a technological choice on the nature of the image: This issue was first highlighted by some of the early works on photography that raised the question of an image's reproducibility (Moholy-Nagy, 1946) and of the possibility of quickly spreading it around the world, thanks in large part to the advent of television (McLuhan and Fiore, 1967). These two media contribute to the image's 'unsustainable proximity',[5] which dramatically challenges the policies of distance that have been imposed since the Renaissance. The digital image is defined by calculations: in addition to the play with light that defines photography and the cinema, the chemical interaction with film is replaced by a computer calculation.

One of the specificities of the digital image is that it is constantly reiterated by the machine. In the case of a drone, this reasoning must be developed further because the image is no longer that which the eye sees and the camera 'captures'. There is a triangulation between the flying machine, the person behind the controls and the landscape, all of which enables the viewer to play with perspective in an unprecedented way. How we make images influences how we feel about them and what we can do with them. Therefore, the relationship between the practical and sensitive dimensions stems from the medium that is chosen and from the three-way relationship between the medium, the author of the image and the place to which the captured image relates.

Placing works in symbolic places could be endowed with an almost literal political weight, as if the position also implied the message or, at least, the existence of a political language attached to the image. As Francis Alÿs suggests in connection with his filmed performance *The Green Line* in Jerusalem: 'Sometimes doing something poetic can become political and sometimes doing something political can become poetic' (Alÿs, 2004). This work is also based on the power of the line: The artist walked around with a can of green paint and concretely marked out the 1967 ceasefire line that Israel's urban expansion has erased from the political landscape. In so doing, both his body and the coloured trail left in its wake materialised the unuttered part the conflict.

The renewal of visual studies and ways of thinking about images has shown that the image exists not in itself but in the way it happens – in a given spatiality and temporality where it can be received. This mediation and the implicit question it raises about the medium conveying the image are consubstantial with an image's political function (Belting, 2005). The act of intervening in a space that is commonly considered to be of geopolitical importance – a space where international power relations are expressed – connects the image that is produced with a framework that both surpasses and pervades it. In my interviews in the West Bank, I have heard someone tell me how a Palestinian still life is, *de facto*, a political work since the house containing the painted vase was under constant threat of arbitrary destruction.

It is not simply because the image is on the line or among the network of border checkpoints or because it depicts one or the other that it becomes geopolitical. Understanding, as Jean Cristofol asks us to, how the border becomes 'a "field" of artistic intervention and not just an aspect of landscape'[6] means considering visual products at the borders not only as single and separate acts but as an iterated object related to the border condition globally. Something essential is at stake in 'inter-visuality' – this implicit link between images anchored in their location on borders around the world.

This modification of a globalised visual order is linked to both the increasing number of closed borders and the renewed aesthetics of the walls as visible surfaces for expression. These interact in two opposing ways, by providing a support both for xenophobic politics and for its denunciation through art. In the media, the vast number of official images showing these barriers gives the impression, first of all, that concrete walls are prevalent at contemporary borders, when in reality they make up only a small percentage of the total number of closed borders (which are mostly constructed with barbed wire because it is less expensive). Although they are increasing in number, they still stand by far in the minority on a global scale (10 per cent of closed borders). The travels by artists making visual interventions at the most famous walls, such as Thierry Noir at the Berlin Wall or Banksy, who invited himself to Bethlehem with fairly consensual media approval, reinforce this perception. Beyond direct intervention at the border, these 'hot' borders are intertwined in the creative processes to the point of being identified by the architect Teddy Cruz as part of a 'political equator' (Cruz et al., 2011; Cruz and Forman, 2011)[7] that links the world's most famous borders (United States–Mexico, Ceuta and Melilla, Israel–Palestine, India–Bangladesh) on the same latitude. This phenomenon was very evident in the first exhibitions organised in response to the wall that the Israelis erected around the West Bank in 2005–6. These exhibitions also featured works from Berlin, Belfast and Cyprus (Al-Hallaj Gallery et al., 2005).

This form of 'geoaesthetics' (Barriendos, 2009), asks us to reflect on the global themes which emerge in contemporary visual arts and questions their possible differentiated expressions in the regional contexts of production. In this context, the various expressions of the border, by being thematic and no longer regional, go well beyond these emblematic geopolitical lines, and shape what can be described of an artistic topos. It is as if a visual creation inspired by a border immediately resonated with all those that preceded it at other international lines around the globe. This connection unfolds through particular forms of aesthetic language – in particular a recurring grammar of moving bodies confronted with the immobility of control facilities, a grammar that is often expressed through moving images (video films and aleatory or algorithmic compositions).

I hypothesise that the resurgence in border security policies sparks artistic excitement at the local level, with processes of art creation appearing on closing as well as opening borders, and seeming to undergo rapid dissemination. Works of art appear on borders that had previously been truly peripheral terrains for contemporary art. This can be the case either on lesser-known segments of a famous border, such as that between the United States and Mexico – as is evident in the diversity of visual products in twin cities like Mexicali and Calexico or in Nogales and Nogales, two towns on either side of the border – or in territories that had previously been little affected, whether in the northern hemisphere (United States–Canada border, for example) or in the southern one (South Africa–Zimbabwe border). It is as if the geopolitical closure were the cause of this creativity, but this interpretation ascribes a militant positioning to the works, not all of which are defined by political intent. They may accompany security mechanisms as much as they condemn them. Another paradox is that works with consensual intentions, especially images from public commissions as well as others produced by militant interventions, are caught up in the same grid of interpretation.

This inter-visuality linked to the location of the works – that is, their functional context, rather than the specificity of their site, the uniqueness of their position – undoubtedly creates the conditions for the renewal of a political regime of images. The artists who operate at the borders are presumably responding to the *visible* order of official images by using *visual* complexity and seeking to restore a form of opacity to geopolitical images that makes it possible to imbue them with forms of resistance to the dominant order (Didi-Huberman, 1990).

A post-politics of images: who is subverting what?

How can one image challenge another? How can it impose a different system of analysing the world? Peircean semiotic analysis has shown that the strength of an image's symbolic content plays only a secondary role in its quality, thus leaving room for artistic intent in a visual product's production of meaning (Houser et al., 1998). The last part of this analysis is also its most complex: that of examining images' political modes of being, understanding *how* art can function as a kind of 'alternative spatiality' (Amoore and Hall, 2010: 305, quoting Keith and Pile, 1997), and not reducing it to forms of 'factual operationality' (Ardenne, 2009: 162), whose aesthetic images would be imbued with politics from the moment the artist conceives it as being disruptive.

Most analyses that return to the link between aesthetics and politics make use of Rancière's notion of 'dissensus' (2000: 70) to show how aesthetic work counters the perpetual quest for consensus in contemporary democratic systems. From this point of view, art is endowed with a political quality as such (because of the aesthetic experience), and one may very well wonder how positioning a work in a geopolitical place can add more to it.

Following Jean-Luc Nancy, who says that '[a]ll space of sense is common space' (Nancy, 1997: 88),[8] we can understand that locating an image at the border means having the potential to amplify the debate. However, for these very particular geopolitical places, we saw that the location plays as much of a role as the site, if not more: not the hazardous location of the successors to Guy Debord's *dérives* (1958: 19–23) but the location in its geographical sense – relative and related. What is likely to be political for an image is as much its position on an international boundary as its integration into a network of interrelated border areas. This visual diffraction underpins the conditions for a renewed geopolitics that is 'agonistic' rather than antagonistic, i.e., according to Mouffe, 'without any possibility of a final reconciliation'.[9]

In many ways, this political dimension renews the question of how the work of art is received. In the aesthetic relationship, it includes a connection to power that is often left implicit. However, these positions often avoid asking the question of who the recipient of the work is. And yet, as

> Joëlle Zask describes in her book on urban sculpture, an outdoor work is perceived by a multitude that is composed neither only of authors and specialists nor strictly of an 'audience'. The work can be received not only by isolated *individuals* but also by *masses* and, possibly, *audiences*. Joëlle Zask distinguishes the *masses* (conglomerates of individuals whose activity is identical, although they do not communicate with one another) (Zask, 2013: 125), *individuals* (isolated individuals who take an individual look at the work without feeling the influence of others, or even by closing themselves to it (*ibidem*), *crowds* (linked by psychological and physical contagion) and *audiences* (characterized by effects of suggestion and communication in the co-construction process of a common object). (Huetz et al., 2019: §9, emphasis original)

In this typology, we can clearly see the important role that the relationship between the individual and the collective plays in constructing the meaning of a work. In the case of an image (all the more so a figurative image), the narrative power of the link to the place contributes to building this possibility of mediation without reducing it to a consensual message.

Participatory works probably produce the most political ambiguity because they encourage communities crossed by borders to revive their images and imaginations. Whether in the northern hemisphere, where the inhabitants of Stanstead (Canada)–Derby Line (USA) appear on stage in a collective performance at a local theatre on the border (Althea Thauberger's performative work for the *Stanstead Project, or How to Cross the Border, Part II*, see Chevalier, 2012), or the southern hemisphere, where Zimbabwean migrant workers in South Africa re-enact their experience of crossing the border in a filmed docudrama (*Border Farm*, a project by Thenjiwe Nkosi and the Dulibadzimu Theatre Group), both the political message within these works and the images they produce are examined. Of course, these are ways of rejecting the security policy leading to the closure of borders and the segmentation of living spaces on either side of international lines that had previously been linked. However, the contradictory expression within the aesthetic system can work in favour of political appeasement (Schmidt Campbell and Martin, 2006) with refusal being channelled into the collective work. In this case, by collecting disapproval and reject which they help inhabitants to express, artists can, often without intending to do so, help to pacify a tensed situation.

It is only by granting this type of experience its aesthetic status that its political potential is preserved: by seeking to never consider the image produced as a representation in order to give it post-political, non-consensual, weight. The goal is to draw an analogy between, on the one hand, the deconstruction of the relationship between the entity represented and the work depicting it and, on the other hand, the political link that is likely to unite citizens with those whom they have elected to represent them. The notion of 'unrepresentability in so far as it implies that there are no given, "natural" political subjects' (Dikec, 2015: 117) restores individuals' full capacity to reinvent themselves as post-political subjects.

How can dissensus be created within a shared 'visibility regime'? In a world dominated by political consensus, artistic subversion makes sense only if it succeeds in giving the keys to an unprecedented visuality. It is by not reducing a creative work to its message in order to renegotiate the link between the images produced at borders – a relationship that is inherently unrepresentable – that artists are beginning to create new geopolitical forms. Consequently, this aesthetic production invites us to build a world that no longer functions in the 'adversarial' mode of us versus them that is rooted in the opposition between good and evil.

Conclusion

By analysing border art and the images it generates, opportunities emerge of building a commons that is not consensual and creates the possibility for politics that go beyond (both political and artistic) representation. There is something essential in what has sometimes been described as 'non-representational' (Thrift, 2008) but that I would rather describe as 'more than representational', because the art here does not entirely do away with the issue of representation. The medium's materiality does not erase its message. It returns a form of agency to the work, which the traditional approach does not allow us to consider – what Mitchell conveys in his question 'What do pictures want?' (Mitchell, 2005) and what Jopi Nyman and Johan Schimanski propose (in their introduction above) to tackle by using the notion of an aesthetical strategy.

The ultimate goal should not be to put these images into words in order to preserve their sensitive energy. However, doing so allows us to formulate proposals that go beyond the moralism induced by condemning others. It also enables us to take nuanced account of borders and emphasise the desire for otherness that they express just as much as the separation of worlds.

International boundaries offer such richness for political and aesthetic thought because they are the source of a range of images whose geopolitical status is complex. It is a matter not only of understanding (figurative or other) images and how they work on borders as sites or, to use Anne Volvey's term, 'artwork places' (2007) but of how they respond 'inter-visually' to each other because of their relative geographical location. It is almost certainly in the unrepresentability of the link between the images that their critical and post-political potential comes into play.

Whilst the central work of Adrien Missika's *Amexica* exhibit is the video I started this text with, the installation is more complex: it also includes several works focused on cacti, including a video captioned 'Saving an agave' and a series of portrait-like photos captioned 'We didn't cross the border, the border crossed us' (see Figure 7.2). In the latter, the plants are isolated from their context and are captured by the photograph in almost anthropomorphic postures: the photos bring to mind the migration of natural species but also human limits. These old saguaro cacti could very well have

7.2 Images from Adrien Missika's photo series *We Didn't Cross the Border, the Border Crossed Us.*

witnessed the first outline of the line before the United States took possession of a territory that had previously belonged to Mexico. It is through the prism of viewing these images that the visitor to the exhibition is able to understand all the elements of complex geopolitics that it would be inappropriate to reduce to contemporary surveillance methods by drone. An image always hides a wide array of others. It is by seizing on this network that the image can revive its geopolitical impact.

Translated by André Crous.

Notes

1 'réconciliation finale' (Mouffe, 2010: 21). My translation.
2 'Le grillage de 280 mètres marquant la frontière entre Constance (Allemagne) et Kreuzlingen (Suisse) sera remplacé par 22 sculptures' (SWI swissinfo.ch, 2006).
3 Some call it the *línea*, THE line par excellence, which exemplifies one of the most violent economic fractures on the planet, also called a 'hyperborder' (Romero, 2008): Although it is one of the most closed borders on Earth (one-third of its length of 3,145 km is now closed off by walls and barriers of various kinds, and the entire route is highly monitored), it sees more than 300 million legal crossings every year.
4 'des pensées sans images seraient vides, des images sans discours seraient aveugles' (Lageira, 2017: 13). My translation.
5 'une proximité insoutenable' (Attia, 2017: 39). My translation.
6 'un "champ" d'intervention artistique, et pas seulement un aspect du paysage' (Cristofol 2012, no page number). My translation.
7 Since 2005, Cruz has organised a workshop with the same name between San Diego and Tijuana (Cruz and Forman, 2011).
8 'Tout espace de sens est espace commun' (2001 [1993]: 139).
9 'sans aucune possibilité de réconciliation finale' (Mouffe, 2010: 21). My translation.

References

Alÿs, F., P. Bellaiche, R.L. Jones and J. Devaux (2004) *The Green Line*. 17 minutes 41 seconds colour HD video. http://francisalys.com/the-green-line. Accessed 27 October 2019.

ABC No Rio (Al-Hallaj Gallery, Bet ha-omanim and 2005) *Three Cities Against the Wall: Ramallah, Tel Aviv, New York*. Brooklyn: VoxPop Press.

Amilhat Szary, A.-L. (2012) 'Que montrent les murs? Des frontières contemporaines de plus en plus visibles', *Études Internationales*, 43(1): 67–87.

Amoore, L., and A. Hall (2010) 'Border theatre: On the arts of security and resistance', *Cultural Geographies*, 17(3): 299–319.

Anzaldúa, G. (1987) *Borderlands / La Frontera: The New Mestiza*. San Francisco: Aunt Lute Books.

Ardenne, P. (2009) *Un art contextuel: Création artistique en milieu urbain, en situation, d'intervention, de participation.* Paris: Flammarion.

Attia, K. (2017) 'Des régimes de l'éloignement à l'abolition des espaces', *Les Carnets du BAL*, 7: 16–47.

Barriendos, J. (2009) 'Geopolitics of global art: The reinvention of Latin America as a geoaesthetic region', in H. Belting and A. Buddensieg (eds), *The Global Art World: Audiences, Markets and Museums.* Ostfildern: Hatje Cantz Verlag, pp. 98–114.

Belting, H. (2005) 'Image, medium, body: A new approach to iconology', *Critical Inquiry*, 31(2): 302–19.

Belting, H. (2009) 'Contemporary art as global art: A critical estimate', in H. Belting and A. Buddensieg (eds), *The Global Art World: Audiences, Markets and Museums.* Ostfildern: Hatje Cantz Verlag, pp. 38–73.

Bredekamp, H. (2018) *Image Acts: A Systematic Approach to Visual Agency.* Image, Word, Action 2. Berlin: De Gruyter.

Brown, W. (2010) *Walled States, Waning Sovereignty.* New York: Zone Books

Chevalier, G. (2012) 'Projet Stanstead ou comment traverser la frontière, volet II / Stanstead Project, or how to cross the border, part II', *geneviève chevalier*, http://genevievechevalier.ca/project/stanstead-ou-comment-traverser-la-frontiere-volet-ii. Accessed 27 October 2019.

Cristofol, J. (2012) 'L'art aux frontières', *antiAtlas des frontières.* www.antiatlas.net/jean-cristofol-lart-aux-frontieres. Accessed 27 May 2019.

Cruz, T., and F. Forman (2011) 'The political equator'. *YouTube.* 3 ninutes 22 seconds video. https://youtu.be/-y6qj_oux5s. Accessed 27 October 2019.

Cruz, T., O. Romo and A. Skorepa (2011) *The Political Equator*, http://politicalequator.blogspot.com. Accessed 27 October 2019.

Debord, G. (1958) 'Théorie de la dérive', *Internationale situationniste*, 2 (December), 19–23.

Deutsche, R. (1992) 'Art and public space: Questions of democracy', *Social Text*, 33: 34–53.

Didi-Huberman, G. (1990) *Devant l'image: Question posée aux fins d'une histoire de l'art.* Paris: Minuit.

Didi-Huberman, G. (2014) *Sentir le grisou.* Paris: Minuit.

Dikec, M. (2015) *Space, Politics and Aesthetics.* Edinburgh: Edinburgh University Press.

Gottmann, J. (1952) *La politique des Etats et leur géographie.* Paris: Armand Colin.

Gruzinski, S. (1990) *La guerre des images: De Christophe Colomb à* Blade Runner *(1492–2019).* Paris: Fayard.

Helias, Y., and A. Jouffroy (1990) 'Portrait idéologique de l'artiste fin de siècle', *Le Monde Diplomatique* (January 1990): 22–3.

Holmes, B. (2009) *Escape the Overcode: Activist Art in the Control Society.* Eindhoven: Van Abbesmuseum / WHW.

Houser, N., C. Kloesel, and Peirce-Edition-Project (eds) (1998) *The Essential Peirce: Selected Philosophical Writings (1893–1913)*, vol. 2. Bloomington: Indiana University Press.

Huetz, A., C. Lehec and T. Maeder (2019) 'What do images in the public space do?', *Articulo: Journal of Urban Research*, 19: §1–24. https://journals.openedition.org/articulo/3847. Accessed 25 May 2019.

Jimenez, M. (2005) *La querelle de l'art contemporain.* Paris: Gallimard.

Kant, I. (1998 [1781]) *Critique of Pure Reason*. Trans. P. Guyer and A.W. Wood. Cambridge: Cambridge University Press.

Keith, M. and S. Pile (eds) (1997) *Geographies of Resistance*. New York: Routledge.

Kester, G.H. (ed.) (1998) *Art, Activism and Oppositionality: Essays from Afterimage*. Durham, NC: Duke University Press.

Lageira, J. (2017) 'Ouverture'. *Les Carnets du BAL*, 7: 5–15.

McLuhan, M. and Q. Fiore (1967) *The Medium Is the Message*. New York: Bantam Books.

Missika, A. (2014a) *Amexica / À l'occasion de l'exposition éponyme, publication un livre d'artiste*. Paris and Lucerne: Centre culturel suisse / Edizioni Periferia.

Missika, A. (2014b) *As the Coyote Flies*. 14 minutes 35 seconds colour HD video with sound. Centre Culturel Suisse Paris. www.adrienmissika.com/projects/as-the-coyote-flies. Accessed 27 October 2019.

Mitchell, W.J.T. (2005) *What Do Pictures Want? The Lives and Loves of Images*. Chicago: The University of Chicago Press.

Moholy-Nagy, L. (1946) *Vision in Motion*. 3rd ed. Chicago: Paul Theobald.

Monahan, T. (2006) 'Counter-surveillance as political intervention?', *Social Semiotics*, 16(4): 515–34.

Mouffe, C. (2010) 'Politique et agonisme', *Rue Descartes*, 67(1): 18–24.

Nancy, J.-L. (1997) *The Sense of the World*. Trans. with a foreword by J.S. Librett. Minneapolis: University of Minnesota Press.

Nancy, J.-L. (2001 [1993]) *Le sens du monde*. Paris: Galilée.

Rancière, J. (2008) *Le spectateur émancipé*. Paris: La Fabrique.

Rogoff, I. (2000) *Terra Infirma: Geography's Visual Vulture*. London: Routledge.

Romero, F. (2008) *Hyperborder: The Contemporary U.S.–Mexico Border and Its Future*. New York: Princeton Architectural Press.

Schmidt Campbell, M., and R. Martin (eds) (2006) *Artistic Citizenship: A Public Voice for the Arts*. New York: Routledge.

SWI swissinfo.ch (2006) 'La première "frontière artistique" du monde', *SWI swissinfo.ch* (17 August 2006). www.swissinfo.ch/fre/la-première–frontière-artistique–du-monde/5386812. Accessed 13 October 2019.

Thrift, N. (2008). *Non-Representational Theory: Space, Politics, Affect*. London: Routledge.

Volvey, A. (2007) 'Land-Art: Les fabriques spatiales de l'art contemporain', in A. Volvey, 'Land Arts: Les fabriques spatiales de l'art contemporain', *Travaux de l'Institut Géographique de Reims*, 33–4 (129–30): 3–25.

Yi, H. (2018) 'Is Trump's border wall art?', *Quartzy*, https://qz.com/quartzy/1182972/trumps-border-wall-prototypes-are-art-argues-artist-christoph-buchel/. Accessed 29 October 2019.

Zask, J. (2013) *Outdoor Art*. Paris: La Découverte.

8

Some cunning passages in border-crossing narratives: seen and unseen migrants

Stephen F. Wolfe

History has many cunning passages, contrived corridors

And issues

T.S. Eliot (2005 [1920]: 402)

Introduction

In this chapter, I will detail how a group of selected migrant writers from 1950 to 2013 have focused on the experience of border-crossing into the city of London, their collective experience of migrancy within that city and their 'burden of representation' of themselves within the current boundaries of the European Union. I will examine how border-crossing narratives and representations of migrant crossings have circulated feelings of displacement created from their imaginative geographies of space and place in the home land, the host land and the context of contemporary public history. Using Susan Stanford Friedman's (2004) 'poetics of home and diaspora' to narrow this focus that emphasises 'the affective body' as a corporeal entity that registers, responds to, and resists socially inscribed boundaries, I will argue that the body is a site of pleasure and pain, as well as a place of resistance (Friedman, 2004: 190–1). I will especially focus on the visibility and invisibility of the migrant body in both its individual and corporate forms specifically in locations within urban 'diasporic spaces' (Brah, 1996).

The border-crossing narratives examined in this chapter always begin with a material border, which invokes a threshold to be crossed or remembered. This border-crossing marks the starting place of my critical interpretation by deliberately fixing the narratives in a specific place and within an aesthetic of writing that 'invests in the artistic processes of imagining, creating, and representing with the spatial idea of a threshold in its material and figurative manifestations' (Mukherji, 2013: xviii). The first section examines the border-crossing narrative as a cultural expression for a community of 'black writers and artists' centred in Britain, during the 1950s to the 1980s, by focusing on their border-crossings via passages aboard ship, or at entry points, as well as in private settings in which migrants lived, or within the working communities in London (see Hall, 1955, 1988). The second section will look at the aesthetic representation of 'the British Isles' and how the physical coastline became policed by a 'Border Force' moving borders to crossing points from air and sea entry points and into the urban spaces of the major cities. This shift was in response to the migrant crisis of 2013. Border-crossers were now 'screened' in these spaces, increasing their visibility under the watchful eye of everyday bordering policies. These policies also facilitated their transfer out of sight into detention centres. The final section will return to the tropes of thresholds and passages to examine reported border-crossings of the Mediterranean Sea to Europe.

Some of the writers analysed in this chapter place their 'precarious lives' (Butler, 2006) and their border-crossings in a set of aesthetic practices based upon the trope of crossing thresholds and moving towards passages to, passages from and passages between their varied experiences of migrancy. I use the word *migrancy* because it denotes the displacement of people and their reterritorialisation, but also applies to their means of travel and the public transformation of ideology about these people in recent cultural or political theory. Finally, the journeys undertaken by the writers and artists discussed here, most of whom were migrants, gains critical force through the aesthetic techniques used in novels, and plays, as well as reportage.

Migration and the figure of the migrant as visible to others and as the Other became problematic starting in the early decades of the twentieth century. This was caused by epistemic disruptions inflicted by colonial legacies and by those who were dispersed in Europe without social networks of reference in the wake of the global movements of peoples taking place after two World Wars. Post-colonial struggles often continued or were resolved by drawing new boundaries for countries and territories. The production of new borders and the sudden appearance of migrant communities seeking to find a place within the borderlands of urban Europe and the United Kingdom are also stable fixtures of early twentieth-century histories of British and European modernism (see Baily et al., 2005; Gilroy, 1995, 2005; Procter, 2003; Walkowitz, 2006). For example, V.S. Naipaul, like a number of other migrant writers, situates his own attempts to begin writing in this disorienting period through the use of tropes of passage: rites of passage, passage as a journey over water from one country to another, and passages of time (Ellmann, 2016: 106). As a youthful colonial migrant from the West

Indies to England (whose family, in its turn, had emigrated to the Caribbean from the Indian subcontinent a century previously), Naipaul sees himself as the product of a disruption whose origins and consequences he is attempting to fully grasp within his fictional autobiography, *The Enigma of Arrival* (1978). In the course of explicating this enigma of his arrival in London, he realises that his task as a writer was to discover a form adequate to 'the worlds I contained within myself, the worlds I lived in' – due to his status as a colonial migrant (Naipaul, 1988: 147). The form is autobiography whether fiction or fact. It is anchored in the tropes of threshold and passage often placed in the public histories of the Middle Passage of transatlantic slavery, or a rite of passage embodied through their exploration of a colonial capital in 'a reverse passage' (Döring, 2002). In this reversal, London becomes the place to be explored and verified against a discourse with which the colonial subject is already familiar through newsreels, films and textbooks.[1] Döring's point is that the migrant must reinvest and renegotiate the signifiers of centralised authority, within the colonial capital. This condition was a product of the material and cultural mobility Naipaul had as son of a prosperous post-colonial family. The writer, by tracing *routes* of migration had also to return to the *roots* of migration in one particular location.

The Middle Passage, cul-de-sacs and community

I will use James Procter's *Dwelling Places* (2003) to develop this argument with a focus on West Indian immigrant writers. Many West Indian migrants took their first passage on ships when they enlisted in the British forces fighting in Europe in the Second World War. With the conclusion of the War, some soldiers returned when they took their second passage in 1948 arriving at the Tilbury docks outside London. They migrated on the MV *Empire Windrush*. The *Windrush* was en route from Australia to England via the Atlantic, having first docked in Kingston, Jamaica, in order to pick up servicemen who were on leave and wanted to return to London. Many former servicemen took this opportunity to return to Britain since the British Nationality Act of 1948 gave British citizenship to all people living in Commonwealth countries, and full rights to settlement in Britain. Attracted by better prospects in 'the mother country', many West Indians took up the offer.

The arrivals were temporarily housed in the Clapham South shelter in south-west London less than a mile away from Cold Harbour Lane in Brixton where they registered and sought employment. This period has received important attention in such novels as George Lamming's *The*

Emigrants (1954), Sam Selvon's *The Lonely Londoners* (1956) and Caryl Phillips's *The Final Passage* (1985). These three novels will be the focus of my analysis in this section.

In George Lamming's novel, the border-crossing journey begins with 'waiting for something to happen' on the docks in Trinidad or Barbados as the characters board the ship to take them to London. In the next section, they are confined to steerage on the boat (Lamming, 1994 [1954]: 105–6). The novel then focuses on the two-week 'passage' to England. It also makes intertextual reference to the Middle Passage of the transatlantic slave trade through the imagery of the 'caging and containment of the men' on board the ship (Lamming, 1994 [1954]: 3–125). The first passage is a journey on a boat or ship as a means of conveyance. But passage also has a figurative meaning which connects their journey to the historical forced migration of slaves in the eighteenth and nineteenth centuries.

But their passages are always dependent upon external forces: boarding the boat, waiting to get to their destination and then waiting to have their papers processed upon arrival, and finally when registering for work and social benefits in London. The border they faced was dependent upon a threshold, marking a modification in place, time and space. Thus, a national border is not merely a line or place, but rather a whole symbolic order with the power to determine who belongs, who can pass through its frontiers, and who will be left waiting on the outside of the legal and security structures of the national state and its institutions. In these modernist novels, the border is defined by a sense of contingency, making the border-crossing narrative into a structuring of desire especially for the migrants who sought to become members of a national workforce with the freedoms of residency, work and social security.

Another form of border-crossing in Lamming's novel is to be found in 'Rooms and residents', containing a long description of lodging houses (1994 [1954]: 129–282). Lamming describes here a dark staircase leading down to a basement room: Fred Hill's Barbershop. As James Procter (2003) has argued, the staircase and the door it leads to are a symbolic threshold to a space between the 'white metropolis (above/outside) that the emigrants have just left, and the black world (below/inside)' (2003: 33). A gate or door in modernist writing, as Gillian Beer (2013: 3–8) suggests, is often used to control threshold spaces. In 'Rooms and Residents', the character Tornado, on his way down the staircase turns the knob allowing himself access to a barbershop decorated as a male diasporic community with photos of American jazz bands, calypso singers, West Indian island scenery and newspapers from the islands. The men in Lamming's novel make a border-crossing down the stairs into a communal social space offering exchange, dialogue and improvised story-telling: 'These men were his immediate community, and any word, attitude, gesture, was an occasion for thinking' (Lamming, 1994 [1954]: 128).

James Procter (2003) has argued that the progression of Lamming's novel is from the communal settings of the basement to the more impersonal streets. The migrant West Indian community begins as 'internally divided and remote' not to be seen from the street, whilst in the final section of the novel, by focusing on 'my London, my street', the author creates 'the new mobile black body' within the wider fragmentation and dispersal of the migrant community (Procter, 2003: 43–4). We have a reversed passage: it is a process of 'turning the inside out'. But overall, the novel uses the trope of passages to emphasise movement towards thresholds with limits, 'doors to tight to open'. Hospitality and inclusion are negotiated in the public spaces of cooking on the landings of lodging houses or later in the cul-de-sacs where pubs and clubs are located.

Late in the novel *The Emigrants*, Lamming uses a threshold to what seems to be a pubic passageway which is in fact a cul-de-sac. A crowd of migrants, who have been in a club, are caught 'remaining in the cul-de-sac ragged and bewildered' (Lamming, 1994 [1954]: 271). 'The cityscape, like the threshold of the basement [...], symbolically confines the emigrants [...] The cul-de-sac signifies their larger confinement within a metropolis of racialised "dead-ends" and limits' (Procter, 2003: 43–4). The cul-de-sac offers a point of entry, a threshold, but with no exit. It represents a failed border-crossing. No final passage is possible. In these bounded and exclusionary locations, little mobility is possible except through the retracing of one's steps: 'The voices of the crowd in the cul-de-sac called for the Strange Man who had remained where he was, silent, self-rebuked' (Lamming, 1994 [1954]: 282).

Rites of passage, disorientation and family

In Sam Selvon's *The Lonely Londoners*, Moses Aloetta, 'Mister London', begins the novel by renaming the immigrant Henry Oliver 'Sir Galahad'. Each character in Selvon's text begins on a threshold between a new and old life with a new name or identity. Moses takes Galahad to 'the Water' (his name for Bayswater) where the Christian symbolism and landscapes not only echo T.S. Eliot's *Waste Land* but also indicate a rite of passage as Moses' boys are rechristened into 'the local black community' (Procter, 2003: 54). Selvon uses basements, as does Lamming, but his passageways across borders and boundaries hinge on inward journeys towards identification with the West Indian community in London and then outward into the wider world of British society. As I shall argue later in this chapter, there is a crucial shift in the trajectory of border-crossing here in which the contact zones must be reimagined, as both an alien or remembered place and a site of cultural hybridity. Another example in Selvon's novel is the migrants' renaming of streets and areas in London: it is a form of remapping in which Moses' boys narrate the complexity of their relocation (McLeod, 2004: 36–7).

Sam Selvon's *The Lonely Londoners* also uses different focalised perspectives on London. The narrative consciousness is split between Moses, a first-generation immigrant to the city of London, and Henry Oliver, who arrives later 'on the crest of the second wave' of Caribbean immigration. Galahad is full of expectations created in the context of grandiose imperial imagery, which he has carried with him from his education in the Caribbean. This is the reverse passage. The novel also follows the passage from winter to summer (McLeod, 2004: 34–35). However, there is another pattern of movement in the novel in which there is a series of contests between action and stasis, leading to enforced disturbances of movement and disorientation within the city. But the tension created between these two forms of manoeuvring also leads to improvised movements of resistance, suggesting opposition to the rigid social discipline of the economics and politics of social control to be found on the streets and in the workplace in London (Wolfe, 2016: 130–6).

Numerous incidents in the novel underscore this dissension and disorientation as a necessary gesture to confront authority with contingency and inventiveness (McLeod, 2004: 26). The novel uses a number of different descriptive techniques and disorienting descriptions of behaviour, all of which are framed as border-crossings or failed crossings. Selvon uses borders that confine as a tool of social analysis: rooms which divide people into little worlds: 'you stay in the world you belong to and you don't know anything about what happening in the other ones except what you read in the papers ... nobody goes into detail; poor man and rich man; old fellows and young fellows' (2006 [1956]: 60–1).

Black bodies: precarious vulnerabilities and locations of contact

For both Selvon and Lammings, Caribbean migrants live their lives both in private spaces, and in the public spaces of their rooming houses where cooking is located on the balcony of each staircase. Many of the characters in both books have no immediate family, and have few friends from whom they might create a 'family' (Moses calls the men he takes in and meets with once a week, his 'boys'). Most of the 'boys' are peripatetic laborers and boarders trying to read political authority in the actions of the police, or in the prohibitions which keep people separated by race in clubs, in pubs and in street meetings in the cityscape, or in regulations administered and shaped by state authority in the labour exchange, and by their landlords. But they are also colonial subjects and their experience of colonialism deeply influences their sense of belonging as it is figured on the borders of their body (on visible images written on the bodies of border-crossers, see also Amilhat Szary's Chapter 7 above)

Selvon's text uses a set of binary oppositions reinforced by visibility/ invisibility and spatial symbolism: visibility is based on a 'communal feeling with the Working Class and the spades (black West Indians), because when you poor things does *level out*, it don't much up and down' (2006 [1956]: 61). For example, the ambiguity of visibility as a racial marker is written on Galahad's body and his consciousness of his inclusion-as-an-excluded-being. This can be studied in detail in an oft-quoted passage when Galahad examines his body, after having just been insulted in public as 'a black bastard' by two white men.

> And Galahad would take his hand from under the blanket [...] Galahad watch the colour of his hand, and talk to it, saying Colour, is you that causing all this, you know ... So Galahad talking to the colour Black, as if is a person, telling it that is not *he* who causing botheration in the place, but Black, who is a worthless thing for making trouble all about. (Selvon, 2006 [1956]: 77)

In this example, Galahad looks at himself in a metaphorical mirror: he sees himself seeing himself as Other. Frantz Fanon in *Black Skin, White Masks* has detailed the consequences of such self-recognition: 'In the white world the man of colour encounters difficulties in the development of his bodily schema. Consciousness of the body is solely a negating activity. It is a third person consciousness' (1986: 110). Galahad's precarious position is caught in his own subjective imprisonment in the economy of the Other, and it is revealed in the border trope of his reified body. The border between safety and danger becomes figured in the vulnerability of his black face and skin (see Brambilla's Chapter 4 above for a theorisation of the notion of the in/ visible and its usefulness in border aesthetics).

Lamming's first novel, *In the Castle of My Skin* (1953), makes this point dramatically, often in terms of the traumatic representations of the male body, but in *The Emigrants* we find a strangely similar dilemma: except with a focus on female characters:

> I was getting the queerest feeling, and then looked in the mirror, and the strangest thing happened [...] My eyes were all right, but I looked and looked, and I couldn't recognize my face. I couldn't. It wasn't my face. I borrowed Queenie's mirror and looked, and it was the same face, but not mine. I wanted to tell Queenie, but I didn't know how to begin. (1994 [1954]: 248)

Later a male character looks into a mirror and sees his face: 'too thick, too black, too everything' (Lamming, 1994 [1954]: 263). Such a trauma is developed from a very different perspective in two more recent border-crossing texts focused on the Finnish–Russian border analysed by Kurki in Chapter 5 above.

In her book *Precarious Life: The Powers of Mourning and Violence* (2006: 20–6), Judith Butler proposes that minorities in a community are subjected to violence, exposed to its possibility, if not its realisation, in part because of their skin colour. In the public sphere, all individuals have a body that is mortal, vulnerable and a possible vehicle of agency. The connection with Friedman's (2004) emphasis on the affective body discussed at the beginning of the chapter is another way of accounting for a poetics of home and diaspora, but Friedman's emphasis is on gendered agency and the violence women face. The feeling body within post-colonial London became a dynamic, affective site where self and home were continuously reconstituted as was the racism that fostered the migrants' hiding in plain sight.

In Caryl Phillips's debut novel, *The Final Passage* (1985), these same types of thresholds and passages are used but with more focus on women. The Caribbean diaspora is exemplified in the lives of a young family from a small island who decide to join the 1950s exodus to the Britain. As newly arrived immigrants, who are looking for suitable accommodation and a regular income, Leila and Michael experience racism by falling prey to unscrupulous lodging-house agents. Michael soon returns to his habit of coming and going whenever he chooses to, and leaving all household chores to Leila. He stops talking to his wife, is frequently drunk and quits his job in London after only a few days, and goes into business with a newly found friend. At the end of the novel, when Leila realises that they have run out of money she finds employment working for London Transport buses. On her first day of work, she has a breakdown and is informed by the examining doctor that she is pregnant. Leila has come to realise that Michael is not going to be part of her future and she must return to 'her small island' with her one child and another on the way. It is Christmas and she gets up early 'catching sight of herself in a mirror. She looked like a yellowing snapshot of an old relative, fading with the years' (Phillips, 1985: 204–5). The mirror is a threshold device making visual her return passage 'home' to a life of resignation and waiting.

Entangled generations, borders and political genealogies

Caryl Phillips argues in *A New World Order: Essays* (2001) that the period from 1970 to 1990 was a reimagining of Black Britain. That could be accomplished only through narratives 'which synthesize different worlds in one body' (Phillips, 2001: 279) while learning to live comfortably with these different worlds in a single body politic (cf. 'Introduction: A little luggage', 241–6). This in turn raised critical questions about identity and 'the burden of representation' within an emergent post-colonial critique. The narrative aesthetic shifts to a cutting and mixing of genres and voices. The 'passage' to Britain had become embodied in an intensified politics of self-representation for groups whose marginal identity and diaspora politics were now to be charted in the borderline areas of British cities, or with the spatial and racial imaginaries of the Other produced by British political culture. The emphasis is on representations of encounter between racial, gendered or generational groups. The border-crossing narrative is becoming a genre of resistance and transformation.

For example, in Hanif Kureishi's *The Buddha of Suburbia* (1990), the fictional border-crossing *Bildungsroman* parodies the post-colonial situation of second-generation migrants from India. Kureishi mixes an intertextual tension between the voice of the post-colonial Karim while echoing the colonial Kim from Rudyard Kipling's novel of that name. Further intertextual references are parodied when Karim plays a part in the theatre company's dramatisation of *The Jungle Book*. In fact, as Bart Moore-Gilbert (2001: 124–6) argues, it is *The Jungle Book* which figures again and again in the commonplace of the city as a jungle as well as being the centre of new communities and new cultural identities for Karim. Karim straddles two cultures and the intersections of two or three social worlds: Kipling's prose and colloquial migrant English, Indian and the white suburban middle class, and the cultural mix-up of punk rock and the Beatles. Karim is 'happy and miserable at the same time', promising the reader he will 'live more deeply', not in the world but in the 'old city' (London) that he loves (Kureishi, 1990: 284).

But for the Indian diaspora living in Britain, the situation was more complex as Kureishi reminds us in his essay 'Under the rainbow sign' (1986). Midnight 14 August 1947 signalled the official beginning of India's independence from Britain but also its division into two separate nations, India and Pakistan. A border was created between the two countries that signalled two new, equitable post-colonial societies. Yet years of chaotic ethnic violence and border conflicts were to follow.

In terms of the trope of passages, the object in Kureishi's novel is to connect the passage of time to newly constructed places where new languages and new representations of identity and ethnicity are formed: these include places such concerts, radical theatre performances and demonstrations. These new languages could present, in the words of the later novel *Midnight's Children* by Salman Rushdie, 'the intertwining of lives, events, miraculous places and rumors' (1981: 3). Thus, the object of Kureishi's novel was to examine the escalation of vicious racist attacks and the emerging popular anti-fascist politics that rose to combat them. Karim, emboldened by countercultural ideas in rock music or in the strikes and marches in the novel (Kureishi, 1990: 62–4), works with immigrants to find sustainable sources of rebellion. The performative experiences outlined in the novel suggest that no deferred passages nor nostalgic revival of the self in the nation state was possible.

Deferred passages into new detention regimes in national border zones

I argue in this section of the chapter that the metaphoric social representations of the 'dehumanisation of the Other' which have developed with new migration policies in Western European states have added to the systematic detention policies in those states. Nation states have now made hostile environments for migrants and refugees approaching their national and international borders. A climate of suspicion greets them, coupled with a lack of knowledge of their history, of their right to apply for asylum, or of the national and international wars and famines that have motivated them, or their aspirations for work and security in a safe environment.

As Andrew Hammond (2018) has argued, the enthusiasm that greeted the end of the Cold War now seems distant. The fall of the Berlin Wall and dismantling of the Iron Curtain promised a more inclusive and united continent, as signalled by the EU's eradication of internal borders by the terms of the Schengen Convention of 1990. Yet the guiding principle of European integration – improved competitiveness in the global market of goods and services – was grounded in a mistrust of the relatively poor East Europeans, not to mention the mistrust of those living in Africa and South-East Asia. In one of the largest acts of reterritorialisation of modern times, the EU refashioned its eastern edge from just an ideological border into what it considered a 'civilizational fault line, adding cultural and ethnic criteria to political definitions' of the threat to a New Europe in populations of people rather than governments (Hammond, 2018: 336–60).

Significantly, the current restrictions on immigration were already being sought in the EU in the late 1990s. These included tightening asylum laws, sharing responsibility for refugees between EU member states and agreeing to measures to restrict so-called asylum-shopping. At the same time, measures were taken to reduce immigration, with an increase in border guards, coastguard patrols, police units, holding centres, and information and surveillance technologies (including radars, sensors and satellite cameras). Now the detainment of migrants is to begin outside the so-called 'smart borders' of Europe in order to prevent asylum claims all coming from within. The

EU frontiers have been moved further out of sight with detention centres and camps in Turkey, Libya, Niger and Eritrea.

Radically new technologies of travel and communication have also heightened global interconnectedness. As such, they have increased diasporic consciousness among migrants because the old home or their imaginary homelands can be so much more present in the lives of migrating peoples. Migration lacks the permanence it once had: the borders between home land and host land have become much more porous and fluid. Arjun Appadurai in his famous article 'Disjunction and difference in the global cultural economy' (1990) calls this phenomenon the global *ethnoscape* of modernity at large, alluding to the globe's rapidly shifting, fluid cultural landscapes enabled by migrating peoples, goods, practices and representations. In positing instability or consistent movement as the central metaphor for the 'new migration', writers have rejected the older brutal binaries, and embattled inheritances. New migration narratives show more fluidity of identity among migrating peoples, more resistance to rapid assimilation, more bilingualism and hybridity. In the words of the best-selling novelist Mohsin Hamid, migrants have 'become more present without presence' (2017: 169). Identity in the 'new migration' has become increasingly reter-ritorialised, a fact that fosters new forms of diasporic consciousness.

The temporality of migration has changed weeks and months of travel to days or hours available for temporary or recurrent visits. The telephone and the Internet (email, listservs, blogs, skype, e-newsletters and so forth) have supplanted letters as means of communication and ongoing connection. These and other transitory forms of cultural expression have made the ruptures of migration less fixed for many, especially the more affluent. Finally, the exponential increase in undocumented migration has also produced other symbols of 'new migration': border patrols shooting at fleeing bodies caught in the infrared lights; leaky boats intercepted or sinking at sea; ship containers or car trunks filled with the dead bodies of the suffocated and frozen in borderscapes; and prison-like detention centres.

A number of these issues can be seen in the complex choices of form, genre and structure that are used in contemporary narratives of migrancy discussed in this volume. These story forms have become mutually constituted by the intersecting itineraries of people and things. In the second part of the chapter I will examine the closed, imprisoning spaces of waiting and confinement within detention centres and the Border Force bureaucracy.

I want to use two examples from *Routes* (2013), a play by Rachel De-lahay, to show how a new border poetics negotiates Europe's 'migrant crises' (2013–19) by focusing on migrants who are living and acting outside mapped spaces or in transitional places. There is a blur of traceable distinctions so important to identifiable political authority and older questions of identity (see Tazzioli, 2015: 4–11). De-lahay's play uses a conflict over imaginary homelands and virtual communities to set into motion new competing representations of attempted border-crossings. The play depicts a border which is not just a line on a map or in a border zone; it is a system for filtering people that stretches from the edges of a national or institutional territory into its centre, affecting the politics of everyday life. Once the migrants in *Routes* cross UK frontiers, their movements are screened and restricted, and their right to work or to access social security is severely limited. The direct historical references in the play are to Theresa May's stated purpose when she was Home Secretary, to make all of Britain a 'hostile environment' for many more legal and illegal migrants. The system places them into categories – refugee or economic migrant, legal or illegal, deserving or undeserving – and these distinctions do not always fit the reality of their lives.

Rachel De-lahay's *Routes* was first performed at the Royal Court theatre in 2013. The play uses border metaphors and the 'contemporary Migrant Crisis' to examine the Conservative government's border politics. *Routes* is a play about migrants for whom the borders of Britain and the EU are central, as is the question of irregular immigration from Africa. The play presents six characters. Three of them are border-crossers, whilst the other three people are working within the border regimes of two different nation states: England and Nigeria. These two groupings are subject to or participate in the political and legal practices of the 2013 Border Force detention industry.

The play begins with a number of short rapid-fire scenes which are central to establishing each character and their power and authority in the border zones of Nigeria or Britain: one is a border guard trying to sell a passport, whilst two others work for social services to assist migrants; in other scenes there are conflicts between a mother and son, and short reports from border authorities at Calais (in Nyman's Chapter 9 below such reports and exchanges are the subject of fictional representation and analysis), whilst the final scenes in the play are set in a detention hostel. Interestingly, mobile phones are central props used by the playwright to build a heterophonic dialogue (two voices simultaneously reforming variations of the same melody). The migrants and the border guards in some of the early scenes each generate their own agency in different voices or melodic lines. But, most importantly in this form of ensemble representation, the protagonists and antagonists are made visible and audible to the audience in another form: as they come before the law.

Routes focuses on a Nigerian woman, Femi, who seeks to re-enter Britain without formal authorisation on a forged passport; whilst the two other female characters, Anka and Lisa, and the male character, Abiola, are workers within the 'Border Force' bureaucracy. The other two male characters are

Bashir and Kola. Bashir is a Syrian refugee seeking to stay in England, despite violating his passport standing. Kola visits the detention shelter and takes Bashir under his wing. The figures of regulation – Lisa, Anka, Abiola and Kola – are seemingly in control through their knowledge of the laws of work permits, social insurance and the new Border Force regime. Migration policy taints all aspects of everyday politics whether for the border workers or their families or between migrants themselves.

In this play, we are in an abbreviated version of *The Trial* (1925) or Kafka's powerful parable 'Before the law' (2003 [1915]). For example, in the play, in a bleak hostel, an orphaned teenage Somalian youth called Bashir is learning to deal with Kola, his truculent, possibly thieving mixed-race room-mate. Bashir discovers, too, that indefinite leave to remain in Britain can be revoked if you have fallen foul of the law, even if you have grown up in Britain. Before long, Kola is his only visitor in a far-flung detention centre. Bashir and Kola try to negotiate this through threat and asymmetrical contests over access to mobile devices: a phone and digital music player. Both of these characters specialise in clipped text-talk; both assert their right to have created several layers of protection for themselves through both their mobile devices and their aggressive language, but that is stripped away at the end of the play as they wait.

In the final scene of *Routes*, Bashir will be removed from England immediately because he has violated the terms of 'his residency permit'. Bashir is to be sent to 'Somalia. Mogadishu' which was his birthplace, but was never his home. To quote the play:

Kola: Show 'em. Go. Carry on nutty. Join Al-Shabaah or something.

Bashir: Shut up, you dickhead!

Kola: What. That's obviously what they want? Moving you off our streets on to theirs!

Bashir: I need to get of that place. And this was the only way.

Kola: No. You wait it out …

Bashir: I'm going home. End of. (De-lahay, 2013: 73–4)

The law locks him into a position inside the territorial laws of a country, in the present, whilst he has to remain waiting outside the society for long periods of time for his papers to be processed. I argue that his state of waiting is a *deferred* passage: the effects of living indirectly and directly before the law while having no immediate recourse to that law except through intermediaries. He is being told, in Kafkaesque terms, 'this Law was made for you' ('Before the law', 1915) although he is not able to come before it.

Bashir, in the words of Kola, has been 'gassed' (De-lahay, 2013: 9, 72), that is, dehumanised by the border officers and the 'new migration' laws. This slang term has a double meaning, of being deceived as well as being destroyed (i.e., gassed in the trenches of the First World War or in the concentration camps of the Second World War). Bashir, while having to wait before the Law, makes himself subject to the affect and dehumanising fact that his own disappearance will leave no trace, at least in Britain: he has been 'gassed' (Houtum and Wolfe, 2017: 129).

Another example from 'Scene Eight: Calais' illustrates this point. Lisa is working as a replacement person on 'the cover shift at Dover', taking phone messages from the border inspectors. The inspectors have discovered 'the smell of clandestines' who have been locked in a refrigerated lorry: five men, one woman, one baby. They are practically frozen solid but still alive:

> Fourteen K fine for the company and driver, bless him, but stock was OK. They'd opened up a couple of the yoghurts from the packages, but starving probably ... They didn't have nothing on them. No papers, documents. The detention centre will just let them go. And we'll see 'em again next week for sure. Same faces ... (De-lahay, 2013: 17)

Here the trapped migrants and the locked-out migrants become the same: the double-jointed sentences suggest this. 'Dave said he saw one fall under yesterday, didn't he? Yeah ...' (De-lahay, 2013: 18). Dave's reporting and Lisa's reporting leave the play's audience with an 'imprisoning and inconsolable heart' at the border as well as facing a language 'swaddled with darkness' (Eliot, 2005 [1920]: 401).

Border tropes and final passages: the threshold between life and death

In the final section of this chapter, I will argue that the events off the island of Lampedusa in 2013 made those migrants seeking passage in small boats across the Mediterranean Sea into another version of the Black Atlantic where the sea has again become haunted by the Middle Passage and death. Now the Mediterranean appears to be a water highway that might lead migrants to escape poverty, disease, dehumanisation and religious oppression in their home countries. The boat trip seems to flow directly into images of the Middle Passage, while now it is the stretch of sea between Libya and Lampedusa. The screening of migrants now is combined with the desire by some European countries to control the processes of migration by processing migrants out of sight, forcing them into the 'frayed seams between patches of governable and waste ground', to use the words of Moshin Hamid's novel *Exit West* (2017: 66). These areas of varied and differential encounters have become an area of darkness and opacity which 'did not reveal what is on the other side, and also did not reflect what was on this side, and so felt equally like a beginning and an end' (Hamid, 2017: 97–8).

In other words, the self-narration determined by memory and circumstances is less central, whether fictional or factual. Time has become chronotropic and space or place have become less cartographic and more imaginary. These new forms bring into focus the social, cultural and political systems where the motion of contravening a border generates a 'complex network of differentiation' which cannot be distanced, neither in time nor in space (de Certeau, 2011 [1980]: 126), as we saw in De-lahay's *Routes*.

I would like now, as a way of ending this chapter, to return to writing the migrant narrative of a border-crossing on the bodies of the migrant and the European *body politic*. Frances Stonor Saunders's often cited essay 'Where on earth are you?' which appeared in *The London Review of Books* on 3 March 2016 suggests that the now familiar news item broadcast on the evening of 3 October 2013 would change the migration discussion in Europe:

> a boat carrying more than five hundred Eritreans and Somalis foundered just off the tiny island of Lampedusa. The boat sank within minutes, but survivors were in the water for five hours, some of them clinging to the bodies of their dead companions as floats. Many of the 368 people who drowned never made it off the capsizing boat. Among the 108 people trapped inside the bow was an Eritrean woman, thought to be about twenty years old, who had given birth as she drowned. Her waters had broken in the water. Rescue divers found the dead infant, still attached by the umbilical cord, in her leggings. (2016: 7)

This particularly well-documented scene helped launch questions, both political and aesthetic, about the haunting of the Mediterranean Sea and the effect of borders that had been created by governments and legal policies both inside and outside the EU. It also fixed in people's memory the boats smuggling people across the Mediterranean Sea and the humanitarian work done to rescue those people, both from the smugglers and from drowning.

As I suggested in the first part of this chapter, a threshold is the mark of the border – an edge, so to speak, which inscribes the difference between one thing and another. 'It's the place where two sides of a solid thing come together', but if we have an 'edge' we also have the advantage (Smith, 2012: 126). Borders, thresholds, edges have marked beginnings, as in the birthing passage into life or towards final passage into death. As we saw earlier, among the migrants who migrated to Britain in the 1950s to 1980s there is a profound sense that everyday reality contains many false openings or thresholds leading to cul-de-sacs and dead-ends. Borders conceal or screen fear of the Other, fear of changes in sovereign control over national territory, over the bodies of its peoples, their laws and their economy.

As Saunders's essay suggests, the young girl who died that night in 2013 while giving birth was trying to get to Europe. She had undertaken 'The longest journey which is also the shortest journey'. As discussed in detail by Horsti and Tucci in Chapter 11 below, Lampedusa is a symbolic site of memory in the European collective imagination: an island full of graves. It makes us think the impossible. A border which does not just screen, veil, or give protection but instead might be

> a death zone, portal to the underworld, where explanations of identity are foreclosed. The boat that sank half a mile from Lampedusa had entered Italian territorial waters, crossing the imaginary line drawn in the sea – the impossible line, if you think about it. It had gained the common European border, only to encounter its own vanishing point, the point at which its human cargo simply dropped off the map. *Ne plus ultra*, nothing lies beyond. (Saunders, 2016: 7–8)

Saunders's powerful essay seeks to map not just the migrant crisis but the crisis which is forcing the need for new cartographies of people and their roots and routes within their own countries and when they cross over their own frontiers. Or, as Brambilla argues in Chapter 4 above, it suggests a citizenship of geographic proximity of Europe and Africa which can be found in the artwork and story-telling of children. In Chapter 11 below, Horsti and Tucci develop this through a detailed analysis of two speakers from the Lampedusa island community and four survivors from 2013 in an attempt to comprehend the tragedy through participatory forms of story-telling and listening.

I have argued that the novels, essays and dramas discussed in this chapter have also contributed to this attempted understanding of risking entrance into the lives of others, especially immigrants, migrants and refugees. Their precarious position needs to be evaluated historically, politically, socially and aesthetically. This is no easy task. We must reject the easy equations offered by the national and international border regimes, regardless of whether the border is one created by cultural criticism, politicians or corporate entities. Those who make identity into identification, and then use identification to document and fix the socially, politically and aesthetically significant within a specific nation state are indeed dangerous.

Many people coming to Europe arrive from already contested border zones where war and poverty are the norm. They want to escape this kind of identification by attempting to travel below the threshold of bordering regimes whose mechanisms of capture, monitoring and containment are the only path to citizenship. Also, people feel compelled to express their identities grounded not in citizenship, or the nation state, but in a historically changing struggle for equality for migrants of all kinds, which does not correspond exactly to a specific geographic location, a national or even ethnic identity; or to discover a spatial presence within the nation states in which they live and work. Thus, these groups have a different 'radically open-ended politics of presence' in the words of Nicholas De Genova (2010). This is a politics of presence that has to be seen and heard to have an authority, as people use and make the spaces and places in which they live. These are places, both real and imagined, in which they can enact their own identities as communities within already existing communities as so many generations of migrants have.

I have also shown that migrants can create connections between their linguistic and social selves through the act of narration in a variety of generic, cyber and expressive forms as acts of identity formation. They will make visible to members of their new and old communities within and outside the nation state links between peoples separated by space and time but united in purpose. But to hear and see this, we must practise and define clearly shared notions of hospitality, and recognise our intertwined history with Others as a way to understand the stated aims of refugee protection and to give rights to displaced people both outside and within our midst.

Notes

1 Lena Mohamed writes in her essay 'The stateless artist' that, from the 1940s to the early 1960s, Britain was contending with the remnants of a once dominant empire, and found the need to reinforce a national identity through focusing on the significance of place, particularly London. During this period many people both from abroad and from other parts of Britain 'were drawn to London as the centre of the world' (2012: 78).

References

Appadurai, A. (1990) 'Disjunction and difference in the global cultural economy', *Theory, Culture & Society*, 7: 295–310.

Baily, D.A., I. Baucom and S. Boyce (2005) *Shades of Black: Assembling Black Arts in 1980s Britain*. Durham, NC: Duke University Press.

Beer, G. (2013) 'Windows: Looking in, looking out, breaking through', in S. Mukherji (ed.), *Thinking on Thresholds: The Poetics of Transitive Spaces*. London: Anthem Press, pp. 3–16.

Brah, A. (1996) *Cartographies of Diaspora*. London: Routledge.

Butler, J. (2006) *Precarious Life: The Powers of Mourning and Violence*. London: Verso.

De Certeau, M. (2011 [1980]) *The Practice of Everyday Life*. Trans. S.F. Rendall. Berkeley: University of California Press.

De Genova, N. (2010) 'Migration and race in Europe: The Trans-Atlantic metastases of a post-colonial cancer', *European Journal of Social Theory*, 13(3): 405–19.

De-lahay, R. (2013) *Routes*. London: Bloomsbury.

Döring, T. (2002) *Caribbean-English Passages: Intertextuality in a Postcolonial Tradition*, London: Routledge.

Eliot, T.S. (2005 [1920]) 'Gerontion', in S.G. Axelrod, C. Roman and T. Travisano (eds), *The New Anthology of American Poetry, vol. 2: Modernisms*. New Brunswick, NJ: Rutgers University Press, pp. 400–3.

Ellmann, M. (2016) 'A passage to the lighthouse', in J. Berman (ed.), *A Companion to Virginia Woolf*. London: Wiley, pp. 95–108.

Fanon, F. (1986) *Black Skin, White Masks*. Trans. C.L. Markmann. London: Pluto.

Friedman, S.S. (2004) 'Bodies on the move: A poetics of home and diaspora', *Tulsa Studies in Women's Writing*, 3(2): 189–212.

Gilroy, P. (1995) *The Black Atlantic: Modernity and Double Consciousness*. London: Harvard University Press.

Gilroy, P. (2005) *Postcolonial Melancholia*. New York: Columbia University Press.

Hall, S. (1955) 'Lamming, Selvon and some trends in the West Indian novel', *Bim* (December): 172–88.

Hall, S. (1988) 'New ethnicities', in K. Mercer (ed.), *Black Film, British Cinema*. London: Institute of Contemporary Arts, pp. 27–30.

Hamid, M. (2017) *Exit West*. London: Hamish Hamilton.

Hammond, A. (2018) 'Lines of conflict: European borders in fiction, 1945–2015', *Modern Fiction Studies*, 64(2): 334–60.

Houtum, H. van, and S.F. Wolfe (2017) 'Waiting', in J. Schimanski and S.F. Wolfe (eds), *Border Aesthetics: Concepts and Intersections*. New York: Berghahn Publishers, pp. 129–46.

Kafka, F. (2003 [1915]) 'Before the law', in *Selected Shorter Writings, transl. Ian Johnston (Before the Law, The Hunter Gracchus, Up in the Gallery, An Imperial Message, Jackals and Arabs)*, *The Kafka Project*, www.kafka.org/index.php?id=162,165,0,0,1,0. Accessed 29 September 2019.

Kureishi, H. (1986) 'The rainbow sign', in *My Beautiful Laundrette and Other Writings*. London: Faber and Faber, pp. 7–38.

Kureishi, H. (1990) *The Buddha of Suburbia*. London: Faber and Faber.

Lamming, G. (1953) *In the Castle of My Skin*. New York: McGraw-Hill.

Lamming, G. (1994 [1954]) *The Emigrants*. Ann Arbor: University of Michigan Press.

McLeod, J. (2004) *Postcolonial London: Rewriting the Metropolis*. London: Routledge.

Mohamed, L. (2012) 'The stateless artist', in L. Carey-Thomas (ed.), *Migrations: Journeys in British Art*. London: Tate Publishing, pp. 78–80.

Moore-Gilbert, B. (2001) *Hanif Kureishi*. Manchester: Manchester University Press.

Mukherji, S. (2013) 'Introduction: Thinking on thresholds', in S. Mukherji (ed.), *Thinking on Thresholds: The Poetics of Transitive Spaces*. London: Anthem Press, pp. xvii–xxviii.

Naipaul, V.S. (1988) *The Enigma of Arrival: A Novel in Five Acts*. London: Vintage.

Phillips, C. (1985) *The Final Passage*. London: Faber and Faber.

Phillips, C. (2001) *A New World Order: Essays*. London: Vintage.

Procter, J. (2003) *Dwelling Places: Postwar Black British Writing*. Manchester: Manchester University Press.

Rushdie, S. (2006 [1981]) *Midnight's Children*. New York: Random House.

Saunders, F.S. (2016) 'Where on earth are you?' *London Review of Books* (3 March): 7–12.

Selvon, S. (2006 [1956]) *The Lonely Londoners*. London: Penguin.

Smith, A. (2012) *Artful*. London: Hamish Hamilton.

Tazzioli, M. (2015) 'Which Europe? Migrants' uneven geographies and counter-mapping at the limits of representation', *Movements: Journal for Critical Migration and Border Region Studies*, 1(2): 1–19.

Walkowitz, R.L. (2006) *Cosmopolitan Style: Modernism Beyond the Nation*. New York: Columbia University Press.

Wolfe, S.F. (2016) 'A happy English colonial family in 1950s London? Immigration, containment and transgression in *The Lonely Londoners*', *Culture, Theory and Critique*, 57(1): 121–36.

9

Borderscapes of Calais: images of the 'Jungle' in *Breach* by Olumide Popoola and Annie Holmes

Jopi Nyman

Introduction

Encounters between border-crossing migrants and their hosts take place in borderscapes, locations that both challenge established identities and transform familiar spaces into locations of difference, generating confusion and conflicts, but also promise what Bhabha (1994) has referred to as 'newness' and transformation. This chapter examines the literary representation of forced migrants in one newly emerged border space, the originally temporary and notorious refugee camp known as the 'Jungle', on the outskirts of Calais, France. The 'Jungle', home to ten thousand people at the time of its closing in October 2016, is portrayed in the recent short story collection *Breach* (2016) by the Nigerian German writer Olumide Popoola and the originally South African author Annie Holmes that is the focus of this chapter. Through fictional narratives telling of forced migrants crossing into Europe and inhabiting the 'Jungle', *Breach* addresses diverse aspects related to migration to Europe and Britain. Its stories, each one written by one author, not in collaboration, emphasise how the Calais refugee camp, known for its poor conditions (see Koegler, 2017: 5), is linked with contemporary global mobility towards Europe and Britain in particular. Telling of life in this now non-existent border town, the stories in the collection show diverse encounters between migrants and hosts, government officials and volunteers, and reveal the agency of the camp's inhabitants in an otherwise hostile space where the border emerges as a key issue governing their identity. The space imagined in the collection is a borderscape where identities are formed and negotiated in conditions that offer moments of both 'belonging' and 'becoming', to use the terms presented by Brambilla (2015: 20). As the borderscape of Calais's 'Jungle' – named so first by the media, but then appropriated by its residents (Godin et al., 2017: 2) – shows, the encounters it provides transform everyone involved and show the fluctuation of identity in conditions of contemporary global migration.

My readings of the stories will pay particular attention to their spatial imaginaries, ranging from the representation of migration as a form of constant movement without an end to the ways in which resident of the camp transform it to their own space of everyday resistance. In a sense, it is through the narrative of their precarious status that we as readers witness their condition. This links the concerns of the present chapter with Karina Horsti and Ilaria Tucci's contribution (Chapter 11 below) that addresses witnessing traumatic events through images and story-telling.

Breach brings together a series of interlinked short stories by two writers, Popoola and Holmes, in which they approach the world of contemporary migration through short narratives focusing on life in an unofficial migrant city. Short story sequences or cycles are often seen to address and foreground issues linked with community (Harde, 2007: 2–3), which is also the case in *Breach*. As Harde (2007: 4) suggests, the looseness associated with stories that are intertwined but not explicitly connected is in this genre often seen as non-hierarchical owing to their open-endedness. In this sense the form appears as an apt mode for representing the borderscape. The borderscape, as well as the narrative strategies used to deal with it, are sites where the new identities ('belongings') come to the world and problematise the alleged fixity of the border. While stories of forced migration may spectacularise the contemporary refugee experience, borderscape narratives can also aim to counter monological representations of the phenomenon and contribute to a multi-sided understanding. By telling different stories of diverse experiences of travel and stay in the borderscape of the Calais 'Jungle', underlining the role of community, *Breach* becomes a borderscape narrative that negotiates the fixity of the border and in so doing challenges all attempts to provide fixed, frozen and objectifying images of migrants and their alleged placement in what Ferrer-Gallardo and Albet-Mas (2016: 527–30) refer to as limboscape.

This chapter has two related aims: first, it will address the different aspects of the borderscape experience as represented in the volume, and second, it will suggest that *Breach*, as a short story composite exploring the thematics of the border and forced migration, narrativises the borderscape. In other words, my reading of *Breach*, rather than examining the book as a mere representation of the borderscape, aims to address the collection in a way that takes into account its generic form and links it with the aesthetics of the borderscape. I will start with a discussion of the relevant concepts and then proceed to an analysis of the text.

Borderscape as concept and narrative

The border is not only a line of separation but it also brings together various actors, and creates new modes and spaces of interaction – these can be seen as new borderscapes where identities, belonging and citizenship can be negotiated (see Brambilla, 2015: 1–14; Newman, 2007: 27–57). These borderscapes are spaces of social and cultural interaction that generate diverse encounters between 'hosts' and 'crossers'. While the concept is approached in different ways by different scholars and sometimes seen as a mere border landscape, today's understanding is more flexible and sees the term in relation to global processes and mobility (Dell'Agnese and Amilhat Szary, 2015: 7–8). In terms of its etymology, the concept is other terms containing the suffix *-scape* such as Arjun Appadurai's (1996: 33) concepts of ethnoscapes, mediascapes and ideoscapes, formed to address the cross-border mobility of people, ideas and media. These terms underline how individuals participate in global processes through their involvement in these diverse imaginary -scapes. For Brambilla, the terms are linked in their concerns, but the particular benefit of using the concept of borderscape is that it 'enables a productive understanding of the processual, de-territorialised and dispersed nature of borders and their ensuing regimes and ensembles of practices' (2015: 22).

Although the earlier usage of the concept does not always take place in the context of migration, migrants' encounters at borders as well as life in the borderlands show how identity is negotiated in relation to the border. Whereas Rajaram and Grundy-Warr understand borderscapes as 'zones of varied and differentiated encounters' (2007: xxx), Brambilla (2015) claims that they are spaces where borders emerge as sites of interaction (see also Brambilla's Chapter 4 above). In her view, they are relational and moving rather than fixed, and reveal that 'bordering processes have impacts, are represented, negotiated or displaced' (Brambilla, 2015: 22), and that through them 'identities [are] negotiated' (Brambilla et al., 2015: 2). The term and its applicability have been widely debated, but it has been seen as capable of addressing processes 'not only on the border, but also beyond the line of the border, beyond the border as a place, beyond the landscape through which the border runs, and beyond borderlands with their territorial contiguities to the border' (Schimanski, 2015: 35). In other words, borderscapes are sites of encounter that extend beyond the actual border and where it may be possible to construct new identities – or prevent their formation. Borderscapes, then, are open rather than closed formations where increased interaction reveals the status of border as a process rather than as a fixed entity.

Studies of borderscapes and borderscaping in literary and cultural narratives have usually focused on the space as imagined in narratives displaying borderscape thematics, including, but not limited to, border-crossings, encounters and the making of new identities in locations that are part of the extended borderscape, if not directly located at the border. This is for instance the case in my own previous work on borderscapes in Finnish migrant narratives (2019) and Jamal Mahjoub's fiction (2017). In the case of *Breach*, however, the book's status as a short story composite – a term that critics such as Lundén (2000) prefer to often-used concepts such as short story cycle or sequence – appears relevant for an understanding of the way in which the aesthetics of the border is generated. In other words, the aim of my following discussion of the genre is to elucidate the ways in which the short story composite explores and embodies identity in the contexts of cultural encounter and bordering.

The form of *Breach*, a collection consisting of intertwined short stories that often use repeated characters or weave the narrative together by using the same narrator or geographical setting, can be described with a number of terms ranging from the short story cycle or sequence to such descriptions as the blend, para-novel or rovelle (Lundén 2000: 12–13). The form and its features have been addressed by several scholars. Whilst 'the short story cycle' is according to Ingram's definition 'a set of stories linked to each other in such a way to maintain a balance between the individuality of each of the stories and necessities of the larger unit' (1971: 15), for Mann a work in this genre is one where '[t]he stories are both self-sufficient and interrelated': they can be understood as self-standing units but also as a whole and generate 'something that could not be achieved in a single story' (1989: 15). What is important is that it is more than a collection of independent texts.

More recent criticism dealing with the genre (Davis, 2001; Lundén, 2000; Smith, 2018) suggests that formal definitions need to be replaced with functional and contextual ones. For instance, Lundén (2000) claims that composites are not necessarily unified texts nor do they provide a single message. Whilst Lundén (2000: 23) associates such refusal to provide a continuous narrative with the fragmentariness of modern life, Smith (2018: 6–7) emphasises that the genre is successful in contexts where identities are in rapid flux, transforming rather than fixed, such as the early twentieth-century United States or the post-colonial Caribbean: 'the genre repeatedly emerges during moments of embattled identity-making' (2018: 7). Both Lundén (2000) and Davis (2001) underline that the form is particularly suitable to address situations of tension and cultural encounters, which makes it relevant from the perspective of border aesthetics. In Lundén's view, the open form is particularly apt for representing the 'contrapuntal' value system of a nation such as the United States whose national culture is full of 'centripetal and centrifugal forces' (2000: 108), that is, paradoxes and contradictions that reveal cultural divisions or what he calls 'biformities', tension between actors at different levels such as ethnicities and the nation (see Lundén, 2000: 108). For Lundén, such perceptiveness to biformities is specific to the genre and makes it the 'literary form of biformal cultural values' (2000: 114). This view resonates well with the characteristics of the borderscape as a site for exploring encounters and conflicts, becomings and belongings. The link between the short story cycle and the border has been made by Sadowski-Smith (2008: 9) who argues that in many Mexican-American texts using the form it is not only the characters or themes but the shared setting of the border that glues the various parts together.

The openness of the genre and its use by ethnic and minority writers to depict such encounters is highly significant. Whilst Smith (2018: 62–3) shows that such texts address diverse cultural negotiations taking place in the borderlands where cultures are enmeshed and generate hybridities, Davis's (2001) work on Asian American and Asian Canadian writing locates in ethnic literatures a process of transculturation that links dominant culture with emergent and migrant cultural processes, showing 'how a traditional literary form converted into a transnational literary phenomenon can cross geographic, cultural, ethnic, and even linguistic boundaries' (2001: 7). For Davis, the genre of the short story cycle contributes to the remaking of community and identity in the in-between conditions of cultural encounters that are similar to those generated by the borderscape. As a 'hybrid form', Davis argues, the genre challenges conventional generic taxonomies and thus resists easy categorisation, making '[t]he ethnic short story cycle ... formal materialization of the trope of multiplicity' (2001: 19).

On the basis of these conceptual discussions, my reading of *Breach* aims to link this short story composite with the borderscape both aesthetically and thematically, building upon the idea that the common setting of the border is crucial for the generic narrative strategies that the collection builds upon. What these generic features mean for my analysis of *Breach* is that its narrated borderscape has parallels with the social structures of the border space of the Calais 'Jungle', extending from a wide gallery of life stories present in both to parallel acts of bordering. Just as the migrants are set apart from visitors in the 'Jungle', the collection sets readers apart from the migrants they meet in the stories, generating two levels of the borderscape that are linked with each other.

Borderscape thematics in *Breach*: spaces, migrants and other actors

This section examines the representation of the borderscape and its different aspects in the stories included in *Breach*, which will be followed with a discussion of the form. My discussion will address questions of migrants' mobility, border-crossings and community making, as well as their life in the 'Jungle' and the responses of the host population.

As is typical of short story composites, the collection focuses on the shared setting of the 'Jungle', the well-known refugee camp near Calais, France, pulled down in March 2016. Recent critical work on the 'Jungle' has pointed to its precariousness as well as its informal and counter-hegemonic functions: Koegler sees it as 'self-organized refuge', a provisional and temporary site of rest (2017: 4–5). This temporariness and precariousness of the camp is picked up in *Breach*, and Sandten suggests that in some of the stories the strategy of using the second person to address the story's audience underlines 'the indelible point that poverty and precariousness play a pivotal role in the creation of humiliation and help to foster an accompanying climate of fear for personal safety' (2017: 10). What I will suggest is that the migrants' sense of precariousness and constant journeying towards safety can be understood in the context of borders and borderscapes that structure their experience in the collection.

What unifies the stories is the border-related setting – the migrants are either on their way to the camp, staying there or trying to leave it. So the collection imagines an extended borderscape that starts during the characters' journey or entry into Europe and in some cases extends to Britain or Germany. To counter a general view of migrants as people entering Europe from outside, *Breach* displays characters who have been forced to leave Britain after lengthy periods of stay and are now barred from re-entering their homes in places such as Leeds and Newcastle (see Popoola, 2016d: 105, 108). The border follows many of the migrants described in the stories from their site of origin to the camp in Calais. Davies and Isakjee suggest that, according to the migrants interviewed in Calais, the 'Jungle' is both a safe haven after 'months of border crossing, danger, and the ever-present violence of transit' but also a mere 'momentary pause on an onward journey of informal mobility' (2015: 93). This issue is addressed by Holmes in stories where the migrants' journeys consist of dangerous border-crossings from Iraq to Turkey, and Turkey to Greece, as in the case of the Syrians Jan and Dlo in Holmes's 'Oranges in the river' (2016b: 129), or from Syria to Turkey, Turkey to Greece, Greece to Macedonia and further to Serbia, Croatia, Hungary and Germany (2016d: 39). The camp is their destination where they 'arrive … with their hopes and plans and justifications and family phone numbers', a point on their journey before crossing 'that last boundary' (Holmes, 2016a: 92). This is indeed a place where most people are, as an older migrant puts it, '*in*volunteer[s]' (Holmes, 2016c: 79, emphasis original). By twisting the phrase ironically the man challenges the discourses of benevolence and authority and shows how the borderscape may generate alternative and critical views.

The thematics of the borderscape permeate the collection. The opening story by Popoola, 'Counting down', follows the movement of a group of migrants in the extended borderscape as it follows a group of young men from the moment they enter Europe in Italy to France. The opening lines locate the migrants at the border: 'GPS tells me it's eleven minutes. I don't think that's right. It's too short. How can you cross a border, go from one country to another, and be there in eleven minutes? It took us two weeks to get here' (Popoola, 2016a: 9). The passage represents the border as an uncanny space of astonishment where time and space transform and challenge the migrant's expectations. The uncanniness of the border-crossing with the related silence and excitement is, however, challenged by the apparent easiness of crossing an intra-Schengen border: 'There is nothing special on the other side. It looks the same. But now we are in France' (Popoola, 2016a: 22).

Encounters at the border are significant and attended to frequently in the collection. The following passage from the first story is indicative of migrant–host encounters as it hints at violence and trauma as emerging from the meeting:

> When I met MG some days ago I looked at him and said to myself, This guy is scared. Sweating too much. It's just a line, I wanted to say, for you to wait in. Nothing can happen here, little brother. You survived the boat, you have been picked up by the coastguard. You survived the crazy people who want to keep their beach clean, free of refugees. They think refugees make their summer income leave through the back door. Tourism does not want to see any dead bodies leaving onto the sand. A man told me this. That man spat in front of my feet. I didn't understand him. That is how I met Calculate. He translated it with his funny Arabic. I didn't spit back. I just nodded. And smiled. (Popoola, 2016a: 13)

The examples above confirm the emphasis given to the border and attempts to cross it in the collection. Several stories describe attempts to leave France for England and thus bring the actual border closer to the camp and locate the 'Jungle' firmly in the borderscape. For instance, 'Ghosts' tells a story of human smugglers operating in the camp, on the one hand emphasising their ruthlessness and greed, on the other hand describing their action as a service for migrants with 'pleading eyes' and 'deserv[ing] the next step' (Holmes, 2016a: 92). Holmes's 'Oranges in the river' (2016b) shows how Jan, assisted by human smugglers, enters a lorry three times and is twice returned to France, with his increasingly more frustrated friend Dlo. The lorry, as such, is a marker of mobility that transports the migrant to a new setting, but owing to police and border control such promises are false for many. In the end, however, Jan is successful. Whilst his friend Dlo abandons attempts to enter Britain after a near-death incident in a refrigerator truck and returns to his family in Germany, Jan's third crossing shows how he manages to cross the border. His entry into Britain, hiding in a lorry, is described in detail:

> He's ready to climb down when they reach the second roadblock, but once more the police ignore their truck. Are they stupid, these police? Are they lazy? This truck might as well bear the slogan *Refugees on board*. And the third roadblock – nothing. Now they sense the incline as their cronky old truck – beloved truck! – drives up the ramp and onto the ferry. Feel that! Jan mimes with his hands they sway of the sea beneath them, explaining to the boy. But it all may come to nothing. How many refugees have been found in Dover and sent back to Calais? Too many to count. 'Be still,' the men in the truck tell each other. 'Not yet.'
>
> As the truck drives out of Dover, Jan's UK SIM card connects and his mobile tells him has 3G. He texts his mother: *Today, I greet you under UK sky*.
>
> They wait until the truck pulls over for fuel, a full forty minutes, before they bang on the sides and the driver – too surprised to be angry – releases them. There's no sunshine as such, but it is daylight, not darkness. And it is UK. (Holmes, 2016b: 138–9; emphasis original)

The passage imagines the crossing into the UK as a transformative moment, almost as a rebirth, as the men enter the country from the womblike lorry and Jan texts his mother. The climactic aspects of the crossing are evident in the fact that the safeness of Britain is associated with daylight, and the traumatising and violent past with darkness: 'Always night … Always darkness … The mortar blowing up the neighbour's house in the night in Hasakah. The boat from Turkey across the sea to Greece. All those nights waiting for trucks or waiting in trucks or running from trucks. Darkness!' (Holmes, 2016b: 138). Jan's border-crossing completes the act of becoming, associated with the borderscape, and the story ends with his performative acquisition of a new identity that brings an end to his liminal position portrayed through the diverse images discussed. As a sign of voicing his new identity, Jan, when stopped by the British police for walking on the motorway, voices his transformation and requests the official to perform as he is expected to: '"I too am illegal," he tells the cop in English. "And this boy is illegal. Arrest us!"' (Holmes, 2016b: 139). The act of naming his identity as 'illegal' is double-voiced in this case: while it designates his official legal status, it also links him with the community of other migrants and in his view provides him with certain rights as an asylum seeker, feeling finally safe and looking for a new life in Britain where, as he thinks, 'Even if you break the law, you have rights' (Holmes, 2016b: 133).

In Jan's dreams, as well in the minds of other characters, the post-crossing space of Britain is indeed associated with safety and the promise of a new life. Mobility and migration are expected to end when entering the promised land. In 'Paradise' by Holmes, Muhib tells Julie that 'London is a place of angels, ... it is my dream' and that 'I will be a new person when I get to London' (2016c: 82). In 'Oranges in the river', Jan's dream of his imaginary room in Birmingham emphasises the importance of setting down roots and starting again. Home, as the passage shows, is treated differently in these migrant narratives than in diaspora writing. Whilst diasporic literature underlines the meaning of home and the memory of the homeland, refugee narratives such as those represented in this collection tend to foreground the impossibility of return and place hope in imagined futures. As Jan puts it:

> While they were moving across Europe ... Jan kept alive an image of their destination, a hostel in Britain, London or Birmingham. He emphasises the last syllable as he pronounces 'Birmingham' in his mind. London, London – everyone wants London, but someone from Jan's home village lives in Birmingham ... The room he pictures is not large or luxurious. He sees a bed, a table where he will prepare for food and eat, and a desk where he will study to improve his English. OK, maybe the desk is asking too much. The desk can come later. In the early days he will study at the table where he eats. He will move the plates to the sink and wash them immediately. Water will flow from the tap and this room will be spotless. (Holmes, 2016b: 132–3)

What the passages share is an emphasis on waiting as an element in the border experience. The moment of border-crossing provides the migrant with an aim and objective in life and thus gives a meaning to waiting. Such waiting, according to Houtum and Wolfe (2017: 134), is an expression of what they label as 'paranoid desire', where homesickness is directed towards the moment following crossing when the dream is finally fulfilled. In their view waiting may be 'liberating' as it equips the waiting subject with 'a task, a meaning, a social function and a potential identity' (Houtum and Wolfe, 2017: 134). In case of Jan, the successful crossing saves him from other parts of such an experience that may include 'emptiness' and 'becoming a stranger' (Houtum and Wolfe, 2017: 134). This is the fate of many migrants portrayed in the stories such as Muhib, his friend Isaac and Jan's friend Dlo. Isaac and Dlo, frustrated with the emptiness offered by the camp and the proximity of the border that appears impossible to cross, choose differently and leave – Isaac opts for resettlement somewhere else in France, and Dlo travels to Germany where some members of his family live.

The Calais camp itself is approached in the collection from different perspectives including those of migrants, hosts and voluntary workers who voice several aspects relevant to the borderscape. The general attitude of the French hosts and people living in Calais exemplifies bordering as it is full of dislike and contempt, seen in the view of the French plumber Luc at work in a guest house in Calais:

> 'Foreign?' he asked and I nodded. Luc snorted. He thinks I'm crazy, allowing strangers into my home. If he'd known these two were not tourists but refugees, dear God, I hate to think what he'd have said. He loses no chance to rail against them, all of them, with their tents and shacks. Trash strewn far and wide, and the noise at night, terrible thumping music distorted on the wind waking his own brother in his own bed. How are his nieces to walk safely with all those men hanging around? Luc holds the bald bowl of his head in his hands when he starts to rage. It burns him. He could spit. Sometimes he does, but not in my bathroom. (Holmes, 2016d: 28)

In addition to showing how the migrants are Othered by using conventional tropes often used in racist discourse such as those of noise, dirt and sexual threat that emphasise migrants' cultural and racial difference, the passage also reveals how the effects are felt bodily and thus are partly non-rational. Other stories reveal the extent to which similar attitudes are present in institutions such as the French police who are never too helpful. In this sense the camp is related to bordering processes and its inhabitants are separated from the host population – armed police officers guard the roads leading to the camp and systematically make their presence known to the residents of the 'Jungle': 'Once in a while they parade in their heavy boots and their helmets with visors through the camp, down the main street and back, showing their presence. A reminder that this is merely an unspoken toleration, the staying here. The empty tear-gas canister another cure' (Popoola, 2016c: 58).

This act of bordering is levelled in some stories by acts of debordering where closer contact with the migrants leads to a larger awareness of them as individuals with personal histories. This is the case of Eloise, the French B&B owner accommodating the Syrian minors Omid and Nalin. Whilst her first visit to the camp site leaves her 'gritty' and is described as 'going too close' (Holmes, 2016d: 37), it initiates a process of transformation that is linked with her own past as the 'figures pacing the high white fence along the railway line' remind her of 'figures from history or documentaries' that are part of culturally mediated 'second-hand memories of war' (37). Her second visit, conducted later when she has learned more about the two adolescents, reveals that her exposure to their experience and the desolate conditions of the camp transforms her ideas and increases her sense of responsibility. Her former understanding of her relationship with them where she is 'the host and cook, not a friend' (Holmes, 2016d: 35) changes and shows a resultant act of debordering where she affiliates with the migrants, rejects her old habits and values, and even decides to lie for them if need be

(47). The Calais borderscape can transform anyone inhabiting it, regardless of their citizenship, gender or status, and generate new affiliations and becomings.

From the perspective of the migrants, the camp provides shelter and community, but its closeness to the harsh realities of migration and the border reminds them also of the violence and oppression that are a part of the border experience. The borderscape as a concept is indeed close to Bhabha's Third Space, a space of in-betweenness that is similarly a space of negotiating tension and constructing new identities in conditions of liminality (1994: 218). For migrants the camp, whilst in principle a temporary stop on a journey towards safety, can be transformed into a community. The stories' descriptions of the 'Jungle' underline that, rather than a temporary shack village, the place has been appropriated by the migrants so that it resembles a town with its barbershops, café-bars and shops selling Red Bull and batteries, a school, a library and the Dome, a club for events and musical performances, all of which bring its residents together and contribute to a sense of belonging in the borderscape. While consisting of ethnic enclaves – Kurds live in one section, Iraqis in another – the camp as a whole is a resource for the migrants and generally welcoming to everyone. Thus it provides, to some extent, an example of Foucault's heterotopia amidst an otherwise hostile space: these spaces of hope are 'real and effective spaces … in which … all the other real arrangements that can be found within society, are at one and the same time represented, challenged and overturned' (1985–86: 12). Accordingly, the space of the camp can be seen to host a community whose values contrast with those of the dominant society but who share a dream of a better life with family and friends in the safety of a new home. As has been noted, the 'Jungle', regardless of its 'abject conditions', offered a 'strong sense of community and mutual help' for residents and volunteers alike (Godin et al., 2017: 2, 3).

While such a view emphasising the role of community within the camp has some basis in reality, it also simplifies and romanticises the refugee experience and disregards potential conflicts. An example of such thinking is presented by one of the French volunteers in Popoola's 'Lineage' who in fact compares the camp to 'a laboratory' where the migrants' ability to live with other people is tested and argued to lead to harmonious coexistence:

> Look at the Muslims. Here we have Sunnis and Shias living side by side, helping each other even. Some of them left their countries because it was dangerous for them there. They decided, I will not live like this, I will go and find a better place where I can survive, where I can build a life for me and my family. When they arrive here they are even closer to each other than at home … They come here to this awful place and they make a life for themselves. Try to keep their dignity. (Popoola, 2016d: 117)

As the passage is attributed to Sébastien, a French volunteer and convert to Islam with highly idealistic views motivated to work at the camp because of his desire to learn more about his new identity from his Sudanese 'brothers', its status is highly questionable. Recent research into volunteerism does in fact show that primary motivations are not always other-directed or altruistic but many volunteers, especially tourist volunteers, combine help with 'leisure seeking or self-developmental motivations' (Sin, 2009: 487).

This transnational community imagined, however, is also temporary and strategic, rather than a permanent one. This is evident in the way in which its members construct temporary alliances that support them in their attempts to escape the camp. It is in fact from the outsider's perspective that the camp appears as a harmonious space of cultural mixing – the following excerpt shows how Julie, a young British student helping at the camp, approaches it as if was a specimen of metropolitan cultural hybridity:

> Julie smiles at everyone she passes on the track. She read on one of the helpful Facebook pages that outsiders should smile, so she smiles at them all: smiles at the young Sudanese men, gangly-tall, whisking along on bicycles; smiles at the Eritrean women darting in and out of the café-bar, even though she can't catch the eye of any of them; smiles at Kurdish families in thick coats, big-eyed children peering out from under their hood; smiles at the Afghan men behind their raw-plank counters of general dealers … Seriously, you'd reconsider all those things you've been saying if you could only see how everyone gets along, how considerate people are of each other. (Holmes, 2016c: 66–7)

Rather than a paradise in any sense apart from the title of the story telling of Julie and her brief affair with Muhib, its representation reveals the underworld of the borderscape, seen in crime, violence and death, associated in particular, but not only, with human smugglers in Holmes's 'Ghosts' (2016a) where abuse and prostitution are present and migrants trade sex for a safe passage. In Popoola's 'Extending a hand' (2016c) the narrator's friend Mariam persuades the narrator to join in a visit to the lorry drivers to make some money to be sent to Mariam's ill mother. The borderscape, as these examples show, is thus also a site of in-betweenness and non-belonging, not merely one of progressive elements.

A group of actors whose presence in the borderscape is occasionally treated with suspicion by migrants consists of the volunteers. In some stories, they are represented as well-meaning helpers who do not necessarily have the relevant knowledge of the background and problems of migrants and whose reasons for entering the camp do not appear genuine. In addition to Sébastien, the blond volunteer with dreadlocks described as looking 'like a little boy, open and trusting and proud' (Popoola, 2016d: 117), other stories provide further representations of volunteers. In 'Extending a hand', the hopelessness of Mariam and Habena, and their decision to resort to prostitution, is not recognised by the volunteer, described as wearing 'practical clothes made for outdoor activities' and suffering from 'the helping syndrome' (Popoola, 2016c: 53). Her condescending approach is from the migrants' perspective only one of many: 'You are tired of visitors who all need acknowledgement, who all need you to engage so that they can feel they are doing the right thing' (Popoola, 2016c: 53). Whilst recognising and appreciating the assistance, the migrants appear to react to the ritualistic reciprocity in the situation, that its 'rules' are 'annoying' (Popoola 2016c: 52). Alluding to the title of the 1984 Band Aid hit 'Do they know it's Christmas', Popoola's story critiques both the spectacularisation of migration, the passive role it attributes to migrants who 'are always the famished skeletons with the kwashiorkor belly' (2016c: 53), and the liberal outlook of many volunteers – or 'optimist[s]' (56) – with their 'five-minute concern' (55). Although mainly told from the perspective of the more cynical Marjorie, who reflects on her motives and decision to allow Julie to travel with her, 'Paradise' discusses the relationships between volunteers and migrants through other characters too. Whilst the case of Julie underlines the naivety of some volunteers by addressing the inexperienced Julie's infatuation with the handsome young womaniser Muhib – an episode alluded to by an English volunteer, one of Muhib's friends, by rephrasing Shakespeare's *Romeo and Juliet* ('Oy Romeo ... you're the one who's meant to climb' (Holmes, 2016c: 74)) – the story ends in Muhib's ambiguous words addressed to a German volunteer, a music teacher, that reveal the border between irregular migrants and their helpers. The borderscape, while bringing them together temporarily and generating belonging, is in the end dominated by the border and its power to divide and restrict mobility: '"All the volunteers go. And you leave us here in the Jungle, thinking about you, missing you. It's painful," he says, "so please, don't love us so much"' (85).

Genre and borderscape in *Breach*

Whilst the previous section has discussed the representation of borderscape phenomena in the collection, this section aims to suggest that in the case of *Breach* its form, the short story composite, is a way of narrating the borderscape. To paraphrase Davis's argument concerning story-telling, I argue that *Breach* 'illustrate[s] the *theme* of' borderscape 'through the *technique* of' borderscaping (Davis, 2001: 13, emphasis original). In other words, the collection narrates the borderscape aesthetically, not only thematically or politically, suggesting that the border and borderscape are tropes that are materialised in the genre. *Breach*'s insistence on problematising the concept of borders is evident in the fact that the stories in the collection have been written by two authors, Popoola and Holmes. While they have not been written jointly, the book is arranged in a way where borders between the individual writers are made invisible: the opening page of each story mentions only the title of the story, and the name of the author is shown only on the copyright page (Popoola and Holmes, 2016: 4).

The borderscape unites the stories, functioning as the site where cultural encounters charactering its various migrant–host encounters take place (cf. Sadowski-Smith, 2008). Resisting unity, it shows the characters' diverse affiliations and transforming identities, their belongings and becomings. Through its attention to bordering and hard borders, the narrative makes the border the site where identities are negotiated and constructed. The migrants of *Breach* interact with the holders of power, construct communities and groups, and in so doing construct their identities anew. As Popoola's 'Counting down' (2016a), the story opening the collection, shows, networks and groups formed during migration are contingent, but the friendships made are long-lasting. Whilst Calculate turns out to lack solidarity as he has stolen MG's money, the others in the group construct a community whose members reappear in the final story – this is significant since in Harde's view community can be associated with the genre's way of promoting 'non-hierarchical and multicultural readings' (2007: 4). 'Counting down' shows their first steps in France, underlining their connectedness through banter and joint laughter and revealing how the border makes them a community. At the same time this can be extended to the narrative level to suggest that the stories are joined like the arms of the character and explore shared meanings of the borderscape:

> Calculate is behind but he is too far gone – he is not part of the group any more.
> MG says, 'Thank you,' turning to all of us.
> I ask, 'For what?'
> He puts his arm through mine [Obama] and through GPS's on the other side and starts walking again.
> 'Welcome to France, Michelle.'
> Suleyman starts laughing, but his chest pushes up too much and holds it, bending over, coughing. Harh-harh-harh. GPS opens his face; the laughter falls out like his hands: beautiful and long. (Popoola, 2016a: 26)

To address the conditions of liminality and in-betweenness as elements of the borderscape, the collection uses a variety of narrative strategies identified by Davis as central facets in ethnic writing and which are linked with the borderscape, including those of 'plurality, multiplicity, polyphony and fragmentation' (2001: 17), as well as carving out an 'empowered narrative

[...] of resistance' (2001: 18). In other words, *Breach* is a narrative of cultural plurality that through its array of different migrants entering Europe calls forth a variety of cultural and ethnic identities that challenge European, French and British hegemonies and the maintenance of hard borders. This polyphony is also a generic feature as the short story composite allows for and actually demands more varied and changing reading positions than the novel as a genre. The stories are also polyphonic, representing a variety of story-tellers of various genders with different linguistic, national and ethnic origins in a way that seeks to resist hegemonic narratives of migration positing it as a threat to the nation state. In so doing it gives a voice not only to migrants but also to those who like the narrator of 'The terrier' represent the host and hold diverse views on increased migration and migrant presence in formerly restricted spaces (Holmes, 2016d). Hence, the collection is an expression of resistance to xenophobic populist discourses and seeks to empower migrants through its provision of an alternative narrative of hope. By inscribing the migrant in the borderscape that is at one level danger-ous and violent, but at another a location offering belonging and becoming, *Breach* participates in what Davis defines as 'a forging and communicating of identity' (2001: 19).

To underline the significance of such narrative strategies, it needs to be remembered that in short story composites the closing story often that generates some kind of epiphany (Davis, 2001: 16). Whilst this is also the case in *Breach*, the collection also works against a simplified closure by refusing to represent the border-crossing as a mere utopia. In its final story, 'Expect me' (Popoola, 2016b), set in Bolton, United Kingdom, and told from the perspective of Alghali, one of the migrants portrayed in the story opening the collection, the representation of life in post-crossing Britain does not generate mere sentiments of happiness, but emphasises the ambiguities of the extended borderscape but closes with a sense of hope and community. The story uses imagery of darkness to portray symbolically the migrant's inability to escape the effects of bordering, and to stress their liminal status. Starting in a 'dark room' with 'drawn' but 'not fully open' curtains where Alghali's 94-year-old English teacher Mr Dishman lives (Popoola, 2016b: 141), the story shows his yet incomplete adaptation to the new homeland. At the same time it also makes evident that many of his friends have not succeeded but remain trapped at the border and keep on 'attempting the journey across the Channel night after night' (Popoola, 2016b: 143). For instance, 14-year-old Adnan has been 'electrocuted' while trying to enter Britain by travelling 'on top of a train' (Popoola, 2016b: 148). The represented loneliness and emptiness associated with the life of a migrant waiting for his papers resembles that of an old man living alone in a small apartment: 'Nothing happens other than in the past. Or in the future, for Alghali. The distant future that could come tomorrow, that could come months down the line. Or never' (Popoola, 2016b: 145). To use the terms of Houtum and Wolfe (2017: 134), this is an example of the paranoid desire to belong, but, regardless of Alghali's successful crossing into Britain, waiting at the border has transformed merely into a different form of waiting where the migrant waits for permission to stay and work, for citizenship and so on, waiting for the possibility of 'becoming' embedded in the borderscape.

Since danger, violence and death are elements of the migrant's border experience and travel with them, whether they want that or not, the story narrates the borderscape as a space of constant struggle where the migrant is a marker of Otherness. This is shown when Alghali returns home from his class with Mr Dishman and is attacked by two men outside the pub. The encounter culminates in an act of racialised violence where Alghali becomes a scapegoat for a terrorist attack by a Syrian in Paris, revealing how easily border-related conflicts may be repeated in the extended borderscape. The division into us and them in such a space confirms the role of the borderscape as a site of re-enacting violence and underlines the precariousness of the migrant. Whilst Alghali's relocation in Britain contributes to the reconstruction of his identity, it also inserts him in discourses of racism and racialised violence and the processes of in/exclusion. The narrative, however, refuses to accept such a position, as the ending of the story, strategically placed as to close the entire collection, hints at an alternative future. The darkness of Alghali's room is at the end illuminated by the screen of his mobile phone when he texts his friend Suleyman, still waiting in Calais:

> *Our lives are this now. Never really home.*
> Suleyman's reply comes in an instant.
> *Expect me. One way or another.* (Popoola, 2016b: 154, italics original)

The final lines of the story show how the borderscape is not only a site of b/ordering and violence but also one of community-making and transformation, and that the act of waiting remains a promise as long as the possibility of a new home is available. If this ending is interpreted in relation to the conventions of the genre where the final story usually generates a reinterpretation of the previous stories (Davis, 2001: 16), in this case the reinterpretation underlines the contradictions of the new space and shows that it is home to both hope and despair. Neither is the message entirely negative, but the SMSs remind the reader that for migrants there are ways of making connections across the border. In so doing the story emphasises the transnational – or transborder – element that adds to the critical and resisting potential of the genre, as Davis (2001) suggests, as the border subject has access to diverse networks (Schimanski and Wolfe, 2017: 155). As the final lines assure both Alghali and the reader, there is hope as long as waiting does not turn into nothingness, revealing that connections, communities and networks play a role in alleviating despair and loneliness. In this sense, the openness of the short story composite and its resistance to fixed meanings and narrative closure make it a form that supports the resilience of the migrant and adds to the agency of the subjects it narrates in the borderscape. In so doing the collection is more than a representation of the borderscape. Rather, it is a part of the borderscape as it is involved in the process of bordering from a perspective that supports inclusion rather than exclusion, and thus has political performativity through the act of making forced migrants visible.

Conclusion

This chapter has discussed the role of borders in the short story composite *Breach* from two related perspectives. Following a critical discussion of the relevant theoretical concepts, the first part of the analysis focused on the volume's political aspects of the borderscape thematics, showing how the stories address problems related to the crossing of borders and the construction of transnational communities in conditions where processes of bordering and Othering play a role in locating the migrant. What I have argued is that the stories reveal moments and encounters that are ambiguous and contested, but also full of hope, showing that borderscapes are sites for reconstructing identity and new affiliations. In the second part of the analysis I have suggested that the form of the short story composite can be seen as a way of narrating the borderscape. As appropriated by Holmes and Popoola, *Breach* is a borderscaping narrative that challenges acts of bordering and fixing the identities of the subjects narrated, and in so doing voices the transnationalism of the experience of forced mobility as a sign of resistance. Whilst the borderscape as a setting uniting the collection is a space of ambiguity and precariousness, it is through mobility that the migrants of the collection may gain glimpses of a better future and become – at least temporarily – members of communities providing safety and hope. This mobility is also a narrative construction characterising the entire collection: the presence of fleeting images and image-like concepts used in the analysis, which range from heterotopia and third space to limboscape and the title *Breach*, emphasise dynamism and challenge the fixedness and one-dimensionality that the discourse of popular media attaches to migrants. It is in this context that we need to understand the title of the collection, signifying the possibility that fiction can perform politically and challenge established conceptions.

References

Appadurai, A. (1996) *Modernity at Large: Cultural Dimensions of Globalization.* Minneapolis: University of Minnesota Press.

Bhabha, H.K. (1994) *The Location of Culture.* London: Routledge.

Brambilla, C. (2015) 'Exploring the critical potential of the borderscapes concept', *Geopolitics*, 20(1): 14–34.

Brambilla, C., J. Laine, J.W. Scott and G. Bocchi (2015) 'Introduction: Thinking, mapping, acting and living borders under contemporary globalization', in C. Brambilla, J. Laine, J.W. Scott and G. Bocchi (eds), *Borderscaping: Imaginations and Practices of Border Making.* Farnham: Ashgate, pp. 1–9.

Davies, T., and A. Isakjee (2015) 'Geography, migration and abandonment in the Calais refugee camp', *Political Geography*, 49: 93–5.

Davis, R.G. (2001) *Transcultural Reinventions: Asian American and Asian Canadian Short-Story Cycles.* Toronto: Tsar.

Dell'Agnese, E., and A.-L. Amilhat Szary (2015) 'Borderscapes: From border landscapes to border aesthetics', *Geopolitics*, 20(1): 4–13.

Ferrer-Gallardo, X., and A. Albet-Mas (2016) 'EU-Limboscapes: Ceuta and the proliferation of migrant detention spaces across the European Union', *European Urban and Regional Studies*, 23(3): 527–30.

Foucault, M. (1985–86) 'Other spaces: The principles of heterotopia', *Lotus International*, 48-9: 9–17.

Godin, M., K. Møller Hansen, A. Lounasmaa, C. Squire and T. Zaman (2017) 'Introduction', in M. Godin, K. Møller Hansen, A. Lounasmaa, C. Squire and T. Zaman (eds), *Voices from the 'Jungle': Stories from the Calais Refugee Camp.* London: Pluto, pp. 1–13.

Harde, R. (2007) 'Introduction', in R. Harde (ed.), *Narratives of Community: Women's Short Story Sequences.* Newcastle: Cambridge Scholars Publishing, pp. 1–11.

Holmes, A. (2016a) 'Ghosts', in O. Popoola and A. Holmes, *Breach.* London: Peirene Press, pp. 87–101.

Holmes, A. (2016b) 'Oranges in the river', in O. Popoola and A. Holmes, *Breach.* London: Peirene Press, pp. 125–39.

Holmes, Annie (2016c) 'Paradise', in O. Popoola and A. Holmes, *Breach.* London: Peirene Press, pp. 65–85.

Holmes, Annie (2016d) 'The terrier', in O. Popoola and A. Holmes, *Breach.* London: Peirene Press, pp. 27–47.

Houtum, H. van, and S.F. Wolfe (2017) 'Waiting', in J. Schimanski and S.F. Wolfe (eds), *Border Aesthetics: Concepts and Intersections.* New York: Berghahn, pp. 129–46.

Ingram, F.L. (1971) *Representative Short Story Cycles of the Twentieth Century: Studies in a Literary Genre.* The Hague: Mouton.

Koegler, C. (2017) 'Precarious urbanity: "The Jungle" (Calais) and the politics of performing the urban', *Postcolonial Text*, 12(3–4): 1–15.

Lundén, R. (2000) *The United Stories of America: Studies in the Short Story Composite.* Amsterdam: Rodopi.

Mann, S.G. (1989) *The Short Story Cycle: A Genre Companion and Reference Guide.* Westport: Greenwood Press.

Newman, D. (2007) 'The lines that continue to separate us: Borders in our "borderless" world', in J. Schimanski and S.F. Wolfe (eds), *Border Poetics De-limited.* Hanover: Wehrhahn, pp. 27–57.

Nyman, J. (2017) *Displacement, Memory, and Travel in Contemporary Migrant Writing*. Leiden: Brill.

Nyman, J. (2019) 'Borders, borderscapes, and border-crossing romances in contemporary migrant writing in Finland by TaoLin and Arvi Perttu', *Journal of Borderlands Studies*, 34: 105–20.

Popoola, O. (2016a) 'Counting down', in O. Popoola and A. Holmes, *Breach*. London: Peirene Press, pp. 9–26.

Popoola, O. (2016b) 'Expect me', in O. Popoola and A. Holmes, *Breach*. London: Peirene Press, pp. 141–54.

Popoola, O. (2016c) 'Extending a hand', in O. Popoola and A. Holmes, *Breach*. London: Peirene Press, pp. 49–64.

Popoola, O. (2016d) 'Lineage', in O. Popoola and A. Holmes, *Breach*. London: Peirene Press, pp. 103–24.

Popoola, O., and A. Holmes (2016) *Breach*. London: Peirene Press.

Rajaram, P.K., and C. Grundy-Warr (2007) 'Introduction', in P.K. Rajaram and C. Grundy-Warr (eds), *Borderscapes: Human Geographies and Politics at Territory's Edge*. Minneapolis: University of Minnesota Press, pp. ix–xl.

Sadowski-Smith, C. (2008) *Border Fictions: Globalization, Empire, and Writing at the Boundaries of the United States*. Charlottesville: University of Virginia Press.

Sandten, C. (2017) 'Representations of poverty and precariousness in contemporary refugee narratives', *Postcolonial Text*, 12(3–4): 1–15.

Schimanski, J. (2015) 'Border aesthetics and cultural distancing in the Norwegian–Russian borderscape', *Geopolitics*, 20(1): 35–55.

Schimanski, J., and S.F. Wolfe (2017) 'Intersections: A conclusion in the form of a glossary', in J. Schimanski and S.F. Wolfe (eds), *Border Aesthetics: Concepts and Intersections*. New York: Berghahn, pp. 147–69.

Sin, H.L. (2009) 'Volunteer tourism – "Involve me and I will learn"?', *Annals of Tourism Research*, 36(3): 480–501.

Smith, J.J. (2018) *The American Short Story Cycle*. Edinburgh: Edinburgh University Press.

10

Seasons of migration to the North: borders and images in migration narratives published in Norwegian

Johan Schimanski

Sublime North, sublime border

Near the beginning of Marie Amelie's *Ulovlig norsk* (2010) ('Illegally Norwegian'), she crosses the border at the northern tip of Finland, travelling into Norway in a car. Her autobiographical narrative describes a border-crossing which is at the same time a journey to the North, and thus provides an introduction to my following discussion of the role of images in border-crossing, combining the methodological approaches of imagology and border poetics.

Amelie's description of the Finnish landscape before crossing the Norwegian border is replete with stereotypical images of Northernness, well-established in studies of historical images of the North and of Arctic discourses (Chartier, 2007; Davidson, 2005; Ryall et al., 2010): the whiteout experienced as 'the white snow continues to merge with the sky',[1] the empty and lifeless surroundings, the deserted waste, sparsely populated with only a few houses and no cars (Amelie, 2010: 16–17). This is a cold place of winter darkness and of snow: 'it is night, and the only bright spot is the snow'.[2] The coldness becomes part of the characterization of human life there: 'the houses and petrol stations we drive past seem cold, unfriendly, and lonely'.[3] It is a place of fear and danger: the possibility that their car might break down 'is even worse thinking about than about the border we are soon going to cross illegally. Who will help us here?'[4]

Fear and danger are markers of the sublimity connected with the North, as in Chauncey C. Loomis's concept of the 'Arctic sublime' (1977), developed by Francis Spufford (1996: 16–40) and others. Spufford follows the eighteenth-century aesthetic thinker Edmund Burke in defining the sublime as a pleasure produced by observing danger from a safe distance (Burke, 1990: 36–7), as might be the case of a geopolitical border to the North today, from a Southern point of view. Spufford also links the Arctic sublime to horror and the gothic (1996: 34–9). The gothic sublime can also be described as a liminal and transgressive state experienced on the outer edge (or border) of society, the world and reality (Aguirre, 2006), often associated with beauty and the fantastic. The imagined North has for a long time been an ambivalent place of extremes, both a hell and an idyll (Davidson, 2005: 21).

In Amelie's text, the fear of the North is mixed with 'the fear and despair'[5] of crossing borders surreptitiously. Not only the North can be dangerous; so can also the border. Since the introduction of a passport union in the Nordic countries in 1954 – supplemented by the later Schengen Agreement – the border between Finland and Norway has had only minimal control facilities, and the crossing between the two is fairly simple and mundane. You drive across the border, and as Amelie's text has it, 'a sign appears: "Norway"'.[6] This relative ease of crossing does not however hinder Amelie's fear of crossing. She describes the phased intensification often associated with approaching the limen or threshold (cf. Aguirre, 2006: 20–1): 'The heart beats harder for each fewer kilometre left'.[7] She also describes the following moment of doubt and elation, marked in the textual discourse with repetitions, exclamation marks and italics: 'We drive through! We *are* in Norway! [...] Can it really go so well? [...] We are really in Norway!'[8] Before crossing the border, there is no help to be had, and the relief of the border-crossing initiates the ascriptions of positive values to Norway which are to follow.

The reality (*virkelig*, 'really') of the crossing, and her joyful surprise, quickly give way to a fantastic and beautiful sublime, perhaps even reinforcing it:

> I stare out of the window in astonishment. Nature has changed so quickly, now it is earthshakingly beautiful. Mountains, mountains, mountains, mountains, tall mountains! Just like at home in the Caucasus! I turn around restlessly in the car, look up and down and left and right and out through the back window. At last I can see mountains again, the mountains which have been part of my life from birth. They didn't have anything like this in Moscow. And not in Finland either. Magical [*eventyrlige*], majestic mountains!
>
> Some kilometres later we even see water. I think of always having dreamt about living a place where there are both mountains and sea ...[9]

Here Maria has left the daunting, entropic flatness she associates with Finland and Russia (Amelie, 2010: 16, 17), and enters into the mountainous and beautiful realm of Norway, combining the alpine, Arctic and Northern in a gothic sublime. The spatial topography of the road to Tromsø (where she ends up) from Finland aids her figuration of the border. Those who have crossed the border at Kilpisjärvi, driving down the valley to the fjord at Skibotn, will know how that highland plateau is broken up by large numbers of increasingly alpine mountains. As the geographer Louis Edmond-Hamelin reminds us in his analysis of Canadian northernness and arcticity, the North is a concept produced by a combination of different semantic fields, and is also associated with winterliness, but also alpinity or mountainousness (see Chartier, 2007: 40–1).

However, Maria sees the mountains not as something exotic but rather as something familiar: in the quotation above, 'Just like home in the Caucasus'. They are still associated with the fantastic – they are *eventyrlige*, precisely 'fairy-tale like' – but, like fairy tales, also connected to positive memories of childhood. They introduce a vertical aspect to border-crossing, also discussed by Wolfgang Müller-Funk and Patricia García (Chapters 1 and 2 above).

To sum up this encounter with the North as a narrative of border-crossing: Amelie figures the border as a movement into the strange and the fantastic (cf. Schimanski, 2015), but also as a place of chiastic (A–B > B–A) mixing (cf. Derrida, 1992 [1980]), in which something homely is projected into a foreign place. Her gaze forwards towards the border, from an 'unorientated' space without frames and limits, is replaced by a disorientating, circular movement often associated with border-crossings (Schimanski, 2015), as Amelie gazes out of the car window at the mountains around her. More generally, her border-crossing exhibits the hopes and fears, and the uncanny elations of thresholds that Stephen Wolfe and Jopi Nyman refer to in Chapters 8 and 9 above. Crossing the border from Finland to Norway becomes interwoven with images of the North as an ambivalent frontier region, invoking both something other and something familiar. The contradictions of this *ulovlig* ('illegal') border-crossing, both dangerous and safe, prepare her for becoming, as the book's title indicates through paradox and oxymoron, *ulovlig norsk* ('illegally Norwegian').

Border poetics and Arctic discourses

Amelie's book, a testimony about her life in Norway as an 'illegal' immigrant, was a best-seller in Norway and contributed to her status as a *cause célèbre*. It tells the story of a child from the Caucasus who is taken by her parents into exile, first to Moscow, then to Finland (the book has also appeared in a Finnish translation), and then to Norway. Their application to stay in Norway is denied, and they take up a life in hiding as 'illegal' migrants; thus the inner paradox of the book's title. The child Marie goes on to complete studies in Norway, all the time without a stay permit, and to write her book, which can be read rhetorically as part of an application for residence. As the title suggests, she is Norwegian, through her upbringing and education.

In Amelie's passage from Finland to Norway, the entropic erasure of the limits between snow and sky is exchanged for the sublime – but strikingly reassuring – juxtaposition of sea and mountains, pointing to similar evocations in other migration narratives, such as those of Romeo Gill and Sara Azmeh Rasmussen, which I will address below. However, as a highly affective and symbolic mobilisation of stereotypes of Northernness, Amelie's description is surprisingly atypical. Most migration narratives like hers published in Norwegian, dealing with first- or so-called 1.5-generation migrants (born abroad but growing up in Norway), tend to avoid images and stereotypes of the North. Whilst staging Northernness explicitly, Amelie's crossing also suggests possible reasons for that lack of Northernness in other texts. Texts based around border-crossings do not look only for the strange; they may also look for the familiar. Indeed, they may also look in other, less stereotypical directions.

In the following, I will examine a selection of novels and autobiographical testimonies published originally in Norwegian and dealing with migrant border-crossings to Norway from other countries, with an eye for how they imagine or image the North – or fail to do so. These readings allow me to bring together two research interests, one focusing on Northern and Arctic discourses, and the second on border poetics – and especially how published migration narratives figure borders and thus produce different conceptions of bordering.

Discourse analysis typically focuses on fixed and reproduced topoi in textual and other forms of discourse (Wodak, 2001), in the form of either motifs or underlying meanings. Interpretation takes place either before or after analysis of discourse, rather than being seen as an integral part of discourse. Border poetics however attempts to understand how texts (con) figure borders on the level of both what is being represented by the text and how it is being represented (Schimanski, 2006). Unlike discourse analysis, it assumes a crossing between textual levels or surfaces. Taking part in a 'border turn' in the human sciences, border poetics does not assume that borders – whether of texts, countries or other phenomena – are purely secondary effects of what they contain (Schimanski, 2017: 63–4).

Border poetics is thus more concerned with the processuality and hermeneutics of narrative than discourse analysis. Hermeneutics is here seen as a cognitive process of reading which circles or switches between different levels of a text: unfamiliar and familiar, part and whole, text and context, present and past, experience and expectation etc. In a hermeneutic process, answers are always seen as provisional, leading to new questions. Hermeneutics first developed as a scientific method for interpreting old and obscure texts, but, within philosophical hermeneutics, interpretation has come to be seen as a part of being (Gadamer, 1990). Not only scholars engage with hermeneutics but also, for example, migrants, as they negotiate the borderscapes they are crossing by constantly creating provisional interpretations of the unfamiliar.

The material of discourse analysis consists of inventories of set images, with 'images' here not necessarily understood as being visual (cf. Beller, 2007: 4). In literary studies, and especially comparative literature, the study of such inventories was pioneered by imagology, the study of literary images of national characters. Imagology has long had an interest in images of the North, though, unlike more recent studies of Arctic and Northern discourses, it has primarily focused on stereotypical images of Northern peoples rather than Northern landscapes (Arndt, 2007; Leerssen, 2016). Classical imagology, marred by Eurocentrism and methodological nationalism (Blažević, 2014: 355–6; Leerssen, 2016; Perner, 2013), has been overtaken by colonial discourse analysis along with gender studies and critical race studies. In the twenty-first century, a new, post-classical imagology – potentially more transdisciplinary, posthuman, intersectional and global (Blažević, 2012; Leerssen, 2016), informed by actor-network theory and discourse analysis (Blažević, 2012, 2014) – points not only towards a dethroning of 'character' as the central figure and 'nation' as the defining frame of the other but also towards a broader 'border turn' in imagology (already hinted at in Leerssen, 1993). Attempts to explain the creation of stereotypes and contradictory images, along with the intimate relationship between images of the other and images of the self (Leerssen, 2016), have necessitated a more processual paradigm, seeing images as a product of the in-between. Developments in imagology connecting it up to translation studies and migration studies (Blioumi and Beller, 2007) – fields in which borders are central, making them difficult to handle within national containers – have prepared the way for appreciating images of both self and other as provisional, interdependent and changing answers (Leerssen, 2016: 22) within the circular interlocutions of a hermeneutic process (Blažević, 2012: 109–11; Świderska, 2013). In terms of border poetics analysis, a migrant will constantly depend on previous – and create new – images of the other and the self, repeatedly crossing epistemological borders (Schimanski, 2006: 56), as they journey through a geopolitical and cultural borderscape.

My challenge here in combining border poetics with Northern or Arctic discourse analysis – necessary, given the image-making involved in border-crossing – is to mobilise the metaphorical potential images of the North, without losing sight of the articulations and entanglements between different surfaces that border poetics make visible. Various border figurations and configurations typical of narratives of border-crossings complicate the border, making it difficult to sustain essentialist and 'boxed-off' images, such as those connected with historical discourses of the North as a sublime place. In migration literature, stereotypes are often relativised and mixed. For the pioneer of border theory Georg Simmel (1997: 141), the border is ideally a manifestation of symbolic differences, but difference posits the possibility of comparison and thus also sameness. The repetitive form that border-crossings often take as they are disseminated across wider topographical and temporal areas – such as Amelie's multiple journeys connecting the Caucasus with Norway – also causes similarity and chiastic mixing, as the migrant border-crossing is dispersed and repeated along the way. Typically, border-crossings involve a paradoxical and chiastic switching of places and supposedly opposed principals.

The violence of the snowball

In *Min drøm om frihet* (2009) ('My Dream of Freedom'), Amal Aden tells the story of how she grew up as a war orphan and child soldier on the outskirts of Mogadishu, and travelled to Norway as a child refugee, slowly becoming integrated in Norwegian society. Apart from the general sense of Norway being an economically rich society and part of the 'global north', there are very few stereotypical images of Northernness in the book.

The image of the North as a place of snow and cold, however, is presented during the second half of the book, when Amal has undergone a downward spiral into drugs, violence and crime after her migration to Norway, and makes friends with a Norwegian woman, Liv, signalling an upward movement to social integration: 'Liv laughs at me when I say I have "snowfright". I think it is scary to walk when there is snow on the ground, but Liv says I must just get used to it. Each time we go for a walk, I learn new words, today I have learnt the words *park* and *minus degrees*. At the same time as I learn new words, I learn a lot about the country. Today I learnt that it is not allowed to carry a knife in Norway.'[10]

Here the narrative focuses on prominent stereotypes of Northernness connected to winterliness. Amal has not only crossed from Somalia to Norway but she is also in the process of crossing the borders of the Norwegian language. The narratives involve a stereotype of Nordic societies, i.e., the people of the North, as well-regulated: knife-carrying is not allowed in Norway. In practice, however, Amal's life has been the opposite of well-regulated, her main problem being that she was not able to leave violence behind in war-torn Somalia. She has found violence, and the clan structures behind it, repeated in the Somalian diaspora in Oslo; like many migrants, she finds herself caught in an extended borderscape after crossing territorial borders.

One previous mention of snow in the book marks snow not as a strange difference between Somalia and Norway but rather as a sign of violence, in the form of the snowballs her classmate Sam – a migrant from the Gambia – throws at her in the playground, to the amusement of three girls standing watching. Sam, who 'tries to be one of the toughest boys in class',[11] gets his comeuppance after school. Amal stands in wait for him and gives him a bloody nose with a punch of her fist, telling him in Somali: 'leave the snow on the ground from now on'.[12] What might be seen as a sign of Northernness and difference is relativised, and instead indicates a similarity created by the violence Amal experiences in Norway and that she has experienced previously in Somalia. Even though the violence in those two different places might take quite different forms, Aden figures them as a repetition and a chiastic mixing across the border, in a negative version of Amelie's repetition of Caucasian mountains in Norway.

The green North

Romeo Gill's novel *Harjeet* (2008) describes the physical and cultural journey of Harjeet, a fictional Indian work migrant, travelling to Norway from India in 1973 (123), and, according to the novel, the first migrant to move into Åssiden, part of the city of Drammen (171). His story is told by his son Akas, and the book ends with Harjeet being joined by his wife and two sons, arriving at Oslo Airport four years after Harjeet has established himself in Norway. The pedagogical, realist style of Gill's book helps give Harjeet's story both before and after his migration to Norway in ethnographic detail, focusing also on expectations about meeting the Other, often fixed in the form of images, before actually experiencing it. The sequel, *Ung Mann i Nytt Land* (2011) ('Young Man in a New Land'), tells the story of Harjeet's sons as they grow up in Norway, with a special focus on Akas, who is the retrospective adult narrator and fictive author of the books.

From the point of view of Indian Punjab, Norway is hidden behind an epistemological border. A lack of images causes characters such as Akas's mother Kaur to grasp for geography books (Gill, 2008: 108). But even after Harjeet arrives in Norway, the North is often subsumed into more general images of the 'Global North'. In accordance with the tendency of realist and mimetic modes to box off and essentialise cultures, the narrative focuses on generalised differences between rural India and a rich, modern and Utopian Norway of cars, factories, tall buildings and work (Gill, 2008:

89–90). Added to this are images of Norwegians as calm, kind and asocial, and speaking a strange language (Gill, 2008: 139). But perhaps surprisingly to Norwegian readers, the Northernness of Norway is not necessarily presented as whiteness and cold, but by another colour: green. For Harjeet, the greenness of Norway in the summer is a symbol of why Norway is better than India (Gill, 2008: 139, 209), and when the brothers Akas and Suraj experience green summer grass for the first time (21), it is as miraculous as their first encounter with snow (57–9).

Norway's tall buildings, especially the apartment blocks in which the family live, are part of Akas's 'vertical axis': 'He had heard that everybody in Norway had cars, and that they lived in houses which were higher that the water tower on the adda [the centre of the village], and that was at least twenty metres tall. Akas had never actually been so high up in the air.'[13] This vertical axis brings together a series of motifs initially established in descriptions of flying a kite during his childhood in India, and wishing he could fly like the kite to school rather than taking the bus (Gill, 2008: 17–19). This axis points upwards, towards the kite, towards the amazingly tall buildings in Norway (Gill, 2008: 16, 24, 160) and to his in-between gaze from above when crossing the border to Norway when arriving there in an aeroplane (251). But it also points downwards, to the dangerous water of the river of his Indian childhood, where his mother has heard that several people have drowned; in Punjab, Akas has seen the sea only in a picture in a book, and wonders whether it is possible to swim in it in Norway, in which case he wishes to learn to swim (Gill, 2008: 163–4). In Norway, deep water and the fear of drowning are slowly replaced by symbols of liberation. Suraj and Akas remember the dangers of the river on the way from the airport, when they see for the first time the Drammen river and fjord of their new home in Norway (Gill, 2011: 10). Later, Akas learns the exotic skill of swimming, a part of his integration into Norwegian society. But the sea also become a symbol of split identity following his break with his father Harjeet, with the book ending as Akas contemplates 'the sea foaming'[14] in a painting by his girlfriend Ida: 'He saw himself being thrown against the rocks which stood up out of the sea, again and again he saw his own body being thrown against the cliff. It will be a struggle against the tide and the waves, he thought, but this struggle will be my struggle'.[15] A topographical border between land and sea, connected to the motif of a transgressive, cross-cultural relationship, symbolises Akas's repeated struggle for survival as a Sikh living in Norway. Akas has just closed the door on his brother Suraj, who has accused him of becoming 'too Norwegian'[16] by rejecting his family, but at the same time reminds him that for Norwegians he will 'always be a brown Indian'.[17] Akas responds by placing himself in a hybrid space, emphasising his individual responsibility: 'I have never thought of being anything but a brown Indian ... I do not know why, but I feel that I have to manage by myself, I must do things in my own way.'[18]

The symbolism of the painting reminds us, as Franco Moretti has stated, that '[n]ear the border, figurality goes up' (1998: 45). Akas's 'vertical axis' constantly disturbs the horizontal border-crossing and the realist mode, and brings with it a corresponding ambivalence of images. Significantly, as the second novel ends, he immerses himself in aesthetic culture; the images of Ida's paintings, and the narratives of Knut Hamsun's novel of a transnational migrant, *August* (1930), part of the 'Landstrykere' ('Wayfarers') trilogy.

In the same manner as Aden's autobiographical text, Gill's second novel focuses repeatedly on similarities between India and Norway, finding the familiar in the strange. On the bus taking them from the airport, described at the very beginning of the book, Akas meets a strong visual difference as he 'studie[s] the other passengers. Some had golden-brown skin, other were so white that he had never seen anything like it. Not all were blonde, but none had as black hair as he did. He got a nasty feeling in his stomach.'[19] However, the unease this perceived 'Nordic' racial difference induces is quickly allayed by similarity after he sees and smells the fields that lie 'like open plains towards the fjord':[20] 'There was a smell here which he had known many times before, but never like today. The smell of newly harvested grain, the same as from the fields around the village at home. The clump in his stomach disappeared. We are at least on the same planet.'[21]

This movement from difference to similarity and from unease to ease is also present in Akas'd first forewarnings of snow, also placed directly at the beginning – and initial textual border – of the book. Harjeet explains the greenhouses they can see from the bus: 'Since the fields are covered by metres of snow in the winter, they grow cucumbers and tomatoes and other vegetables inside these greenhouses'.[22] A few pages later he explains to Akas why all the houses have sloped roofs: '"It's so the houses do not collapse when it snows in winter." He [Harjeet] was used to houses with sloped roofs from Kashmir, where he had been stationed as a border guard in the military.'[23] Suddenly, Norway is not the sole repository of snow and Northern-ness: snow is also typical of a Northern, mountainous part of the Asian subcontinent, in a moment which bears comparison with the border-crossing scene in Amelie's *Ulovlig norsk*.

Gill's novels figure images across the border in a chiastic fashion, with polar oppositions constantly being reversed and relativised. In Norway, Harjeet feels that he has been treated 'like being from a lower-caste family',[24] but as a respected man when he visits India from Norway (Gill, 2008: 200, 210). His wife Kaur worries about receiving strange looks when she wears her Indian clothes in Norway (Gill, 2011: 15, 50), whilst in India she is admired for her beauty (Gill, 2008: 82). Indians not only have images of Norway but they also have images of the images Norwegians have of Indians; these can put into question their own positive image of Norway and of the North. As we have seen, Akas assimilates to Norwegian cultural norms, but knows that he can never be seen as Norwegian. Harjeet idealises Norway, but is critical when his sons shows signs of becoming 'too Norwegian',[25] thinking they can live by Norwegian rather than Indian rules (Gill, 2011: 271). India is repeated in Norway, but the Norwegian is also repeated in Indian. The images of both are chiastically articulated upon one another and cannot be separated.

Polar hallucinations

My final example is Sara Azmeh Rasmussen's semi-autobiographical novel *Skyggeferden* (2013 [2012]) ('The Shadow Journey'). Unlike Amelie's, Aden's and Gill's books, it describes the border-crossing not of a child migrant but rather that of a young woman – her name, 'Sara Azmeh Rasmussen' (Rasmussen, 2013: 428), is revealed in full at the very end of the book – who after a troubled upbringing in Syria converts to Christianity and seeks refugee status in Norway. She becomes integrated into Norwegian society, but is not happy; the book ends after a suicide attempt.

As in Gill's books, Rasmussen's protagonist combines the horizontal movement of migration with a strong vertical imaginary, including fantasies of flying: as a child, on a bicycle, in a school bus or on a flying carpet (Rasmussen, 2013: 7, 10–11, 16). From an early age, Sara feels limited by gender roles, along with social and religious rules, and wishes to cross the boundaries they bring with them. An early image of borders and verticality involves looking at a jasmine bush 'higher than me'[26] within the fenced courtyard of a church. She is too scared to go in through the open gates of the courtyard to get closer to the bush, but a priest tells her she can come inside when she likes (Rasmussen, 2013: 8, see also 236–7). Her wish to play with the boys at school rather than the girls makes her an outsider, and she begins to spend time in a border space: 'On one side of the schoolyard was a wall. In the breaks I balanced on the edge of the wall.'[27] This image is recreated in the photograph taken by the author that is reproduced on the front cover of the novel (see Figure 10.1), showing a child dressed in T-shirt and shorts walking along the top of a concrete wall, arms outstretched for balance. Later, Sara uses the image of balancing on the narrow edge of a wall to explain to the Norwegian police her difficulties with living with the cultural contradictions in Syria (Rasmussen, 2013: 290). Soon her urge to inhabit and move across boundaries is combined with images of mountains

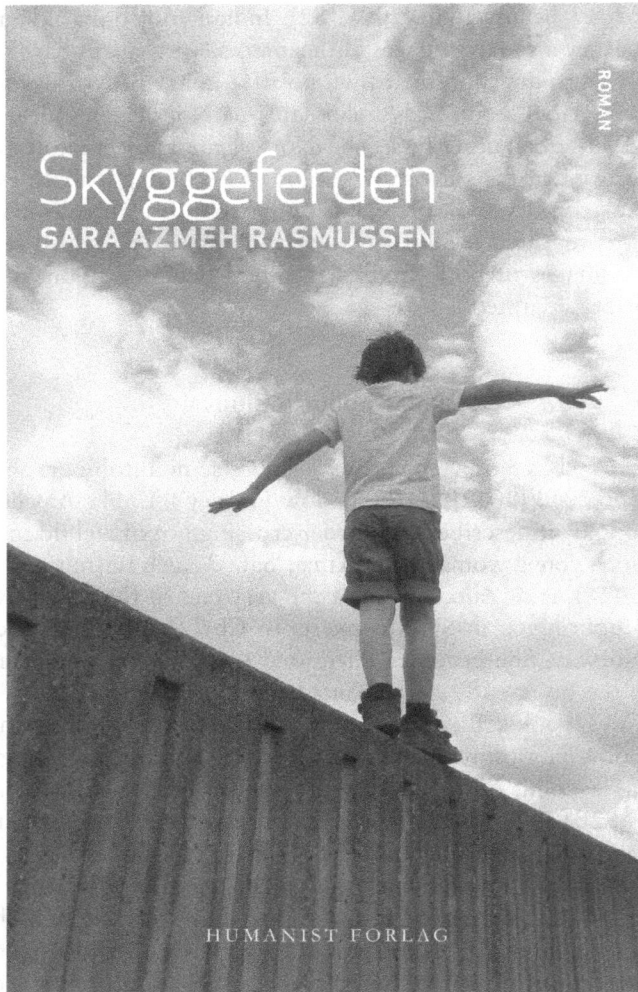

10.1 Front cover of Sara Azmeh Rasmussen's *Skyggeferden* (2013 [2012]).

(Rasmussen, 2013: 21). The vertical axis, as in Gill's novels, also stretches downwards, involving images of deep water (Rasmussen, 2013: 25, 232), drowning (362, 234) and falling (85, 361, 362). When Sara attempts suicide, it is by trying to drown (Rasmussen, 2013: 425–6).

Sara also connects images of flying to national borders, which are crossed by the wind: 'In the spiral notebook I once wrote that the wind did not have a nationality. It crosses the borders of countries without being stopped at control points. It did not have a passport or a proof of identity. It was everywhere, crossing the globe's latitudes and caressing both white and dark cheeks with the same fresh warmth.'[28] Borders being figured as 'latitudes' indicate that they are primarily borders between South and North (despite Sara coming from the Middle East). But after arriving in Norway, Sara realises that wind is not the same everywhere, falling back on contrastive imaging of a new country with a country of origin we also find in Romeo Gill's novels: 'But I wrote that before I had myself explored the world. The wind was alien in Bergen. I had been mistaken. The wind was no longer mild and warm, but howling and cold. I froze, buttoned up my coat and sat with my arms crossed.'[29] Her surprise may be seen as odd, given that she later tells a Norwegian friend that she has learned at school 'that winter in this country is long and cold' (Rasmussen, 2013: 288, in English in original). Sara needs experience to understand the implications of pre-learned images. Being in Norway shows her that illustrations in children's books of pine forests and the sea are not just exoticising fantasies (Rasmussen, 2013: 251). Like Amelie, she feels there is something fairy-tale-like about Norway; but it is not a magical place, rather she is 'in the middle of a sad fairy-tale',[30] invoking a typical image of the North as melancholic (Leerssen, 2019: 18). Magic is involved however: oxymoronically, 'the distant became, as if by magic, close'.[31]

At one point, long after Sara's move to Norway as a refugee, Rasmussen's book utilises a very specific image of Northernness and a common 'nodal point' (a signifier that structures a particular discourse, see Laclau and Mouffe, 2001: 113) in Arctic discourses, the North Pole. After the break-up of her marriage to a Norwegian man she experiences a series of hallucinatory images during sleepless nights, featuring falling off cliffs or down slides, houseplants dying, a threatening forest, oozing liquids, drowning in a car in the sea (Rasmussen, 2013: 361–3), and a journey to the North Pole: 'I am grown up. My mother says we are going to the North Pole, that I must go there, that I am going there. Only she and I are on the enormous ship. When we arrive at the North Pole, she has disappeared without a trace. I get off on to the ice. The ship disappears. It is big, white, empty.'[32] This entropic and melancholic vision of whiteness and emptiness combines on the one hand a Northern imagery conveying a non-pleasurable sublime (in her mental state, she does not have the safety of distance) and on the other a border figuration of a liminal state at the edge of the world, bordering on to infinity. The image of the enormous, empty ship disappearing at the pole is sublime, absurd and fantastic, and comes close to the border figure Patricia García describes as 'horizontal vertigo' in Chapter 2 above. The North is a place of Arctic ice and whiteout.

The imaginary journey with her domineering mother to the Arctic is also an image of migration to the North, and refers back to earlier border figurations in the book. In Syria, the mountains are a space of liberation for Sara and refuge from her problems growing up as a woman in a society with strict norms where gender and sexuality are concerned. Trips with her father to a mountain farm near the border to Israel (Rasmussen, 2013: 395) signify a borderlessness, a place without barriers. '*The stream flowed freely in the open landscape in the mountains. The fresh wind met no hindrances. It was open around me. I could spin round and round and round. My hands met no walls. My gaze ran all the way to the horizon*'.[33] As in Amelie's book, the mountains cause the body to engage in a turning motion, suggesting a heady freedom. The horizon does not limit so much as suggest an unreachable romantic sublime. Sara daydreams of setting out like some legendary hero – 'Abu Batuta, Aladdin or some Arabian knight'[34] – to find the origins of the stream, which she imagines as 'the magical lake I knew must be at the top of the mountain',[35] and she repeatedly sets out towards the mountain. However, she never reaches it, as the following passage confirms:

> However far I went, the mountain moved away the whole time. Its top, which was covered by a white layer of snow, and sometimes white clouds, must have been a hiding-place for robbers, or perhaps even aliens. It must have been that they moved the mountain just as I was about to reveal their dwelling-place. For I walked for hours, for whole days, and it could not be so completely impossible to reach the foot of the mountain, at least! But I never arrived there.[36]

The mountains are a place of no rules or limits (Rasmussen, 2013: 20–1). Their boundlessness is paralleled, if negatively, in the entropic borderlessness of the North Pole in her later hallucination.

The Arctic is a place of mountainousness, and the image of the North Pole has often been associated with that of mountains, whether because of its Alps-like cold and snowy conditions, its status as being at the top of the world (Schimanski and Spring, 2003), historical imagery of mountains or volcanoes at the North Pole, or the verticality of the image of a pole. But the echo of the snow-topped Syrian mountain in the Arctic parallels also the chiastic mixings between Norway and origin countries involving mountains in Amelie's and Gill's books, if not in such a comforting fashion.

As a child trying to reach a magical snow-clad mountain, Sara never gives up seeking liberation from the limitations of her Damascus upbringing: 'In spite of this, I never gave up. I just had to delay it to some other time. I had to think up a better plan.'[37] The mountain is an object of desire, and snow is something she has loved as a child (Rasmussen, 2013: 130). As an adult migrant in Norway, however, she has reached the snowy North Pole in her imagination, but finds herself alone, in a mountainless flatness, with nowhere to go. In Norway, snow has become an ambivalent force: visiting a plant nursery, she imagines it as 'the land of summer, a piece of summer preserved inside a limited area in the middle of the white and snow-heavy landscape'.[38] Only momentarily, when she feels comparatively secure, does Sara see snow as neutral. As a student studying history of religion and Arabic in the same building where I wrote parts of this chapter – 'at the northernmost border of the campus' of the University of Oslo – she watches from a café window as 'people walked and bicycled in drizzle, rain, snow and sunshine'.[39]

The motif of walking towards a potential endlessness is repeated in Norway – for example after Sara drives a car by herself for the first time, then walks on a pier and looks out at the horizon (Rasmussen, 2013: 410) – but is also treated in an ambivalent manner. Just before news of her father's death in Syria, Sara remembers the stream that previously promised her limitlessness as a child, but now becomes an image of loss: throwing sticks into it and following them (downhill, away from the mountains), she must always give up as they disappear. The sticks continued 'to float downwards towards a point I never managed to discover. I always had to stop somewhere and see the stick disappearing. The terrain became too difficult to move in. But the water in the stream ran unhindered. Towards a point I never reached.'[40] This version of the unreachable point is unknown and unimagined, lacking the romanticism of the mountain with its magical lake on the summit. Continually, her images of liberation are revised and negated during her life in Norway.

The whiteout image of the North Pole also points forwards towards the end of Rasmussen's book and the final scenes in a hospital, after a suicide attempt, when Sara takes pills and jumps into open water as mist closes in. She awakens in the intensive care unit: 'It was white. A white ceiling. At her side was a white curtain, which was drawn.'[41] She is given a room at a psychiatric institution: 'The walls were white'.[42]

Mists and whiteouts, typical phenomena in the polar regions, are usually experienced as disruptive spaces without reference points (cf. Frost, 2011a, 2011b). The whiteout could be called a 'meta-image', being a place without images, or a space in which distances cannot be judged, making any images present difficult to situate and thus impossible to understand properly. In Rasmussen's book, such spaces are paradoxically seen as limits to Sara's freedom rather than spaces of liberation. The text ends with a description of the view from her window on to a car park below. The entropic whiteness of her room is transformed into barriers: 'On the ground, white lines were painted. Straight lines.'[43] Read against the positive image of the snow-topped mountain in Syria and the negative whiteness of the room and the parking lines, the image of North represented by the empty, open, white borderspace of the North Pole becomes ambivalent, both bordered and borderless.

Images on borders, images as borders

As in Amelie's, Aden's and Gill's texts, Rasmussen's novel presents images of the North at parts of a process of crossing the border and negotiating the borderscape. Contradictory images worry the border to the North, creating continuities with the 'global South' and life before migration. Chiastic switchings of North and South, circling disorientations, entropic whiteouts, and liberating and destructive verticalities figure the border as a place in which migrants create new images of the North at different points of their physical and symbolic journeys.

The imagologists Aglaia Blioumi and Manfred Beller write that it is 'the representation of migrants' experiences as they cross political, linguistic, cultural, religious, and social frontiers, which evokes images, prejudices, and stereotypes about Others in particular' (2007: 366). For migrants, images of the Other become part of hermeneutic processes predicated on narratives of bodily experience. Each border figuration of the North is subject to redefinition as the migrant continues their extended border-crossing, constituting a temporary 'tidemark' (Green, 2018). The specific combinations of images and narratives in Amelie's and Aden's performative testimonials, in Gill's ethnographic pedagogies and in Rasmussen's (post)modernist life-writing each constitute a partition of the sense-able (cf. Rancière, 2004) in the borderscape, making experience visible and invisible in diverse ways. Each text in different ways includes its own articulation of the narrative and hermeneutic configurations of images in its narrative, since they all tell the story of migrants who become writers, and also involve forms of per-formative self-reflection typical of migrant testimonies (also in other mediums – see Karina Horsti and Ilaria Tucci in Chapter 11 below).

Migration narratives come from many different contexts; they can ascribe contradictory values of beauty or fear to border-crossings, and convey diverging affects, whether they be of reassurance, integration, liberation or melancholy, as in the texts examined here. Approaching the ambivalence of images when crossing borders into an entropic and sublime North through a border poetics informed by post-classical imagology points to the status of images not just as something often involved in border-crossings but as borders in their own right: epistemological borders to be negotiated in bodily and hermeneutic processes. Such epistemological borders 'distribute the sensible' (Rancière, 2004) of the migratory situation according to the way they figure borders as mixings, as verticalities and horizontalities, as swirling disorientations or as entropies. Analysis of such figurations can contribute to our understanding of the binarities, hybridities and aliena-tions that have for so long been central to post-colonial approaches to migration.

Acknowledgements

Part of the research for this article was carried out as part of the EU FP7 project EUBORDERSCAPES (FP7-SSH-2011–1, Area 4.2.1, project 290775) Working Package 10 'Border-Crossing and Cultural Production'. I would like to thank Ulrike Spring for her careful reading and comments.

Notes

1 'Den hvite snøen går fortsatt i ett med himmelen' (Amelie, 2010: 16). My translations from the Norwegian texts of the novels and autobiographies throughout.
2 'Det er natt, og det eneste lyspunktet er snøen' (Amelie, 2010: 17).
3 'husene og bensinstasjonene vi kjører forbi, virker kalde, uhyggelige og ensomme' (Amelie, 2010: 16).
4 'er enda verre å tenke på enn den grensen vi snart skal krysse ulovlig. Hvem vil hjelpe oss her?' (Amelie, 2010: 16)
5 'frykten og fortvilelsen' (Amelie, 2010: 17).
6 'kommer det et skilt: "Norge"' (Amelie, 2010: 17).
7 'Hjertet banker fortere jo færre kilometer er igjen' (Amelie, 2010: 17).
8 'Vi kjører gjennom! Vi *er* i Norge! [...] Kan det virkelig gå så bra? [...] Vi er virkelig i Norge!' (Amelie, 2010: 17, emphasis original).
9 'Jeg stirrer forbløffet ut av vinduet. Naturen har forandret seg så fort, nå er den rystende vakker. Fjell, fjell, fjell, fjell, høye fjell! Akkurat som hjemme i Kaukasus! Jeg snur meg rastløst i bilen, ser opp og ned og til høyre og venstre og ut av bakvinduet. Endelig ser jeg fjell igjen, fjell som har vært en del av livet mitt fra fødselen av. Slike hadde de ikke i Moskva. Heller ikke i Finland. Eventyrlige, majestiske fjell! / Noen kilometer senere ser vi til og med vann. Jeg tenker at jeg alltid har drømt om å bo et sted hvor det var både fjell og hav ...' (Amelie, 2010: 17, ellipsis in original).
10 'Liv ler av meg når jeg sier at jeg er 'snøredd'. Jeg syns det er skummelt å gå når det ligger snø på bakken, men Liv sier at det må jeg bare venne meg til. Hver gang vi går tur, lærer jeg meg nye ord, i dag har jeg lært *park* og *kuldegrader*. Samtidig som jeg lærer nye ord, lærer jeg også mye om landet. I dag fikk jeg vite at det ikke er lov til å gå med kniv i Norge' (Aden, 2009: 94).
11 'prøver å være en av de tøffeste guttene i klassen' (Aden, 2009: 42).
12 'La snøen ligge på bakken fra nå av' (Aden, 2009: 43).
13 'Han hadde hørt at alle i Norge hadde bil, og at de bodde i hus som var høyere enn vanntårnet på adda, og det var i hvert fall tjue meter høyt. Akas hadde faktisk aldri vært så høyt oppe i lufta noen gang' (Gill, 2008: 160).
14 'havet som bruste' (Gill, 2011: 314).
15 'Han så seg selv bli slengt mot fjellet som stakk opp fra havet, igjen og igjen så han sin egen kropp bli slengt mot klippen. Det blir en kamp mot tidevannet og bølgene, tenkte han, men den kampen blir min kamp' (Gill, 2011: 313).
16 'for norsk' (Gill, 2011: 312).

17 'alltid være en brun inder' (Gill, 2011: 312).
18 'Jeg har ikke tenkt å være noe annet enn en brun inder … Jeg vet ikke hvorfor,
    men jeg føler at jeg er nødt til å klare meg selv, jeg må gjøre tingene på min
    måte' (Gill, 2011: 312).
19 'studer[er] de andre passasjerne. Noen var gyllebrune i huden, andre var så hvite
    at han aldri hadde sett maken. Ikke alle var blonde, men ingen hadde like svart
    hår som ham. Han fikk en ekkel følelse i magen' (Gill, 2011: 9).
20 'som åpne sletter mot fjorden' (Gill, 2011: 9).
21 'Det var en lukt her han hadde kjent mange ganger før, men aldri slik som i dag.
    Lukten av nyslått korn, som fra markene rundt landsbyen hjemme. Klumpen i
    magen forsvant. Vi er i hvert fall på samme planet, tenkte han' (Gill, 2011: 9).
22 'Siden jordene er dekket av metervis med snø om vinteren, dyrker de agurker
    og tomater og andre grønnsaker inni disse glasshusene' (Gill, 2011: 10).
23 '"Det er for at husene ikke skal rase sammen når det snør om vinteren." Han
    var vant til hus med skråtak fra Kashmir, hvor han hadde vært stasjonert som
    grensevakt i militæret' (Gill, 2011: 14).
24 'som fra en lavkastefamilie' (Gill, 2008: 251).
25 'for norske' (Gill, 2011: 130).
26 'høyere enn meg' (Rasmussen, 2013: 8).
27 'På den ene siden av skolegården fantes det en mur. I friminuttene balanserte
    jeg på murkanten' (Rasmussen, 2013: 12–13).
28 'I spiralboken skrev jeg en gang at vind ikke hadde nasjonalitet. Den krysser
    landegrenser uten å bli stoppet ved kontrollpunkter. Den hadde ikke pass eller
    identitetsbevis. Den var overalt, krysset klodens breddegrader og strøk både
    hvit og mørke kinn med den samme friske varmen' (Rasmussen, 2013: 246).
29 'Men det skrev jeg før jeg selv hadde utforsket verden. Vinden var fremmed i
    Bergen. Jeg hadde tatt feil. Vinden var ikke lenger mild og varm, men hylende
    og kald. Jeg frøs, kneppet jakken og satt med armene i kors' (Rasmussen, 2013:
    246).
30 'Midt i et trist eventyr' (Rasmussen, 2013: 251).
31 'Det fjerne ble, som ved et trylleslag, nært' (Rasmussen, 2013: 251).
32 'Jeg er voksen. Moren min sier at vi skal til Nordpolen, at jeg må dit, at jeg
    skal dit. På det enorme skipet er det bare meg og henne. Når vi ankommer
    Nordpolen, er hun sporløst borte. Jeg går av på isen. Skipet forsvinner. Det er
    stort, hvitt, tomt' (Rasmussen, 2013: 362).
33 *Bekken rant fritt i det åpne landskapet på fjellet. Den friske vinden møtte ingen
    hindringer. Det var åpent rundt meg. Jeg kunne snurre rundt og rundt og rundt.
    Hendene møtte ingen murer. Blikket fløt hele veien til horisonten'* (Rasmussen,
    2013: 107, italics in original).
34 'Abu Batuta, Aladdin eller en arabisk ridder' (Rasmussen, 2013: 21).
35 'den magiske innsjøen jeg visste måtte finnes på toppen av fjellet' (Rasmussen,
    2013: 21).
36 'Uansett hvor langt jeg gikk, flyttet fjellet seg bort hele tiden. Toppen, som var
    dekket med et hvitt lag av snø, og iblandt hvite skyer, var sikkert et skjulested
    for røvere, eller kanskje til og med romvesen. Det måtte være slik at de flyttet
    fjellet når jeg var rett ved å avsløre tilholdsstedet deres. For jeg gikk jo i timer,

i hele dager, og det kunne bare ikke være så umulig å nå foten av fjellet, i det minste! Men jeg kom aldri frem' (Rasmussen, 2013: 21).

37 'Jeg ga meg alikevel ikke. Jeg måtte bare utsette det. Jeg måtte finne på et bedre plan' (Rasmussen, 2013: 21).

38 'sommerlandet, et stykke sommer som var konservert innenfor et avgrenset område midt i det hvite og snøtyngede landskapet' (Rasmussen, 2013: 366).

39 'ved universitetsområdets nordlige grense'; '[f]olk gikk og syklet i yr, regn, snø og solskinn' (Rasmussen, 2013: 384).

40 'å flyte nedover mot et punkt jeg aldri klarte å oppdage. Et sted måtte jeg stoppe og se pinnen forsvinne. Terrenget ble for vanskelig å bevege seg i. Men vannet i bekken rant unhindret. Mot et punkt jeg aldri nådde' (Rasmussen, 2013: 311).

41 'Det var hvitt. Et hvitt tak. På siden var et hvitt forheng som var dratt for' (Rasmussen, 2013: 426).

42 'Veggene var hvite' (Rasmussen, 2013: 428).

43 'På bakken var det malt hvite linjer. Rette linjer' (Rasmussen, 2013: 429).

References

Aden, A. (2009) *Min drøm om frihet: En selvbiografisk fortelling*. Oslo: Aschehoug.

Aguirre, M. (2006) 'Liminal terror: The poetics of gothic space', in J. Benito and A.M. Manzanas (eds), *The Dynamics of the Threshold: Essays on Liminal Negotiations*. Madrid: Gateway Press, pp. 13–38.

Amelie, M. (2010) *Ulovlig norsk*. Oslo: Pax.

Arndt, A. (2007) 'North/South', in M. Beller and J. Leerssen (eds), *Imagology: The Cultural Construction and Literary Representation of National Characters: A Critical Survey*. Amsterdam: Rodopi, pp. 387–9.

Beller, M. (2007) 'Perception, image, imagology', in M. Beller and J. Leerssen (eds), *Imagology: The Cultural Construction and Literary Representation of National Characters: A Critical Survey*. Amsterdam: Rodopi, pp. 3–16.

Blažević, Z. (2012) 'Imagining historical imagology: Possibilities and perspectives of transdisciplinary/translational epistemology', in D. Dukić (ed.), *Imagology Today: Achievements, Challenges, Perspectives / Imagologie heute: Ergebnisse, Herausforderungen, Perspektiven*. Bonn: Bouvier, pp. 101–13.

Blažević, Z. (2014) 'Global challenge: The (im)possibilities of transcultural imagology', *Umjetnost riječi*, 58(3–4): 355–67.

Blioumi, A., and M. Beller (2007) 'Migration literature', in M. Beller and J. Leerssen (eds), *Imagology: The Cultural Construction and Literary Representation of National Characters: A Critical Survey*. Amsterdam: Rodopi, pp. 365–71.

Burke, E. (1990) *A Philosophical Enquiry*. Oxford: Oxford University Press.

Chartier, D. (2007) 'Towards a grammar of the idea of North: Nordicity, winterity', *Nordlit*, 22: 35–47.

Davidson, P. (2005) *The Idea of North*. London: Reaktion Books.

Derrida, J. (1992) *Acts of Literature*. Trans. and ed. D. Attridge. New York: Routledge.

Frost, S. (2011a) 'White in. White out. The noticeability of text: Conspicuous text', *Nordlit*, 23: 89–101.

Frost, S. (2011b) *Whiteout: Schneefälle und Weißeinbrüche in der Literatur ab 1800*. Bielefeld: transcript.

Gadamer, H.-G. (1990) *Hermeneutik I: Wahrheit und Methode: Grundzüge einer philosophischen Hermeneutik*. Tübingen: J.C.B. Mohr (Paul Siebeck).

Gill, R. (2008) *Harjeet: Roman*. Oslo: Oktober.

Gill, R. (2011) *Ung mann i nytt land: Roman*. Oslo: Oktober.

Green, S. (2018) 'Lines, traces and tidemarks: Further reflections on forms of the border', in O. Demetriou and R. Dimova (eds), *The Political Materialities of Borders: New Theoretical Directions*. Manchester: Manchester University Press, pp. 68–83.

Hamsun, K. (1930) *August*. Oslo: Gyldendal.

Laclau, E., and C. Mouffe (2001) *Hegemony and Socialist Strategy: Towards a Radical Democratic Politics*. London: Verso.

Leerssen, J. (1993) 'Europe as a set of borders', *Yearbook of European Studies*, 6: 1–14.

Leerssen, J. (2016) 'Imagology: On using ethnicity to make sense of the world', *Iberic@l*, 10: 13–31.

Leerssen, J. (2019) 'The North: A cultural stereotype between metaphor and racial essentialism', in S. Halink (ed.), *Northern Myths, Modern Identities: The Nationalisation of Northern Mythologies Since 1800*. Leiden: Brill, pp. 13–32.

Loomis, C.C. (1977) 'The Arctic sublime', in U.C. Knoepflmacher and G.B. Tennyson (eds), *Nature and the Victorian Imagination*. Berkeley: University of California Press, pp. 95–112.

Moretti, F. (1998) *Atlas of the European Novel 1800–1900*. London: Verso.

Perner, C. (2013) 'Dislocating imagology – And: How much of it can (or should) be retrieved?', in M. Munkelt, M. Schmitz, M. Stein and S. Stroh (eds), *Postcolonial Translocations: Cultural Representation and Critical Spatial Thinking*. Leiden: Brill, pp. 29–44.

Rancière, J. (2004) *The Politics of Aesthetics: The Distribution of the Sensible*. Trans. G. Rockhill. London: Continuum.

Rasmussen, S.A. (2013) *Skyggeferden*. Oslo: Humanist.

Ryall, A., J. Schimanski and H.H. Wærp (2010) 'Arctic discourses: An introduction', in A. Ryall, J. Schimanski and H.H. Wærp (eds), *Arctic Discourses*. Newcastle: Cambridge Scholars Publishing, pp. ix–xxii.

Schimanski, J. (2006) 'Crossing and reading: Notes towards a theory and a method', *Nordlit*, 19: 41–63.

Schimanski, J. (2015) 'Reading borders and reading as crossing borders', in I. Brandell, M. Carlson and Ö.A. Çetrez (eds), *Borders and the Changing Boundaries of Knowledge*. Stockholm: Swedish Research Institute in Istanbul, pp. 91–107.

Schimanski, J. (2017) 'Reading from the border', in J. Lothe (ed.), *The Future of Literary Studies*. Oslo: Novus, pp. 61–71.

Schimanski, J., and U. Spring (2003) 'Austro-Hungarian and other mountains in Arctic discourse', *Trans*, 15:10.

Simmel, G. (1997) 'The sociology of space', trans. M.R.D. Frisby, in D. Frisby and M. Featherstone (eds), *Simmel on Culture: Selected Writings*. London: Sage, pp. 137–70.

Spufford, F. (1996) *I May Be Some Time: Ice and the English Imagination*. London: Faber and Faber.

Świderska, M. (2013) 'Comparativist imagology and the phenomenon of strangeness', *CLCWeb*, 15(7): 1–8.

Wodak, R. (2001) 'The discourse-historical approach', in R. Wodak and M. Meyer (eds), *Methods of Critical Discourse Analysis*. London: Sage, pp. 63–94.

11

Performance of memory: testimonies of survival and rescue at Europe's border

Karina Horsti and Ilaria Tucci

Introduction

On 3 October 2013, an overcrowded fishing boat carrying mainly Eritrean refugees shipwrecked close to the Italian island of Lampedusa. At least 366 of the people on the boat died, but 155 people survived the approximately three-hour struggle in the sea until a group of Lampedusans on Vito Fiorino's leisure fishing boat *Gamar* heard the cries of the survivors. This disaster, like so many other mass deaths at the border, is accounted in public by the number of the victims: 366, 368 or 369 depending on the count; some bodies were found washed ashore later. The anti-racist organisation United added the figure 373 to its List of Deaths at Europe's borders that it has updated since 1993 on the basis of media reports (United, 2019). The differing numbers of the victims circulating in the public sphere are characteristic of the difficulty involved in the attempt to count border deaths. Despite the impossibility of presenting the exact numbers, exercises of border fatality metrics have proliferated. For civil society actors such as United, counting is a form of critical activism: quantifying demonstrates the *many*, the masses of the dead. In recent years, International Organization for Migration, Frontex and several academics have compiled lists and developed methods of counting border deaths. Quantification, in other words, has become the dominant way of representing border deaths.

Scholars have also criticised the nature of the knowledge acquired by fatality metrics. Martina Tazzioli (2015) argues that counting reinforces a governmental gaze at the border by creating a sense that the border and its fatality are merely issues of management. Such a gaze normalises death at the border, flattens the dead and does not pay attention to the families of the victims. Migrants – dead or alive – turn into objects of governmentality.

The knowledge produced by this gaze escapes humanity and social life that are lost or are in danger. Jennifer Hyndman (2007), who writes about fatality metrics in relation to the Iraq war, argues that metrics are incapable of accounting for the destruction of life as they produce a removed and distanced representation of border deaths.

Artists, authors and activists, in particular, have resisted such distanced representation prevalent in the academic, administrative and journalistic fields and sought alternative ways of producing knowledge concerning border deaths. Examples can be found, for instance, in the documentary *Sortir du noir* (Liénard and Jimenez, 2019), the ethnography-based theatre project *Miraculi* (Zagaria, 2016), and the art installation *Love Story* (Breitz, 2017). One of the methods suggested is critical optics, a macro lens that focuses on the specificities and details of single disasters, instead of treating border deaths as generic events. For example, Forensic Oceanography (Heller and Pezzani, 2012) is an artistic-forensic project that traces the particularities of disasters in the Mediterranean Sea. This project, like many others, seeks to gain knowledge through details and particularities rather than generalities. Here the testimonies by those who have intimately lived through a disaster at the border – by witnessing death and surviving the disaster – are central. Such approaches account for the embodied spatiality of the border zone and the consequences of the fatal border by listening.

In this chapter, we contribute to this alternative engagement with border deaths and argue that a key to critical knowledge is a careful and detailed telling and listening: the *work of listening*. For the Nobel literature laureate Svetlana Alexievich, who works with oral histories, history is found in little details, and the most interesting knowledge about life is in what she calls 'mysteries': the memories that appear when people speak to each other and tell stories of what has happened (Alexievich, 2017). Such work of listening, we argue, is a critical means of producing knowledge on the humanity of disasters at the border. Listening is not the only mode: seeing, being in places and doing things with those who have survived the border are equally significant ways of gaining embodied and situated knowledge. Seeing border deaths for what they are is obstructed because they appear as accidents, while, in fact, they are disasters that have been produced: they are results of a combination of political, structural, social and individual action and inaction (see, e.g., Albahari, 2015; De Genova, 2017).

The work of listening that we examine in this chapter is situated in the project *Remembering Lampedusa* (2017–18) during which a group of academics, media professionals, activists and refugees documented the disaster of 3 October 2013 by archiving testimonies and documents, and producing short documentary films based on the memories of the witnesses of the disaster. The project, in which the authors of this chapter also worked, is

predicated on a participatory approach involving academics, media professionals, activists, refugees and civil rescuers. The testimonies were edited
by Anna Blom (a professional film director), Adal Neguse (a human rights
activist) and Dominika Daubenbuchel (a professional movie editor) into
ten-minutes-long short films. The survivors watched the edits, commented
on them, and the editing team worked through the proposed changes. The
team discussed the role of 'participation' extensively, seeking to constantly
balance and horizontalise power between those with professional film-making
knowledge and those with knowledge and experience of survival and
witnessing.

From early on, the telling and listening of witness testimonies became
the core methodology for approaching the disaster and producing critical
knowledge about it: this is embodied knowledge that would bring the
humanity of the disaster to the foreground. To generate such knowledge,
Diana Taylor (2011: 272–3) has argued for the use of 'presence' as an active
verb (Sp. *presenciar*). Whilst being with the witness in the place of events,
seeing the sites where violence took place and the embodied feelings and
reactions of revisiting the place and the memory are central to 'presencing',
it also requires listening to what is being recalled and how the story is
performed. 'I participate not in the events but in his transmission of the
affect emanating from the events', Taylor (2011: 273) writes in the context
of presencing the testimony of a torture victim in Villa Grimaldi, Chile.

The *Remembering Lampedusa* project team began to document the stories
of four survivors and two Lampedusan civil responders by recording and
filming testimonies. However, witnessing and testimony turned out to be
complex group–individual practices. As soon as a witness starts telling about
the act of experiencing or seeing something, the act turns into a moral act
of bearing witness: an act of taking responsibility for the knowledge one
has gained (see e.g., Durham Peters, 2001; Felman, 2000; Tait, 2011; Zelizer,
2007). Whilst each testimony is unique, a personal account that cannot be
repeated by any other witness, it is also a critical and a political act: the
story is told for a particular reason and with implicit consequences in mind.
Moreover, a witness testimony is performative, as Shoshana Felman has
argued, it is a *'performance of a story'* (Felman, 2000: 41, emphasis original).
The story is shared with those who are present in person or who are imagined
to be present through mediation: its primary or secondary audience (de
Jong, 2018: 40–6). In the case of the documentary film project, while telling,
the witnesses knew that their story would be shared with the public. Furthermore, for those who become witnesses *through* mediation (both the
film-makers and the audiences of the films), witnessing is inherently 'a mode
of listening' (Wake, 2009: 82). So, for us, the argument that testimony is
a performance of a story is to highlight that testimony does not equal to

'real' but moves between 'pretend and new constructions of the "real"' (Taylor, 2016: 6). By using the term *performance*, we acknowledge that the notion has been used across different fields to describe and analyse a wide range of social behaviour. Our use of the term follows Diana Taylor's (2016) work, which highlights that performance creates effects and affects: it is important to analyse what performance does, 'what it allows us to see, to experience, and to theorize, and its complex relation to systems of power' (Taylor, 2016: 6). A testimony documents the disaster, and it does so in a specific relationship between those who tell and to whom they tell it, or imagine they tell it.

In this chapter, we argue that the witness testimonies of the Lampedusa disaster are 'performances of a story', and that careful attention needs to be paid to the complexities of the production of the 'performance'; this is the context in which the story is told and listened to. We analyse the process of creating a listening context as well as the relationships that are generated by the act of telling and listening the testimonies. This chapter explores how understanding testimony as performance of a story allows us to be more attentive to the contexts of telling and listening. Whilst we focus on telling and listening in this chapter, we acknowledge that other non-verbal communication and the place of the telling are equally important to the performance of the story. Specifically, we focus on the participatory production of the context in which telling and listening are made possible. These practices are crucial in developing a critical optic required to gain an alternative representation of the fatal border, one that is currently unavailable because of the dominating forms of representation, particularly the quantification of deaths.

We first discuss previous literature on witnessing and listening, and position the *Remembering Lampedusa* project in relation to these. In the analytical section, we examine how we created an empathetic listening context for the two witnesses, and how the relationship to the listeners shaped the performance of the story. Our aim is to examine witnessing and testimony as methods needed to gain knowledge of fatal border and its human consequences, and argue for the potentiality of these methods in providing alternative representations through arts. Nevertheless, we conclude that these are highly contested and complex practices, which need careful scrutiny and ethical reflection.

Politics of witnessing and of listening

Attention to the context of listening is highly significant in the field of cultural production, particularly because artists, authors, theatre makers, activists and journalists often use story-telling and testimony in their work with refugees. In addition to journalism and civic activism, arts and culture have recently become central fields in documenting the crisis of the reception of refugees in Europe. There is a strong understanding that art can bear witness to politics, as Lindroos and Möller (2017) have argued (see also Brambilla's Chapter 4 above). For example, Belfiore and Bennett (2008: 10) have claimed that art can be a source for 'ethical vision' in societies engaging with difficult presents and pasts. One fundamental debate about art that engages with traumatic events has focused on representation of the Holocaust. Michael Rothberg (2000) identifies two contradictory yet coexisting approaches to the demands regarding representing the Holocaust: realist and anti-realist. By the realist approach, Rothberg (2000: 3–4) means 'both an epistemological claim that the Holocaust is knowable and a representational claim that this knowledge can be translated into a familiar mimetic universe'. The anti-realist position, on the contrary, means 'both a claim that the Holocaust is not knowable or would be knowable only under radically new regimes of knowledge and that it cannot be captured in traditional representational schemata' (2000: 4). Rothberg presents a third mode of representation that engages with both the realist (or documentary) and the anti-realist (or radically new aesthetic), that of traumatic realism. This approach combines the banal everyday and the extreme horrific experiences of Holocaust survivors. Whether the artwork speaks using 'realist', 'anti-realist' or 'traumatic realist' aesthetics, it is uniquely capable of illuminating structures and processes in European societies that produce violent borders. The borders and their consequences are often not seen or felt by the citizens.

In all three modes of knowing concerned with the traumatic event, however, testimony and the first-hand eyewitness experience are central. Whilst feminist and post-colonial scholars have criticised the idea of 'giving voice' to marginalised communities for several decades (see, e.g., Spivak, 1988), it is still oftentimes debated in the field of the arts; this critique is currently accompanied by attention to listening and the right to be heard. The contemporary positions on this issue underline that ethical listening is an attempt not to cognitively understand and explain the Other or what is different but to understand unequal relationships and power dynamics. Instead of providing explanations, listening means presence at the telling of the event and openness to recognise the incompleteness and unsettledness emerging in encounters across differences (see Dreher, 2009, 2012; Husband, 1996; Ong, 2014; Rovisco, 2015; Sreberny, 2006).

There is often little attention paid in the actual artwork or activist *Kunstaktion* to the ways in which the story has been produced and listened to, that is, to the performance of the story. The notion of performance includes the presence of a spectator or a listener. The people who listen to the testimonies through mediation become 'secondary witnesses' (Wake, 2013) or 'mediated witnesses' (Frosh and Pinchevski, 2009) to the events. Those who have not been in the moment of disaster in person and, thus, have not witnessed the events in the 'flesh'[1] (Harari, 2009) can nevertheless be moved by the testimony in profound ways. This is sometimes triggered by the artwork itself in the tradition of postmodern aesthetics (Rothberg, 2000: 13), so that the performativity and the power relations in the situation of the telling and listening become audible or visible to the viewer.[2] The self-consciousness of representation may also occur through other means such as websites, talks, articles and 'the making of' videos produced along-side the main project. The documentary film *Come un uomo sulla terra* directed by Andrea Segre, Riccardo Biadene and Dagmawi Yimer (2008) is an exemplary project that reflects the listening context at multiple levels. The film is a manifestation of participatory film-making, as it is visible to the viewer that Yimer is simultaneously a protagonist and a film-maker (see Horsti, 2019b). In addition, the DVD version of the film is accompanied by a book that reflects on the production process and what one of the project's collaborators, the historian Alessandro Triulzi (2015: 215–17), has termed the 'empathic listening context'. The essential elements of this listening context are a willingness to speak but also its participatory setting, where the stories are shared as a joint effort that assures both confidence and empathetic listening (Triulzi, 2015). Within the broader project of *Remembering Lampedusa*, this chapter sets out to do something similar: we discuss the complexities of testimony and witnessing by examining the listening context of the project, and, in doing so, we aim to contribute to the practice of critical assessment of the production and performance of the story.

Creating an empathetic listening context

Our analysis focuses on two testimonies that narrate the 3 October 2013 disaster in Lampedusa. Solomon Ghebrahiwit, from Eritrea, is one of the 155 survivors of the disaster and Vito Fiorino is the first Lampedusan civil responder who saved 47 people in the early morning in his leisure boat, including Ghebrahiwit. Both the witnesses of the disaster told their stories in their native language, Tigrinya and Italian, in their living rooms to a Finnish-Swedish-Italian-Eritrean research and documentary film crew in 2017. Ghebrahiwit lives currently in Sweden as a refugee and Fiorino in Lampedusa where he has his second home. The testimonies lasting approximately one hour were filmed and transcribed in their original language, and then translated into English.

The situations where the memories of the disaster could be evoked and shared took place in the project in an organic and participatory way: none of us academics, media professionals or refugees was in charge of the moment of the telling. The survivors or the rescuers might express a detail or two about the disaster in the middle of conversation as we spent time together, but the act of remembering meant going into a specific emotional state. Trust was the essential element of that state, particularly so to the survivors, who decided on telling their testimonies collectively. They explained to the non-Eritreans of the project that the lack of public narratives of Eritrean refugees in Europe was due to the fact that Eritreans have kept details about their suffering and personal emotions in the private sphere. The media in Eritrea were controlled by the regime. The 'culture of secrecy' that the survivors refer to is echoed in scholarship addressing Eritrean responses to decades of violence and war. The anthropologist Victoria Bernal (2017) writes about the broader cultural 'unspeakability' concerning personal losses among the Eritreans, also among those in diaspora, and sees it as 'a secondary form of violence' (Bernal, 2014: 7, 27–9). The violence that Eritreans have experienced through generations, during the struggle and war for independence from Ethiopia, during the harsh regime of President Isaias Afewerki, and during the escape from the country leading to the refugee experience are not talked about in public. In the official discourse, those who have died in wars are considered to be 'heroes' and those who have died while fleeing the regime are 'traitors'. This is the context in which the participating survivors performed their stories. Eritreans, like many other refugees, have often experienced traumatising events before escaping; and border-crossing, including seeing others dying, is a further traumatic experience. These layers of traumatic events and delayed responses to them shape – or may even prevent – the narrative of the border-crossings (on border, narrative and trauma, see Schimanski, 2006: 49–50; 2019; and Wolfe's Chapter 8 above). There are various geographical, social and cultural borders that refugees have encountered before leaving Eritrea, during the journey and while in Europe. In the *Remembering Lampedusa* project, the act of recalling the journey and the disaster as a group was essential to piece the memories together into a narrative. The decision to do so also publicly was made as a group, which was necessary since in the Eritrean diasporic setting to tell one's testimony is a critical and a radical act.

The *Remembering Lampedusa* project involved two stages of producing the listening context empathetically: one was collective and the other individual. In his definition of the empathetic listening context, Triulzi (2015) emphasises confidence and empathy, which are both founded on trust. Different but equally important layers of relationships of trust were developed in the project, including the relationships among the survivors, those between the survivors and Adal Neguse, the two Lampedusan responders and the survivors, those among the international and multidisciplinary team members, and those between the non-Eritrean team members and the Eritrean survivors. The survivors had created a familial and trustful relationship between the Lampedusan civil rescuers during their return to Lampedusa to commemorate the disaster. Adal Neguse had become an important figure for the survivors in Sweden, where he has helped many of them in their new everyday lives. Karina Horsti who directed the project, had collaborated with Adal Neguse and Anna Blom, the co-directors of the films, and she had built relationships with two of the four survivors during collaborative research in Lampedusa. These earlier encounters and friendships were fundamental for the trust needed to embark on the project.

The survivor testimonies were developed in two encounters with the team. The first phase was a memory workshop where the survivors collectively recalled and shared their memories about the disaster within the group. The second was focused on the individuals' testimonies, and it was shared through the camerawork. However, instead of progressing in a linear way from one stage to another, the process was circular. Individual shootings, meetings and edited version of conversations were entangled with group meetings, which provided us with the opportunity to confirm and strengthen the feeling of collective trust and safety when sharing the testimonies and working with them. This circular process facilitated the production of informed consent. Each participant signed an informed consent form, but that took place only after the collective workshop and the first shootings, when it was clear to everyone how the project was to be carried out. Informed consent, therefore, is a process, rather than a mere formal act of signing a paper; it is founded on a deep accomplishment and commitment of sharing personal memories, and it is a conscious decision to take a risk through telling.

The memory workshop took place at the home of one of the survivors in Sweden.[3] We first prepared and ate an Eritrean meal with *injera*, and then the host prepared an Eritrean coffee ritual. During the three or four hours of preparation, eating and drinking coffee, we chatted about our lives in general, about Swedish, Finnish and Eritrean cultures, and watched Eritrean and Ethiopian music videos. After the host had collected the coffee making equipment from the living room floor, she sat on a large sofa with the others. It was clear to everyone that this was the moment for speaking about the disaster. The listening context had been created in a joint process of *being together*. The conversation in Tigrinya lasted for two hours. Every now and then, someone would summarise the conversation in Swedish for those without a command of Tigrinya, but nothing was recorded. This was the stage of sharing memories, remembering collectively, but also a stage for collective preparation and decision-making: would some of them want to share their memories with broader publics through the mode of documentary film and filmed testimony?

The second phase of remembering took place six to twelve months later, when the survivors present in the first workshop narrated their stories to Adal Neguse in the presence of the camera and the other team members in their own homes. Solomon Ghebrahiwit's testimony, under analysis in this chapter, took place six months after the first workshop. Again, we prepared *injera* and enjoyed a meal together. Ghebrahiwit participated in the setting up of the filming equipment in his living room and, when that was ready, he sat on the sofa and said when he was ready to start. Ghebrahiwit decided what constituted a testimony – where the disaster began and who were the protagonists in the story. The narrative started with Adal's question: Could you tell me your name and where you come from? After that, Solomon Ghebrahiwit directed the telling, and Adal Neguse made some clarifying questions only. Solomon had the story to a certain extent 'ready' in his mind. The testimony had some of the same elements that he had narrated in the days immediately following the disaster in an interview with Zed Nelson for Channel 4's 'Dispatches' programme Europe's *Immigration Disaster* (2014) and some of the elements he had shared in the collective memory workshop.

Creating the listening context with Vito Fiorino was different. When Ilaria Tucci first contacted him by telephone a few months before our actual meeting, the team already knew he was willing to speak openly about his experience and opinions concerning the disaster. He had released numerous interviews about what had happened on 3 October. We noticed that his interviews had the same narrative elements, word-for-word. Fiorino argued in many of the interviews, including the one conducted in this project, that the rescue operation was inefficient and that the arrival of the Italian Coast Guard after his friend's emergency call took longer than was officially reported. He also reminded repeatedly that the survivors had witnessed large military vessels passing by them without stopping for rescue.

Although Vito Fiorino had been interviewed several times before, he was eager to participate in the documentary film project without hesitation. Our willingness to listen to his story and share it with a wider audience was enough to motivate Fiorino to give his testimony once more, he said. So, on a day with heavy rain, he waited for the authors and the film-makers Anna Blom and Ditte Uljas in his home in Lampedusa. He had bought his house in Lampedusa seventeen years previously after a summer holiday spent there. We had already spent time together during our two days in Lampedusa before the filming of the testimony.

After the filming equipment had been set around his dinner table in the living room, Fiorino asked: 'Do you want the short version or the long version of my story?' He was about to perform a story that he had told numerous times before, and he had created different versions of it. Nevertheless, after his one-hour testimony, Fiorino said, the retelling of the long version was always emotionally tiring and he had to get into a specific emotional state in order to perform the story. Fiorino, like Ghebrahiwit, signalled the moment when the performance of the story started. It started when he had gained the emotional confidence. For example, Ghebrahiwit sat on the sofa in front of the camera that had been placed on a tripod, but he sat still and did not speak before everyone else had also taken their seats. A still moment signalled the beginning of the telling. He also signalled where the story of the disaster started and where it ended, and what aspects were not to be shared – the silences were deliberate.

Relationship with the listener(s)

A crucial element in the listening context of the survivor's testimony concerns the primary listener of the testimony, Adal Neguse, who had a personal connection with the survivors. His brother had died in the shipwreck, and Neguse had travelled to Lampedusa in the days following the disaster to look for his missing younger brother among the survivors. Neguse's motivation for evoking the memories and encouraging the public to listen to them was crucial to the project. Towards the end of the testimony, Solomon Ghebrahiwit recalls the moment he saw Neguse holding a photograph of his brother at the refugee reception centre and asking: 'Do you know this person? Was he on the boat?' For Solomon, the memory of Adal Neguse searching for his missing brother prompted another memory that becomes a part of the former's testimony: the difficulty of calling his own brother, who also had escaped Eritrea, to let him know that he had survived. The difficulty was that, at the same time, he would have to pass the news about those who had not survived. On the boat, there were ten friends whom he knew from Dekemhare, Eritrea, and he was the only one who survived the disaster:

> Wasn't the disaster on Thursday? I didn't call on Thursday. It was Friday evening when I called. They had given us a phone card so we could call our relatives. But, you know, I felt ashamed that I had survived. To say that I have survived, I didn't call. I kept quiet. I didn't tell my family, no one. Nevertheless, my brother had heard somehow that I was on that ship and people had already started to console him. He thought I was dead. Some others had already called on Thursday. Then, I called and said 'Hello Musie', my brother said 'Selie' and fainted. He was gone. That was it. And then, soon after, you came with

your brother's photo. I felt your emotion so strongly, and I saw my brother in you. We should forget, but honestly, this is what I always remember. When I remember my brother, I remember you and your brother. (Solomon Ghebrahiwit's testimony)

The person to whom Ghebrahiwit narrated the story shaped its performance. The memory of their first encounter brought to the surface the memory of the delayed telephone call to his own brother. This memory also demonstrates how the disaster did not end in the events at sea, and how survival necessitated certain practices in the afterlife as a survivor. These practices became parts of the testimony. What this means is that survival resulted in complex and contradictory feelings as the above quotation illustrates: guilt and grief are stronger than the survivor's potential happiness of being able to tell his brother the news of his survival.

Adal Neguse's presence as a primary listener shaped the story also in other ways. Solomon Ghebrahiwit mentions the names of various places – schools he went to in Eritrea, Mendefera where he worked as a DJ, a mixer in a nightclub and an announcer in a movie theatre before he was forcibly enslaved in Dekemhare by the army. Ghebrahiwit and his friends prepared for the trip to Libya in Sudan, doing their shopping in Shuq-Ashaebi, a place that Google maps does not recognise. He also talks about a place in Sudan where he was tortured by the kidnappers. All these details would make no sense to those listeners in the room who are not familiar with Eritrea. Possibly, Ghebrahiwit would not have shaped the story in the same detailed way if Neguse were not among listeners. However, it does not mean that those details would not matter to those who are not familiar with Eritrea and the places along the escape route. On the contrary, since those details are in the transcribed testimony that we read in an English translation, they influence us. We become aware that the disaster did not happen only at sea in sight of Lampedusa, but that it began much earlier, before the European border, and that there are many places and worlds we are not familiar with, but which exist as important sites of memory for the survivors. In the European collective imagination, long before the disaster happened, Lampedusa had already become recognised as a symbolic site of memory (Nora, 1996) for death and suffering at the border. It is unquestionably a significant memory site for thousands of migrants who passed through the island, including the survivors of the 3 October 2013 disaster. However, as Ghebrahiwit's story demonstrates, there are other borders that remain unacknowledged in the European public sphere. The border zone that produced the fatality extends far beyond the actual European Union border at sea, and the impact of the disaster continues to be present in the life of Solomon Ghebrahiwit in Sweden.

Adal Neguse has the ability to listen to a story told in this way. For the majority of the European public, those places become visible and audible through this testimony and the act of narration (see Wolfe's Chapter 8 above), as well as through its translation, potentially. Consequently, the places become meaningful sites of memory also in the small Swedish town where Ghebrahiwit performed his story on a Saturday, the day off from his work as a bus driver. Furthermore, his testimony is shaped by his life in Sweden: when explaining what kind of bread they were able to buy at one smugglers' holding place in Libya, Solomon refers to a Swedish grocery store: 'it was the same long white bread that we can buy here at Hemköp'. The temporality and spatiality of the disaster – as it enfolds in Solomon's testimony – extends beyond 3 October 2013 and the specific site right off Lampedusa. The testimony is a manifestation of transnational memory that connects different sites and people in Eritrea, Ethiopia, Sudan, Libya, Italy and Sweden. Similarly, Solomon Ghebrahiwit's motivation to narrate his story has multiple temporal and spatial layers. His memory of Neguse in Lampedusa encourages him to collaborate in the project. His sense of 'survivor citizenship' (Horsti, forthcoming), that is, his acting upon his experience of survival, necessitates that he recalls the disaster for two main reasons: first, for the memory of the dead, and, second, for the rights of the living present-day refugees who have suffered along the journey, particularly in Libyan detention centres.

In addition, Vito Fiorino has a strong need to share his testimony by recalling publicly what he had witnessed. Part of Fiorino's (often-repeated) testimony criticises the Coast Guard's slow response to the disaster and the lack of public investigation into the disaster. Fiorino was obliged to repeat his testimony because of the aim of finding justice, he told us. For Fiorino, stating facts of what he had seen on 3 October 2013 is not enough. The emotional state, embodying the memory, is crucial for the *performance of the story*. Each time he narrates the story, he does so in a specific emotional mode. During his testimony, Fiorino recognised how the act of remembering intensifies emotions. He said: 'you amplify this ... this moment hundred times more'.[4] This takes place in interaction with the listeners: the emotional power of the testimony is produced in the relation to those who are willing to listen. While for Fiorino the telling of the story is repetitive, for us, as listeners, it takes place for the first time. His presence and telling *embody* his claims concerning the injustice that he witnessed both in the scene and after the disaster.

For Fiorino, repeating the public testimony is also a tool for self-exploration: despite having rescued 47 persons during that night, he feels the frustration of being unable to save more lives. Sharing his memory about the disaster is also a way of living with the experience of having witnessed the deaths of so many people, similar to Ghebrahiwit's sense of survivorship. Fiorino describes his first reaction to the disaster site as 'a stab wound', and retelling his experience in different contexts has become a way of living and honouring the memory of those who died. In some way, through his testimony, the dignity of the lost human lives can survive.

Vito's testimony emerges as a personally needed act of healing and at the same time as an act advocating justice. The two levels – personal and public – are strongly interconnected in his telling: 'What happened that morning, what we experienced, is something that ... sooner or later I should ask some help. Institutional support performed really badly. No one has thought that we would need some psychological support.' In Vito's eyes and words, the disaster appears not only in the deaths he has witnessed but also in the absence of co-operation and support from the institutions that manage the border.

Conclusion

This chapter has examined how a conceptualisation of witnessing and testimony as a 'performance of a story' contributes to the production of a context where telling and listening to experiences of the border become possible. Instead of 'giving voice' to those who have experienced the violence of the border, we have highlighted the ability to listen and to *presence* to those experiences. The analysis of the *Remembering Lampedusa* project demonstrates how at least two aspects are crucial for this end. First, telling and listening are founded on mutual trust and commitment. They need to be nurtured throughout and after the project. Privileges and power relationships are to be taken into consideration constantly, and they need to be discussed and negotiated in order to locate ways of balancing and horizontalising power.

Second, teamwork and intermediaries allow for different kinds of details and memories to appear. This does not mean simply that cultural intermediaries such as Adal Neguse in the project would function as those who translate and explain 'differences' to 'us', a group whose understanding would form the norm. It is more about learning to listen to accented stories – stories that have places, names and events that are not familiar to those who listen. In addition, the motivations of those who ask others to narrate their stories need to be scrutinised. Those who tell have the right to justify of their motivations.

Thus, what is fundamental is self-reflexive thinking concerning the motivation of the scholars, activists, authors and artists who become 'secondary witnesses' by documenting and mediating the testimonies of others. In

Remembering Lampedusa project, we asked the question of what is our right to ask for a testimony. Our motivation was founded on the idea of rethinking the 'cultural' and 'national' memory of the Nordic countries. We took the responsibility of offering our expertise in archiving the testimonies as evidence of the present-day mass death. The governments of the Nordic countries have contributed to the production of the violent EU border, and a majority of those who survived the disaster in Lampedusa live in Sweden and Norway. The memory of the disaster is central to 'Swedish' history (and that of other European countries), we argue.

Finally, both Vito Fiorino and Solomon Ghebrahiwit had their motivations to tell their stories. In both cases, this did not take place for the first time. Onn the contrary, both had told their experiences before, and, in fact, constructed 'a story' (with a short or a long version, as Fiorino noted) that they were able to perform again. Fiorino stressed that the fact that someone wanted to listen to his experience was enough to motivate him to tell – and to embody, presence his claim. He was driven by a sense of justice – he would continue to tell the story until the victims and survivors receive justice, he said. Fiorino has continued to remind the public that the disaster has not been investigated. The high number of deaths resulted from an inefficient rescue operation, he says. In a similar vein, in his public appearances, alongside telling his story, Ghebrahiwit advocates for refugees who are currently held in Libyan detention centres. The mutual interest in engaging with the memories of the disaster, although articulated in different ways, has been central to the ability to produce a context for telling and listening testimonies.

Notes

1 By analysing Erich Maria Remarque's *All Quiet on the Western Front*, Yuval Noah Harari (2009) makes a distinction between two different forms of witnessing that claim distinct modes of authority – eye-witnessing that claims to be objective observation and flesh-witnessing that draws from experiential authority.
2 In another example, Candice Breitz successfully brings the meta-representational level and the politics of celebrity and attention visible in her installation *Love Story* (for an analysis see Horsti, 2019a).
3 In the workshop there were present four survivors (three men and one woman), the husband of the woman, a relative of one victim and the Swedish-Eritrean human rights activist Adal Neguse, the Swedish director Anna Blom and Karina Horsti.
4 'Voi amplificate questa … questo momento cento volte di più in quel momento'. All translations from Italian to English are by Ilaria Tucci.

References

Albahari, M. (2015) *Crimes of Peace: Mediterranean Migrations at the World's Deadliest Border*. Philadelphia: University of Pennsylvania Press.

Alexievich, S. (2017) '"Our own memory": A Q & A with Svetlana Alexievich and Phillip Gourevitch', *Samsoniaway: An Online Magazine for Literature, Free Speech & Social Justice* (13 March). www.sampsoniaway.org/interviews/2017/03/13/our-own-memory-a-qa-with-svetlana-alexievich/. Accessed 30 June 2020.

Belfiore, E., and O. Bennett (2008) *The Social Impact of the Arts: An Intellectual History*. Basingstoke: Palgrave.

Bernal, V. (2014) *Nation as Network: Diaspora, Cyberspace, and Citizenship*. Chicago: The University of Chicago Press.

Bernal, V. (2017) 'Diaspora and the afterlife of violence: Eritrean national narratives and what goes on without saying', *American Anthropologist*, 119(1): 23–34.

Blom, A., and A. Neguse (2018) *Remembering the Tragedy of Lampedusa*, https://Rememberinglampedusa.com. Accessed 29 September 2019.

Breitz, C. (2017) *Love Story*. Installation at National Gallery of Victoria, Melbourne.

De Genova, N. (ed.) (2017) *The Borders of 'Europe': Autonomy of Migration, Tactics of Bordering*. Durham, NC: Duke University Press.

De Jong, S. (2018) *The Witness as Object: Video Testimony in Memorial Museums*. New York: Berghahn Books.

Dreher, T. (2009) 'Listening across difference: Media and multiculturalism beyond the politics of voice', *Continuum*, 23(4): 445–58.

Dreher, T. (2012) 'A partial promise of voice: Digital storytelling and the limit of listening', *Media International Australia Incorporating Culture and Policy: Quarterly Journal of Media Research and Resources*, 142: 157–66.

Durham Peters, J. (2001) 'Witnessing', *Media, Culture & Society*, 23(6): 707–23.

Felman, S. (2000) 'In an era of testimony: Claude Lanzmann's *Shoah*', *Yale French Studies*, 97: 103–50.

Frosh, P., and A. Pinchevski (2009) 'Introduction: Why media witnessing? Why now?', in P. Frosh and A. Pinchevski (eds), *Media Witnessing: Testimony in the Age of Mass Communication*. London: Palgrave, pp. 1–19.

Harari, Y.N. (2009) 'Scholars, eyewitnesses, and flesh-witnesses of war: A tense relationship'. *Partial Answers: Journal of Literature and the History of Ideas*, 7(2): 213–28.

Heller, C., and L. Pezzani (2012) 'The left-to-die boat'. forensic-architecture.org/investigation/the-left-to-die-boat. Accessed 29 September 2019.

Horsti, K. (forthcoming) 'Afterlife of a disaster' (unpublished book MS).

Horsti, K. (2019a) 'Refugee testimonies enacted: Voice and solidarity in media art installations', *Popular Communication*, 17(2): 125–39.

Horsti, K. (2019b) 'Temporality in cosmopolitan solidarity: Archival activism and participatory documentary film as mediated witnessing of suffering at Europe's borders', *European Journal of Cultural Studies*, 22(2): 231–44.

Husband, C. (1996) 'The right to be understood: Conceiving the multi-ethnic public sphere', *Innovation: The European Journal of Social Sciences*, 9(2): 205–15.

Hyndman, J. (2007) 'Feminist geopolitics revisited: Body counts in Iraq', *The Professional Geographer*, 59(1): 35–46.

Liénard, B., and M. Jimenez (2019) 'Sortir du noir: Who will remember them?', *Atlas of Transitions*, www.atlasoftransitions.eu/indepth/sortir-du-noir-who-will-remember-them/. Accessed 29 September 2019.

Lindroos, K., and F. Möller (eds) (2017) *Art as a Political Witness*. Opladen: Barbara Budrich Publishers.

Nelson, Z. (2014) *Europe's Immigration Disaster*. London: Channel 4. https://vimeo.com/126935104. Accessed 29 September 2019.

Nora, P. (1996) *Realms of Memory: The Construction of the French Past. Vol. 1: Conflicts and Divisions*. Trans. A. Goldhammer. New York: Columbia University Press.

Ong, J.C. (2014) '"Witnessing" or "mediating" distant suffering? Ethical questions across moments of text, production and reception', *Television & New Media*, 15(3): 179–96.

Rothberg, M. (2000) *Traumatic Realism: The Demands of Holocaust Representation*. Minneapolis: University of Minnesota Press.

Rovisco, M. (2015) 'Community arts, new media and the desecuritisation of migration and asylum seeker issues in the UK', in C. Kinnvall and T. Svensson (eds), *Governing Borders and Security: The Politics of Connectivity and Dispersal*. London: Routledge, pp. 99–116.

Schimanski, J. (2006) 'Crossing and reading: Notes towards a theory and a method', *Nordlit*, 19: 41–63.

Schimanski, J. (2019) 'Migratory angels: The political aesthetics of border trauma', in K. Horsti (ed.), *The Politics of Public Memories of Forced Migration and Bordering in Europe*. Cham: Palgrave Pivot, pp. 37–52.

Segre, A., R. Biadene and D. Yimer (2008) *Come un uomo sulla terra*. Rome: Infinito Edizioni.

Spivak, G.C. (1988) 'Can the subaltern speak?' in C. Nelson and L. Grossberg (eds), *Marxism and the Interpretation of Culture*. Chicago: University of Illinois Press, pp. 271–313.

Sreberny, A. (2006) '"Not only, but also": Mixedness and media', *Journal of Ethnic and Migration Studies*, 31(3): 443–59.

Tait, S. (2011) 'Bearing witness, journalism and moral responsibility', *Media, Culture & Society*, 33(8): 1220–35.

Taylor, D. (2011) 'Trauma as durational performance: A return to dark sites', in M. Hirsch and N.K. Miller (eds), *Rites of Return: Diaspora Poetics and the Politics of Memory*. New York: Columbia University Press, pp. 268–79.

Taylor, D. (2016) *Performance*. Durham, NC: Duke University Press.

Tazzioli, M. (2015) 'The politics of counting and the scene of rescue', *Radical Philosophy*, 192: 2–6.

Triulzi, A. (2015) 'Roaming to Rome: Archiving and filming migrant voices in Italy', in E. Bond, G. Bonsaver and F. Faloppa (eds), *Destination Italy: Representing Migration in Contemporary Media and Narrative*. Oxford: Peter Lang, pp. 431–48.

United (2019) 'List of 36 570 documented deaths of refugees and migrants due to the restrictive policies of "Fortress Europe"', *UNITED for Intercultural Action*. www.unitedagainstracism.org/wp-content/uploads/2019/07/ListofDeathsActual.pdf. Accessed 29 September 2019.

Wake, C. (2009) 'After effects: Performing the ends of memory', *Performance Paradigm*, 5(1): 5–11.

Wake, C. (2013) 'Regarding the recording: The viewer of video testimony, the complexity of copresence and the possibility of tertiary witnessing', *History and Memory*, 25(1): 111–44.

Zagaria, V. (2016) 'Performing Lampedusa in Miraculi: Thoughts on theatre and research in a saturated field-site', *Journal of Migration & Culture*, 7(2): 193–208.

Zelizer B. (2007) 'On "having been there": "Eyewitnessing" as a journalistic key word', *Critical Studies in Media Communication*, 24(5): 408–28.

Epilogue: border images and narratives: paradoxes, spheres, aesthetics

Johan Schimanski and Jopi Nyman

Answering our three questions about border images and narratives

In our Introduction we framed the work in this book in terms of three questions: First, how does the choice of form, medium, genre and aesthetical strategies help form and potentially transform the borderscape? Second, how do these different forms, discourses and genres cross the borders into the public sphere? Third, what paradoxes can make problematic simple perceptions of making visible and giving voice? We accompanied each of these questions with a series of other questions suggesting the many different ways in which the contributors to the book might understand these queries.

In this epilogue we attempt to link our different chapters by summing up how they deal with the central concepts in each question. However, as we exit the book we aim to do so in the opposite order: *paradoxes*, *spheres*, *aesthetics*. The chapters use specific cases in order to provide a number of provisional answers to the three main queries we started with, but here we reflect further on the theoretical issues that span the chapters and pose possible questions for future research. In so doing we will thus not only circle around these central concepts but also ask how the narrative will continue in the future, beyond the borders of this book.

For convenience, in the following we refer to the other chapters in this volume just by the names of the contributors, without year numbers (Müller-Funk, García, Pötzsch, Brambilla, Kurki, Konrad and Hu, Amilhat Szary, Wolfe, Nyman, Schimanski, Horsti and Tucci).

Paradoxes

Much of the inspiration for this book goes back to work in a previous research project, *Border Aesthetics* (2010), and more specifically one chapter in the book that resulted from that project: the chapter addressing the key word 'in/visibility', by two of our present contributors, Chiara Brambilla and Holger Pötzsch (2017). The theme of in/visibility suggests that a central problem of politics and aesthetics in contemporary borderscapes is a contradiction, an ambiguity or a paradox concerning the role of aesthetics in the political sphere. To have agency in democracies is a question of being visible, of not being marginalised, or of having a voice, and being heard: the contradictory term 'in/visibility' could be accompanied by the term 'in/audibility', the two pairs suggesting the two main themes of this book, images and narratives. As Brambilla and Pötzsch (2017) argue with reference to Marieke Borren's (2008) interpretation of Hannah Arendt (1958: 178–9, 198–9; 1973: 295–6, 299, 302), visibility can both give and take away agency, as can invisibility. So for example, migrants, being marginalised, are often made invisible or inaudible, and would have to be seen and heard to gain political agency. But at the same time, migrants are often made visible and audible in ways detrimental to them: they are criminalised and subject to the imaging which is part of surveillance regimes either at the border or within the state, or they are imaged in the media as anonymous, brown masses. The contradictions between pathological and non-pathological visibility becomes a paradox when visibilisation is both pathological and non-pathological at the same time; for example when a photograph of dead bodies in the Mediterranean gives agency by awakening sympathy and the need for action, but at the same time as those bodies have been silenced and made visible as racialised others. Such paradoxes are the source of political ambiguity in media and cultural discourse.

In the 1970s, 1980s and 1990s, 'paradox' was a buzzword in critical and post-structuralist theory, along with related terms such as 'deconstruction' (often presented as the contradiction of meaning by expression) and 'aporia' (a situation of irresolvable choice). In some cases it was as if it was enough for a close analysis of some literary text, philosophical theory, cultural phenomenon or political ideology to show that it contained some unavoidable paradox or contradiction which resisted its own underlying master narratives. Eventually, the suspicion arose that, by implying that every sign or representation was per se ambivalent, all possibility of political agency had been neutralised, leading to a strong critique of such theory. However, to reclaim political ground by referring to the realities of power and oppression does not mean that paradox and its companions have been somehow magicked away, and several of the contributors to our volume set store by complexity as a corrective to simplistic narratives (see among others chapters by Brambilla; Amilhat Szary; Schimanski). Complexity can suggest alternative concepts of the border as a place of encounter rather than purely a place of division and solidification (Müller-Funk; Brambilla), and of borderscapes as spaces of plurality and polyphony (Brambilla; Nyman). Political theorists such as Jacques Rancière (2010: 37–9) and Chantal Mouffe (2013) emphasise another form of complexity by giving contradiction, or, as they frame it, 'dissensus' or 'agonism', a central role in the realisation of a truly political democracy (Brambilla; Amilhat Szary). We would suggest also that it is precisely when social or cultural contradictions begin to be formulated as paradoxes that they matter the most. It is then that the political is truly approached. Paradoxes can be seen as starting points, and, indeed, paradox and similar terms are figurations of borders, pointing to internal differences, interference between centres and margins and, in the case of aporia, to the way in which a fork in the road can function as a threshold and a place of (paradoxical and disorientating) stasis in movement.

As already implied, the paradoxes and ambiguities of in/visibility run as a red thread through this volume. The pathological border spectacle of 'the migration crisis' occludes by simplifying and creating ahistorical bias (Brambilla); the visibility of bodies on urban streets both marks communal solidarity among between migrants and the working class and leads to the racialisation of migrants (Wolfe; Nyman); visibility implies not only representative power but also the 'burden of representation' (Kurki; Wolfe); and traumatisation, with its peculiar erasure of past experience combined with fixed, substitute narratives and images, makes something visible, but not the original trauma (Kurki).

What this volume makes clear is that the paradoxical workings of in/visibility are accompanied by other ambiguities, such as those between subversion and complicity, legality and illegality, presence and absence, motion and stasis, abjectness and creativity, stereotypical and unfamiliar, and so on. As a response to the overheating of borders and migration control, border art often mimics the workings of Net-based surveillance apparatuses and border control regimes, partly using the same technologies as those used by state power. The paradox here is that artists intend to subvert power, but can end up reinforcing it (Pötzsch; Amilhat Szary). We are forced to ask: 'How can one image challenge another? How can it impose a different system of analysing the world?' (Amilhat Szary). This ambiguity is not just the concern of artists resisting power: the technologies involved in themselves both subvert and extend state power as they cross national borders; they function as 'pharmakons', to use Jacques Derrida's deconstructive term (1981: 70) designating both a remedy and a poison (Pötzsch; Müller-Funk). Since such technologies are mostly ways of revealing and indeed visualising different kinds of border-crossing, the paradox of subversion/complicity becomes intimately connected to that of in/visibility in the borderscape (Pötzsch), and often also with another paradox, that of il/legality.

Migrant deaths in the Mediterranean make us aware of another contradiction already hinted at, that between existence and annihiliation. The dead cannot speak: they are present and absent at the same time, hinting at what Nicholas De Genova (2010) has called a 'politics of presence' (Horsti and Tucci), and to risk one's own self when crossing the Mediterranean is to situate oneself on 'the threshold between life and death' (Wolfe).

In/visibility, presence/absence, il/legality, motion/stasis and abjectness/ creativity often come together in a powerful figuration of the border, the threshold (Müller-Funk). The threshold is often a border zone where one can be seen and also see across the border, quite possibly a place of standstill where one cannot not reach what lies beyond (Müller-Funk). Migrant border-crossings can be seen as rites of passage (Wolfe), and migrants traversing the Mediterranean or the Mexico–USA border live on the threshold to death, often ending up waiting by the border in Kafkaesque limboscapes (Ferrer-Gallardo and Albet-Mas, 2013; Houtum and Wolfe, 2017), urban labyrinths and prison camps, caught in a disorientating and uncanny ambiguity between motion and stasis (Wolfe; Nyman). On the thresholds of nations and states they exist in states of exception (Agamben, 2005), experiencing the ambiguities of il/legality (Wolfe). But such threshold places – such as the 'Jungle' by Calais – can also function as heterotopias (Foucault, 1986), third spaces or in-betweens (Bhabha, 1994). They either annihilate the border subjects that inhabit them or, conversely, allow them to refashion their identities and image their futures, and become places of cultural polyphony and creativity (Wolfe; Nyman). This principle of hope and agency applies not only to border-crossers, but also to borderland dwellers (Brambilla).

Border images and narratives may be stereotypical and thus familiar and simplifying. They can also give voice to outsiders, yet this does not mean that we should ask them to be unfamiliar or defamiliarising in every case or on every level. Migrant and borderland narratives may indeed defamiliarise the trope of the other country by unexpectedly focusing on familiarity and similarity rather than on unfamiliarity and difference (Brambilla; Schimanski). Narratives can also present striking alternatives to our normal expectations where borders are concerned (García).

Spheres

Theories of in/visibility (we continue here to use the visual as a stand-in for a whole number of ways of experiencing the world) fit well with Jacques Rancière's (2004) attempt to bring together politics and aesthetics through the notion of the *partage du sensible*, the sharing or dividing of that which can be sensed. This *partage* takes place precisely on the border between the private and the public spheres, where we may attain agency if we are privileged enough to make ourselves seen or heard in the political arena, in the mass media, in the arts and sciences etc. It remains to be asked how this actually happens, and how effectively it happens in each case (Amilhat Szary).

What becomes clear in the present volume is also that we must also ask where, and in what spaces. The public sphere is not a single or homogeneous space, even during historical periods when the borderings between nation states have been more absolute and it was possible for Europeans at least to imagine that they lived in a specific space or 'society', and that other such spaces were unimportant (today, politicians and journalists will still talk about 'relevance to society' meaning relevance to their own national space). Neat, bordered national public spheres are now disturbed by global and transnational publics, diasporic cultures, minorities, in-betweens, gated communities, subcultures, political 'bubbles' or 'echo-chambers' and internal borderings in terms of class, gender, ethnicity and so on. At the same time it is important to emphasise that many public spheres have been subject to a 'national orders' that can erase certain forms of border narrative (Kurki), that national power can still stand in tension with deterritorialised global technologies of communication (Pötszch) and that global cultures can 'seemingly transcend traditional borders but confirm them in a second step' (Müller-Funk). The focus on dissensus as an essential part of democratic culture also points to the importance of imagining the public sphere as a heterogeneous and dynamic space.

As noted earlier, our contributors tend to agree that images and narratives that convey complexity are better than those that simplify. We need however to investigate further the mechanisms by which contradictory images and narratives can coexist, either contesting each other in dissensus or aligning with each other in consensus. Contradictory images and narratives can be apparent on different levels or scale of the borderscape, but they can be aligned from the viewpoint of state power (Konrad and Hu). Negotiation and moderation between different interest groups may be necessary, in a process of 'borderation' that still allows for polyphony and hybridity, and for dissensus to compete with consensus (Konrad and Hu). Similarly, images of global multiculturalism can act as harmonic veneers covering global 'power asymmetries' and 'structural violence' (Müller-Funk).

How then do images and narrative cross from the private and into the public, for example where migrant border-crossers are concerned? Such crossings involving various forms of exposure: publication, exhibition, performance, signage, internet posting and so on. Some such processes, such as surveillance, only cross from the private and into a very limited and even secret 'bubble'. Some involve spectacularisation, in which the private becomes so public that it tends to lose contact with the original experience. One can observe forms of 'border discourse cycles' in which top-down and bottom-up narratives and images of the border alternate (Konrad and Hu). Some crossings are not easy to make, as when 'national orders' erase traumatic border narratives (Kurki) and experiences of migration trauma have to be teased out by witnesses in order not to remain erased (Horsti and Tucci). Border images and narratives must then traverse any number of epistemological and media borders before they become visible or heard. It is not enough to give voice to migrants; one must also be able to hear them (Horsti and Tucci).

Border images that resist power can also be also dependent of the frameworks of power in order to become visible in the public sphere (Pötzsch). One way of sorting out the ambiguities around such images and narratives we have discussed above is to attend in hermeneutic detail to their positioning in the political sphere, ask whether they contribute to a true political dissensus, and compare 'the analysis of political anthropology with an aesthetics reading of the works' (Amilhat Szary). Border narratives and images are regulated by their reception, and we must be aware that processes by which they are produced and circulated become part of what they make visible and what they perform (e.g., Müller-Funk; Kurki; Pötzsch; Amilhat Szary; Horsti and Tucci).

Migrants and borderland dwellers, as border subjects and bodies, often live in border zones. In these in-between spaces they can have a key role as 'importers and exporters from one space to another' (Müller-Funk) or they can fall between identities (Kurki). They can acknowledge or overcome limits (Müller-Funk); they risk losing their status as human subjects, but they can also be in a position to utilise the flux of the border zone and their 'multiple senses of belonging' in order to shape 'new political subjectivities and agency', or even new forms of transnational citizenship (Brambilla).

Aesthetics

In/visibility, or the *partage du sensible*, involves both sharing and division; it both crosses and creates epistemological borders between what is visible and what is invisible, and thus partakes in acts of bordering and borderscaping (Schimanski, 2017/2018). 'Aesthesis', the process of making something accessible to the senses, is another name for this sharing and division. Given that there exist a large variety of aesthetic strategies – e.g., choice of medium, mode, genre, style, rhetorical trope and narrative technique – how do these afford or hinder the *partage du sensible* in different ways? To take for example the two main aesthetic strategies focused on in this volume – image and narrative – is one 'better suited' to crossing the border from private border experience into the public sphere than the other?

Our volume addresses a wide variety of media (text, cinema, video, television, architecture, painting, drawing, performance, ritual, park, landscape, installation, monument, sign, dress, data cloud, drone surveillance, photography, dream, mirror), modes (realism, the fantastic, fiction, documentary, ethnography, autobiography, political vision, participation), genres (novel, short story cycle, drama, essay, border studies, map, photograph series, land art, exhibition), styles (grotesque, montage) and rhetorical figures (metaphor). As the volume makes clear, this wide spread of aesthetic strategies goes beyond traditional works of art, literature or entertainment, including also academic research practices (Brambilla), political discourse and not least, a range of ways in which we as bodies sense our surroundings through buildings and road surfaces (García), border walls (Amilhat Szary), border crossing points (Konrad and Hu), coach windows and membranes (Müller-Funk) and our own and other bodies (Wolfe; Nyman) – and indeed also our inner worlds of traumatic memory (Kurki; Horsti and Tucci) and 'inter-visual' cultural imaginary (Konrad and Hu; Amilhat Szary; Schimanski). The different strategies are often mixed in hybrid forms, and in the volume we often discuss how one strategy simulates, enables or portrays another, such as when a border wall becomes art (Amilhat Szary), a film simulates a global aesthetic space (Müller-Funk), a television series conveys psychasthenia (García) or a painted or a metaphorical, mirrored or dream image figures in an autobiographical novel (Kurki; Schimanski; Wolfe).

To a certain extent, the present volume privileges narrative, with its complex temporality, focalisation techniques, situatedness and capacity for being heard, before image. However, it is important to emphasise that probably all media, modes and genres have the potential to enact complexity – as do for example membrane-based artworks (Müller-Funk) or the short story cycle in its polyphony (Nyman) – and to mix with and mimic other aesthetic strategies. It would not be a good idea to throw out the image as an invalid border aesthetic strategy, initially associated with solidification, with objectification and with authoritarian propaganda (Amilhat Szary); rather, we need to understand how also images can situate themselves in relation to their means of production (Pötzsch; Amilhat Szary; Horsti and Tucci), make visible different experiences, and convey complex temporalities. Some aesthetic forms, such as the fantastic, are perceived as being transgressive and border-orientated in their own right (García), and even the image can be seen as a product of the border between self and other (Schimanski). As Matteo Stocchetti and Karin Kukkonen argue in the volume *Images in Use*, images have no inherent value independent of the way they are used, and thus cannot seen as powerful or dangerous in themselves (2011: 1–2). The corollary is that images will always have power, because they are always used in some way (Stocchetti, 2011: 35).

An aesthetic strategy that actually does something – in other words, that is performative, or that engages in borderscaping (Brambilla) – is highly valued, and especially participatory strategies (Brambilla; Horsti and Tucci) seem to promise a way out of the pathologies of in/visibility. However, we need to ask whether certain media (e.g., texts, artistic forms) have a much more limited impact and more difficulties in crossing into larger public spheres than others (e.g., visual forms, entertainment, spectacle), raising questions of reception and performativity (Amilhat Szary). A concrete and visual intervention into a public space of gathering or transit – e.g., public art or cultural signs at a border (Amilhat Szary), border crossing (Konrad and Hu), tourist landscape, urban space (Müller-Funk) or street – may have a wider impact than for example a migration novel, and still convey the complexity of border experience. We may also hypothesise that aesthetic strategies of the border (e.g., 'border art') are caught in a paradox because of their origins in various acts of bordering. Borders can be taken as either simplifying the world (dividing it into boxes) or making the world more complex (creating in-between spaces of encounter and hybridity), and this will influence any aesthetics of the border.

Openings

We hope that this volume will inspire further investigations of the border aesthetics of images and narratives, firstly purely because it inevitably fails to cover all forms of border image and narrative. Such research could also focus on other primary media than the visual and linguistic, for example the sense of taste involved in border cuisine (Nyman, 2017).

We would also suggest other openings for future research following up aspects outlined here and in the rest of the volume. One would be to focus more on the mechanisms by which border images and narratives cross into the public sphere, needing both careful readings of images and narratives, but also research on how they act in the world. Another would be to trace on the complex temporality of border images and narrative in order to counteract the ahistoricism of media spectacle (Müller-Funk; Brambilla), to account for changing temporalities of border-crossing, communication and travel (Wolfe) and more specifically to give a more sustained accounts of the border aesthetics of utopia, dystopia, instability (Müller-Funk), histo-riography, memory, trauma, justice (Horsti and Tucci), transgenerational phenomena (Kurki) and border/borderland heritage (Konrad and Hu; Amilhat Szary). A third would focus on the emotional and affective dimension of border images and narratives: what desires, hopes, pleasures and fantasies they mobilise (Brambilla; Müller-Funk; Nyman; Wolfe), how they deal with trauma (Kurki; Horsti and Tucci), melancholy and pain (Wolfe), how they may both attract and repulse (Müller-Funk; Kurki), and how they are integrated in a 'cognitive assemblage' (Pötzsch, using N. Katherine Hayles' (2016) term). Here precisely an investigation of 'border feeling', focused on the sense of touch (Müller-Funk), might be revealing: it would attend to aesthetic strategies such as rhythm, musicality, immersion, virtual reality and the already mentioned participation, in order to understand the role of embodiment and empathy in the borderscape.

References

Note: References without year numbers to Müller-Funk, García, Pötzsch, Brambilla, Kurki, Konrad and Hu, Amilhat Szary, Wolfe, Nyman, Schimanski, and Horsti and Tucci are to the chapters in the present volume.

Agamben, G. (2005) *State of Exception*. Trans. K. Attell. Chicago: The University of Chicago Press.
Arendt, H. (1958) *The Human Condition*. Chicago: The University of Chicago Press.
Arendt, H. (1973) *The Origins of Totalitarianism*, new ed. New York: Harcourt Brace & Company.
Bhabha, H.K. (1994) *The Location of Culture*. London: Routledge.
Border Aesthetics (2010) 'Border Aesthetics', *UiT The Arctic University of Norway*, http://uit.no/hsl/borderaesthetics. Accessed 27 November 2019.
Borren, M. (2008) 'Towards an Arendtian politics of in/visibility: On stateless refugees and undocumented aliens', *Ethical Perspectives: Journal of the European Ethics Network*, 15(2): 213–37.
Brambilla, C., and H. Pötzsch (2017) 'In/visibility', in J. Schimanski and S.F. Wolfe (eds), *Border Aesthetics: Concepts and Intersections*. New York: Berghahn, pp. 68–89.
De Genova, N. (2010) 'Migration and race in Europe: The Trans-Atlantic metastases of a post-colonial cancer', *European Journal of Social Theory*, 13(3): 405–19.
Derrida, J. (1981) *Dissemination*. Trans. B. Johnson. Chicago: The University of Chicago Press.
Ferrer-Gallardo, X., and A. Albet-Mas (2013) 'EU-limboscapes: Ceuta and the proliferation of migrant detention spaces across the European Union', *European Urban and Regional Studies*, 23(3): 527–30.
Foucault, M. (1986) 'Of other spaces', *Diacritics*, 16(1): 22–7.
Hayles, N.K. (2016) 'Cognitive assemblages: Technical agency and human interactions', *Critical Inquiry*, 43(1): 32–55.
Houtum, H. van, and S.F. Wolfe (2017) 'Waiting', in J. Schimanski and S.F. Wolfe (eds), *Border Aesthetics: Concepts and Intersections*. New York: Berghahn, pp. 129–46.
Mouffe, C. (2013) *Agonistics: Thinking the World Politically*. London: Verso.
Nyman, J. (2017) 'Culinary border crossings in autobiographical writing: The British Asian case', in I. Goodson, A. Antikainen, P. Sikes and M. Andrews

(eds), *Routledge International Handbook on Narrative and Life History*. London: Routledge, pp. 190–201.

Rancière, J. (2004) *The Politics of Aesthetics: The Distribution of the Sensible*, trans. G. Rockhill. London: Continuum.

Rancière, J. (2010) *Dissensus: On Politics and Aesthetics*. Trans. S. Corcoran. London: Continuum.

Schimanski, J. (2017/2018) 'Frontières de verre / Glass borders', *antiAtlas Journal*, 2: 1–27.

Stocchetti, M. (2011) 'Images: Who gets what, when and how?', in *Images in Use: Towards the Critical Analysis of Visual Communication*. Amsterdam: John Benjamins, pp. 11–37.

Stocchetti, M., and K. Kukkonen (2011) 'Introduction', *Images in Use: Towards the Critical Analysis of Visual Communication*. Amsterdam: John Benjamins, pp. 1–7.

Index

EU authorised representative for GPSR:
Easy Access System Europe, Mustamäe tee 50,
10621 Tallinn, Estonia
gpsr.requests@easproject.com